GW00363294

THE BEST OF MODERN BRITISH COOKERY

THE BEST
OF
MODERN
BRITISH
COOKERY

SARAH FREEMAN

LITTLE, BROWN AND COMPANY
BOSTON NEW YORK TORONTO LONDON

A LITTLE, BROWN BOOK

First published in Great Britain in 1995
by Little, Brown and Company (UK)

Text copyright © 1995 by Sarah Freeman
Illustrations copyright © 1995 by Christopher Wormell
The right of Sarah Freeman to be identified as the Author
of this work and the right of Christopher Wormell to
be identified as the illustrator have been asserted in accordance
with the Copyright, Designs and Patents Act 1988

A CIP catalogue record for this book
is available from the British Library

ISBN 0-316-91392-8 (Hbk)
ISBN 0-316-91389-8 (Pbk)

10 9 8 7 6 5 4 3 2 1

Designed by Bernard Higton
Printed and bound by Mackays of Chatham

Little, Brown and Company (UK)
Brettenham House
Lancaster Place
London WC2E 7EN

CONTENTS

SALADS AND VEGETABLE SIDE DISHES

FISH DISHES

MEAT, POULTRY AND GAME DISHES

SWEET DISHES

INDEX

INTRODUCTION

So completely has British cooking been out of fashion in recent years that when I first thought of writing this book, several younger people asked, quite sincerely, 'What exactly is British cooking?'. It was a good question. Like any nation's cookery, ours is a mixture of native and foreign elements. In the past, foreign styles of cooking were introduced chiefly by the aristocracy and, to a lesser extent, by immigrants and through foreign trade. New ingredients, such as sugar and spices, rice, potatoes, and tea, were eagerly utilized as soon as they became available. It is therefore a mistake to try to identify it either as a particular style or in terms of specific ingredients, although, as anywhere, native ingredients have played a leading part in its evolution. Thanks to the rain and relatively early advancement of agriculture, the excellence of many of these ingredients was acknowledged: certainly by the middle of the last century, British beef and mutton were accepted as the best in the world. Salmon was wild, oysters unbelievably cheap, and virtually all fruit and vegetables organically grown. As elaborate cooking and flavourings were not needed, the style which developed was relatively plain. Modern conditions have altered the quality of ingredients and our cooking is changing accordingly, but I would still describe it as designed to flatter rather than disguise or distort ingredients.

The fact that it has been out of fashion is nothing new: to a greater or lesser extent, it always has been. The aristocracy, the leaders of fashion of their time, established the custom of employing foreign chefs (this was how the famous nineteenth-century chef Alexis Soyer started his career). The introduction of restaurants, which initially were by definition upper-class and foreign, was merely a continuation of this trend, which perhaps still partly accounts for the popularity of eating-places serving foreign food today. A second factor which has discouraged the serving of British-style food is that a number of favourite traditional dishes are difficult to present in a restaurant context: roasts, for instance, take a long time to cook and suffer from being kept waiting; the same applies to boiled meats and hot pies (as opposed to cold tarts). Of course, there are many other items which could be, and now being served, but it demands imagination and (it takes some courage to say this) more culinary care and skill than is often the case with dishes from other countries.

Another historical circumstance which has affected British food in a wider sense is that the food trade in this country was industrialized at a time when price was the first (and often the customer's only) consideration. It is easy to overstate and impossible to assess the influence which this has had on its subsequent development and our tastes and expectations, but I at any rate choose to bring it to mind when I see gravy-browning, British so-called ice-cream, and other similar products on supermarket shelves. Soggy cabbage and tough, overcooked meat are not so obviously attributable to the same cause but can also be traced to past social conditions.

Even by Mrs Beeton's time, the future of mutton was threatened and the nutritive value of beef versus bread had become a topic of dinner-party conversation (though neither would have been served at a fashionable meal). Today, economic pressures have led farmers and market-gardeners to raise produce which undermines the basis of traditional cooking as it evolved. Recipes, which only fifteen or twenty years ago would have given pleasing results, are now obsolete because of the tastelessness of ingredients: as well as horror on humanitarian grounds at the way in which the majority of calves, pigs, and chickens are reared, I sometimes feel that one might as well eat soya on gastronomic grounds as well. Warnings about excessive protein intake and concern about saturated fats in particular have added to the incentive to turn against native cookery and seek culinary inspiration elsewhere.

Neither the altered quality of ingredients nor modern nutritional ideas, however, are really as threatening as they might appear: as with restaurant food, they merely call for the exercise of skill and imagination, plus a little time in which to collect and adapt our ideas. While we (the public) have been experimenting with pasta, coriander, ginger and chillies, and lemon-grass, a new generation of committed, imaginative, and liberal-minded chefs has been at work on the home front and evolved a school of modern British cookery which holds a promise unique in our history. Not only are these chefs now producing dishes which can stand comparison with any in the world, but they have elevated cooking to the same status as other creative arts or sciences such as architecture or fashion design. An outward sign of the change is the open-plan restaurant where, instead of kitchens hidden from view in the basement on the Victorian pattern, they are visible from the dining-room so that customers can watch the drama of their meal being prepared. More importantly, the chefs' response to economic pressures has been to free top-class cooking from its former association with top-bracket incomes and offer it at moderate, democratic prices. You may not be cosseted in the old style at their establishments: you go there specifically to sample excellent food. If this leads more of us to enjoy it more often and in turn to produce it in our own homes, there is every reason for standards in British gastronomy and British cooking to soar in the future.

INGREDIENTS

As I have commented on particular ingredients where necessary in my introductions to the recipes, I have only a few general points to make here. The first is simply the importance of quality. I suppose that almost every cook of every nationality says the same, but in British cooking it is crucial, for the reasons I have tried to make clear in the introduction. The chefs who have contributed recipes to this book are rigorous, and sometimes almost fanatical, about freshness and quality and tend to plan their menus according to the best produce they can find. With vegetables and fish, I particularly recommend this approach, which is why I have included quick, simple recipes which do not require pre-planning.

While on the subject of quality, I should perhaps explain that my choice of dishes has been narrower than corresponds to modern British cookery in general because I wanted to highlight certain British ingredients which are excellent but seem to me undervalued, such as hard cheeses other than Cheddar, smoked haddock and smokies, and grey (as opposed to red) mullet. I have also included several recipes for venison, of which we make far less use than we might, partly because of current prices (the supply, however, is there: if demand rose, prices might fall).

Similarly in the interests of quality, all the relevant ingredients in the recipes, except frozen peas, are fresh or unground: this includes herbs and salt as well as meat, vegetables, and spices. Cut herbs are expensive: much more sensible than buying them is to grow your own either in the garden or on the window-sill. Bay and rosemary really need a garden, but both can be grown in a large pot: fortunately, dried bay-leaves are one of only two kinds of herb which in my view are worth using dried (the other is oregano). Basil will be killed by frost but is an annual which will probably die in the winter anyway; chives, marjoram, mint, parsley, rocket, sage, and thyme are hardy perennials.

Spices lose their flavour very quickly after grinding: I have therefore suggested crushing or grinding them yourself just before use. This is impossible with a few, notably mace, which features in a number of old recipes and I have given in one or two. Here and there, I have also used hot chilli powder and ground ginger, both of which have a completely different effect from the fresh vegetable. Elsewhere, I have followed the Indian practice of using spices whole, partly to save time but also because they add an agreeable, nutty texture to the dish. Unless otherwise stated, I have taken freshly ground black pepper for granted; salt measurements are based on roughly crushed or flaked sea-salt rather than finely powdered table-salt. I especially recommend Malden sea-salt flakes, which can be crushed with the back of a spoon or left whole and have a soft, almost herb-like taste.

All the recipes were devised and tested with free-range or at any rate outdoor-reared meat, including gammon and bacon (free-range bacon is stocked by at least two major supermarket chains). The eggs I used were also free-range; unhappily, however, this does not guarantee freedom from salmonella. As the fresher they are, the less time there is for bacteria to multiply, choose the freshest possible: this applies with particular force where they are used raw. Everyone harbours some salmonella bacteria in their intestinal tract: for most people, taking in a few more will have no effect, but dishes containing raw egg, or egg which has not been sufficiently heated to kill the bacteria, should be avoided by small children or anyone else who may be vulnerable.

With one exception, as little fat or oil as is consistent with easy cooking and optimum results has been used throughout. Traditionally, because cheap, pleasant-tasting oils were not available, the British cooked with animal-fats, including clarified butter: usually, I have compromised by adding a little butter to olive oil. Unsalted or only lightly salted butter and ordinary, relatively cheap, olive oil should be used. The more expensive virgin or extra-virgin olive oils have a much stronger flavour which would sometimes interfere with the taste of the dish: where they, or another kind of oil (e.g. groundnut) are needed, they have been specified. I have also assumed that you will use unsalted butter elsewhere, notably for pastry.

Finally, I feel obliged to say something about stock, a subject on which chefs and cookery writers are at odds with everyone else. Nobody who works has time to make it during the week, but for soups in particular there really is no substitute. Stock cubes to my mind are only one step up from gravy-browning (although I have used them in one recipe). I cannot understand why supermarkets who offer fresh washed vegetables and ready-prepared meals do not fill the gap by selling at least fresh chicken and vegetable stock. Here, I have treated stock as an integral part of the recipe and given directions for it as needed; I have only used it where it is essential and suggest that you simmer it at the weekend. You can keep it for two to three days in the refrigerator and then for another two if you re-boil it for ten minutes. Chicken stock can also be frozen, either as it is or reduced until it is very concentrated, when you can store it in the compartments of an ice-tray: this is useful when you need only a little, as for braised celery or other vegetables.

COOKING EQUIPMENT

Here again, the operative word is quality; this is partly offset, however, by the fact that only a few serious items are needed. Apart from the basic essentials of oven and refrigerator, my entire equipment consists of a blender with mincing and mixing attachments, scales, sugar- and oven-thermometers, five saucepans of varying sizes, a large non-stick wok, a frying-pan, rolling-pins (pastry and pasta), pastry brush, sieve and colander, a rotary egg-whisk, pestle, mortar, pepper-mill, knives, including an oyster-knife, kitchen-scissors, a perforated spoon, skewers, string and gardeners' twine, plus baking trays and sheets, casseroles, pie- and soufflé-dishes, patty-tins, and assorted basins, bowls, a measuring jug and various spoons.

The saucepans are stainless steel, with lids and U-shaped stainless-steel handles which do not conduct heat. The lids are an extra expense but indispensable for simmering rice, stock, and soups. I have also come to find a wok indispensable, partly because of its large capacity and lightness, but also because the bowl-shaped bottom means that items which cook too quickly can be pushed up the side; this too has a lid.

I have no pastry-board, but use a 75 by 75-cm/ 30 by 30-inch piece of melamine-coated shelving, the surface of which is easy to clean, conveniently non-stick, and apparently impervious to knives. Anyone buying a board is now recommended to choose plastic rather than wood for reasons of hygiene. (I am a little sceptical about this, however, since I am told that wood has lately been found to have natural anti-bacterial properties.)

A pestle and mortar is essential not only for crushing spices but also herbs: pounding extracts the flavour far more effectively than the cutting action of a machine. A pepper-mill is also virtually essential, but I long ago abandoned salt-mills because of the irritation of round tops rolling on to the floor and being lost. If you use Malden flakes, you do not need a mill.

Good knives, like saucepans, are an investment worth making: you need a heavy, largish knife for chopping meat, a smaller, thin-bladed one for boning, and a very sharp, thin-bladed one for filleting fish, plus a small vegetable-knife; if you plan to serve oysters, you must also buy an oyster-knife, which has a spike-like blade to insert between the shells. A sharp pair of kitchen-scissors saves much time: in particular, I recommend them for dicing bacon. The gardeners' twine is one of the most useful products that I have ever come across: I use it for hanging jelly-bags and tying half-empty packets, of which I always have far too many to put the contents into jars (items which are to be cooked or will become hot, however, must be secured with string, since the plastic coating on the twine may melt).

Ovens present a problem to any cookery writer because of their diversity. I have made allowances for the difference between fan- and non-fan-operated, and also for integrated and separate grills; in addition, however, is the fact that very few ovens are completely accurate (mine is not: hence my oven-thermometer). To some extent, therefore, you must use your own judgement: cook something for a little less time or longer than is given in the recipe if necessary. Roasts or pastry which brown too quickly can be covered with cooking foil; cover loosely, however, so that air can circulate underneath. As hot air rises, a non-fan-operated oven will be hotter at the top than the bottom; a tray placed across it may impede the passage of heat. Opening the oven door lowers temperature: except when this really matters (as, for instance, with soufflés), turn items round from time to time to ensure even cooking.

BASIC TECHNIQUES AND RECIPES

Just as ingredients really matter in British cookery, so does attention to detail. The precise balance of seasoning is vital to soups; just a single tablespoonful of cream can have an almost magical effect on a sauce; a dish can be transformed by the way in which vegetables are cut.

Partly because of my concern for detail, the directions given in the recipes are more precise and inclusive and hence look rather longer than usual. Many readers will not need all my instructions and to them I apologize; however, I am anxious to ensure that those with less culinary experience will be able to produce the dishes successfully. To avoid the need for cross-referencing, I have explained every technique with the recipes except for those which follow; sauces and other additions have also been given where they apply rather than collected into a separate chapter.

The first part of this section consists of a few basic techniques, most of which occur too often to be repeated elsewhere every time; in the second, I have given basic recipes for pastry, cooking rice, and polenta, all of which are called for in the book but which I hope will also be independently useful.

Skinning tomatoes

Immerse the tomatoes for 20-30 seconds in boiling water; you will then be able to peel off the skin easily.

Skinning red peppers

If you have a gas hob, you can char the skin of a pepper over the flame; otherwise, you can use the grill or oven. For salads, a gas flame or grill is preferable to the oven because the pepper will not be cooked through; after baking, it will be soft and difficult to slice. To char on a hob, place the pepper (whole) in the middle of the smallest ring and turn the heat to medium. Leave until the part in contact with the flame is black and blistered. Turn off the ring. It is important to avoid piercing the pepper or it will dry out: turn it with tongs or your hand (use an oven glove). Re-light the ring and char another section. Repeat until the whole pepper is black. Allow to cool for a moment or two, seal in a food-bag, and leave for 10-15 minutes. The skin will peel off easily but in pieces: wipe off remnants with damp kitchen paper. If the flesh underneath the skin is also slightly charred, it is an advantage rather than otherwise, since it will add flavour to the dish.

To grill, paint the pepper with oil and grill 5-6 minutes or until the top is black or deep brown; turn with tongs or an oven glove and seal in a bag as before.

To bake, set the oven to 225 C, 425 F, Gas Mark 7, and cook for 20-30 minutes; continue as above.

Separating eggs

At the risk of being thought over-cautious, I suggest washing eggs before separating them in case pieces of shell fall into the whites. Set ready two bowls: crack the egg sharply in the middle on the edge of one, pull it apart, holding it over the bowl, and tip the yolk from half of the shell to the other until all the white has fallen out. Turn the yolk into the second bowl.

It is always advisable to wash your hands after handling raw produce but especially necessary in the case of poultry and eggs. Knives, bowls, and other utensils used for preparing them should also be washed up promptly.

Opening oysters

It is obviously possible, and no doubt becomes easy with practice, to open oysters with a penknife; however, as far as I am concerned an oyster-knife is essential. The knives either have short, strong blades or clippers and a spike with which to open the shells: some people clip the shells sufficiently far back to make an opening, but I find it simpler to insert the spike between them at the side. Once inserted, twist the knife and prize the shells apart.

Preparing and boiling vegetables

Vegetables have infinitely more flavour if boiled in only just enough water to cover; in addition, this has the advantage of preserving more of their vitamins. They will also retain more of their vitamins if not cut until directly before use (from this point of view, vegetables bought ready-trimmed or shredded are a bad bargain).

Simmering

To simmer is to cook in liquid which is not quite boiling: the top should be only just moving, or if it is a fast simmer, throwing up the occasional bubble. It takes a little care to adjust the heat accurately, particularly if items are to be simmered covered, which raises the heat inside the pan; however, it means setting your ring nearly at its lowest. Some ovens have specially adapted simmering-rings: these are especially useful with a gas hob, since a very low flame is often blown out (e.g. by the draught from another ring).

Poaching is cooking at a slightly lower heat still but can be counted as a very slow simmer.

Baking rusks

Rusks are in effect toast: the bread is baked in the oven until brown, dry, and very crisp. They are excellent served with patés or soups; if cut smaller and cooked with a little fat, they become croûtons.

Slice the bread to medium thickness, trim the crusts, and cut into fingers or (for croûtons) small squares; bake at 200 C, 400 F, Gas Mark 6 for 8-10 minutes or until golden.

Making pastry

Many people find pastry a problem: shortcrust crumbles, becomes sticky, or breaks when they try to lift it, and puff refuses to rise. In fact, pastry is very easy to make provided that you remember two rules: to keep it cool and be lazy. Use very cold water to bind the dough and (except with puff pastry) fat straight out of the refrigerator. The dough should be made quickly, with little handling, and similarly rolled swiftly and lightly: this is not only because working it will warm it but because if the pastry is to be crisp, the gluten in the flour must not be stretched (the opposite applies to pasta, which is made by stretching and strengthening the gluten). For crisp pastry, it is also important not to add too much liquid: you need just enough to take up the flour and form a cohesive dough, but no more.

The flour must be ordinary household rather than strong bread flour (which contains more gluten); in general, it should also be plain rather than self-raising. For shortcrust pastry, you can use wholemeal or a proportion of wholemeal if you wish: entirely wholemeal flour tends to be crumbly but is easier to handle if you substitute olive oil for 1 tablespoonful of water. Particularly good flaky pastry can also be made with a proportion of wholemeal or malted brown flour.

The fat should be butter for sweet pastry and butter, or butter mixed with a little lard, for other types. In the interests of flavour, it is essential to use unsalted or only slightly salted butter. The addition of lard is traditional in this country and I think makes the pastry crisper and lighter.

Shortcrust Pastry

For this, the proportion of fat to flour is 1 to 2. Up to a third of the flour can be replaced by ground nuts or another grain, e.g. ground almonds or oatmeal: both of these produce pastry with a delicious, melting texture but make a crumbly dough which is relatively difficult to handle.

The quantities needed are given with the recipes: here, I have taken 175 g/ 6 oz flour because this amount is enough to line a standard 22-cm/ 8½-inch tart tin.

175 g/ 6 oz plain flour plus a little extra for dusting
Salt
25 g/ 1 oz lard straight out of the refrigerator
50 g/ 2 oz butter straight out of the refrigerator

Mix the flour with a small pinch of salt. Add the lard and butter (unchopped) and cut them into the flour with a knife until the pieces are too small to be visible; then rub with your fingertips until the mixture is like fine breadcrumbs. The reason for this method of mixing is that the narrow blade of a knife and your fingers will work the flour less than a spoon. Make a well in the centre and add 1½ tablespoonsful of iced or very cold water: draw the dough together with your hands and if necessary add more water by degrees until it coheres and all the flour is taken up. Wrap in foodwrap and chill for 20-30 minutes.

To roll out the dough, lightly flour the rolling-pin and board and roll it with short, brisk strokes to a thickness of 3-4 mm/ about ⅛ inch.

Lift and place it loosely over the tart tin. If it sticks to the board, gather it up and roll it out for a second time, sprinkling the board and pin with just a little more flour; if the same thing happens again, chill it for at least 30 minutes. Gently ease it into the tin, pressing it loosely but firmly round the edges. Trim, patch any breaks or cracks with pieces of the trimmings, moistening both the surfaces to be stuck, and prick the bottom.

For tarts with a moist filling, the pastry is usually blind-baked, i.e. partly cooked, before the filling is added to prevent it from becoming soggy. To blind-bake, set the oven to 200 C, 400 F, Gas Mark 6 and completely cover the pastry and rim of the tin with cooking foil. As the empty pastry-case will rise as it cooks, it is desirable, although not absolutely essential, to weight it down. If you have china baking-beans (designed for the purpose), scatter them over the cooking foil; alternatively, use rice or pulses. Bake for 10 minutes; remove the weight and foil and bake for a further 5 minutes or until the pastry is very slightly coloured.

SWEET PASTRY

Sweet pastry is similar to shortcrust but contains egg yolks and sugar.

4 size 2 eggs (yolks only)
250 g/ 8 oz plain white flour
Salt
125 g/ 4 oz butter straight from the refrigerator
125 g/ 4 oz caster sugar

Separate the eggs (see page 17). Mix the flour with a small pinch of salt and make a well in the middle. Chop the butter into very small pieces, place in the well, and work until slightly softened with your fingertips. Add the yolks and sugar, cover the well with flour, and stir gently with a spoon until the eggs are absorbed. Work with your hands to a smooth dough, then work gently for a minute or two longer, until plastic and shiny (this is important, since if you do not, the dough will be too crumbly to roll). Wrap in foodwrap and chill for at least an hour. Continue as for short pastry.

FLAKY PASTRY

This is half-way to puff pastry: it is less rich and quicker to make. The proportion of fat to flour is 3 to 4. A pie must be full enough to hold up the pastry. Traditionally, an egg-cup was put into the middle to support it: this should not be necessary, but if the dish is too big for the filling, a small ramekin or other ovenproof bowl or dish can be put in the centre and the filling piled round it.

175g/ 6 oz plain flour
Salt
40 g/ 1½ oz lard straight from the refrigerator
75 g/ 3 oz butter straight from the refrigerator
1 egg or a little milk for glazing

Blend the flour and salt. Cut in the lard and 40 g/ 1½ oz of the butter as for shortcrust pastry; then rub with your fingertips until the mixture is like fine breadcrumbs. Make a well in the middle, add 1½ tablespoonsful of very cold water, and draw together to form a dough, gradually adding more water if necessary until all the flour is taken up. Wrap in foodwrap and chill for 20 minutes.

Chop the rest of the butter into very small pieces. Lightly flour the rolling-pin and board and roll out the dough to an oblong. Sprinkle very lightly with flour, distribute 20 g/ ¾ oz of the chopped butter evenly over half of it, and fold into two. Seal the edges and re-roll: use short, brisk strokes and be careful to avoid dragging or stretching. Repeat. Roll out and fold (without butter or additional flour) twice more; chill for another 20 minutes.

Set the oven to 225 C, 425 F, Gas Mark 7. Add a pinch of salt to the egg if you are using it and beat smooth. Roll out the pastry fairly thickly, fold in half, and re-roll to 4-5 mm/ less than ¼ inch thick. Cut strips of dough to cover the rim of the pie-dish; wet both sides and place over the rim. Turn the pastry over and cover the pie loosely; trim underneath the rim to allow for possible shrinking, stamp the edges with a fork, and make an air-hole in the middle. Brush with egg or milk and bake for 20-25 minutes, until golden.

PUFF PASTRY

Pastry rises because hot air becomes trapped either underneath it, as with shortcrust tart-cases, or between the layers, as with puff and to a lesser extent flaky pastry. For puff pastry to rise successfully, the layers must be kept separate: the only way to achieve this is to keep the dough and the butter it contains very cold throughout rolling. This means returning it to the refrigerator after every couple of so-called 'turns', which is time-consuming but less so if you make it while you are cooking other items.

For this pastry, the proportion of fat to flour is equal.

Allow 3-4 hours for the butter to soften before you start.

225 g/ 8 oz plain white flour plus a little extra for dusting
Salt
50 g/ 2 oz lard
½ lemon
175 g/ 6 oz butter
1 egg for glazing

Take the butter out of the refrigerator and do not start until it is as soft as firm dough. If the kitchen is cold, soften it with a pestle and mortar. It is completely necessary that it should not be harder than the dough when you have made it or it will break through it when covered and make it impossible to roll. Blend the flour and salt; cut the lard into it as for shortcrust pastry. Rub with your fingertips until it is like fine breadcrumbs. Make a well in the middle and squeeze in a few drops of lemon juice. Add 4 tablespoonsful of very cold water and draw the dough together gently with your hands. Gradually add 2-2 ¼ more tablespoonsful water until it coheres and has taken up the flour. Lightly flour the rolling-pin and board and roll it out to a rectangle large enough to enclose the butter (unchopped) with a wide margin when folded. Place the butter on one half of it, fold, and seal the edges. Lightly sprinkle with flour, cover loosely with foodwrap or a piece of kitchen paper, and leave to rest for 15-20 minutes.

Roll out to about double its size; flour it very lightly, fold in half, and re-roll. Wrap in foodwrap and chill for 30 minutes. Roll out slightly thinner than before, dust lightly with flour, fold in half, and repeat. Chill again. Repeat the rolling and chilling twice. Then roll out to 5 mm/ less than ¼ inch and continue as for flaky pastry; glaze with the egg.

Cooking rice

I have included this because, although everyone knows how to cook rice, not everyone cooks it this way, which is both the kindest to the rice and the easiest. The rice is washed, simmered in just as much water as it will absorb, and then left to rest for 10-15 minutes; during this time, any surplus liquid evaporates in its heat. It comes out perfectly separate-grained and, because of the relatively small amount of liquid used, with much more flavour than when boiled.

About twice the volume of water to the weight of rice in metric measurements is needed: for 425 g/ 15 oz, you need 900 ml/ 1½ pints; for 275 g/ 10 oz, 600 ml/ 1 pint; or for 225 g/ 8 oz, 500 ml/ 17 fl oz. As brown rice takes longer to cook than white, it may need more (although not much more, since it is also less absorbent): look at it after it has simmered for 20 minutes and if the pan is dry, add just enough to moisten.

Rinse the rice under the cold tap until the water runs clear to remove surplus starch and put into a saucepan with a lid. Add the appropriate amount of water and, if you wish, a little salt (many people prefer it without). Bring to the boil, stir, cover, and simmer 18 minutes for white Basmati, 20 minutes for other types of white rice, or 30 for brown. Leave to rest in the pan, covered, for 10-15 minutes.

Cooking polenta

Polenta goes particularly well with a number of British dishes, notably game, and is extremely easy to make; however, if it is to be cooked sufficiently, you must ignore the instructions on some of the packets. There is a quick-cook kind which is claimed to take only 5 minutes: allow 20. The ordinary kind takes an hour.

You can use milk, skimmed milk, water, or a combination, with or without a little cream: for a creamy but fairly low-fat result, use a mixture of milk and skimmed milk.

Do not attempt to scrape off any porridge stuck to the bottom of the saucepan: leave the pan to soak. You can simmer the polenta up to 2 days in advance.

FOR 6-8

1 litre/ 1¾ pints milk and skimmed milk, mixed
175 g/ 6 oz polenta meal
½ teaspoonful salt
15 g/ ½ oz butter

Put the milk into a saucepan and bring almost to the boil; while it heats, transfer the polenta to a jug or other vessel from which it can be easily poured. When the milk is on the point of boiling, reduce the heat to a simmer. Add the salt and butter and dribble in the polenta in a slow stream, stirring continuously. Continue to stir for 3-5 minutes or until it has thickened. The quick-cook sort will probably be smooth, but the ordinary kind will form lumps, which should be pressed out with the back of a spoon; more will form, but the subsequent ones will disappear as the porridge cooks. Simmer for 20 minutes or an hour, depending on the kind, stirring at intervals. Lightly butter a tart dish or shallow baking dish, pour in the porridge, and leave to cool. If made in advance, cover and store in the refrigerator.

To serve, cut into slices and either grill under a moderate/hot grill until crisp and brown or bake at 225-230 C, 425-450 F, Gas Mark 7-8, for 25-30 minutes.

For polenta chips, make the porridge as above but pour it into a very large, shallow dish so that it forms a layer about 4 mm/ ⅛ inch thick; smooth the top if necessary. When cold, cut out circles with a small pastry-cutter; set a large plate lined with kitchen paper to hand by the hob, warm a little oil over high heat, and fry the chips until brown and crisp (1½-2½ minutes). Set on the plate to drain off surplus fat; serve promptly.

PATÉS AND
SOUPS

SMOKED COD AND PARSLEY PATÉ

Rather in the style of William Kitchener, a 19th-century food enthusiast and cookery writer who gave tasting-parties to test his recipes, I recently gave a dinner party at which I served three smoked fish patés, salmon, mackerel, and cod: once they had tasted this cod paté, nobody bothered with the others. It is an outstanding example of the difference between crushed or pounded and blended ingredients: if the flavourings are blended, the paté tastes mildly pleasant and is white with green flecks, but when they are crushed it is sharp, refreshing, and green. Crushing is really not very hard work: even when I am feeling lazy, it takes me only five or six minutes. Once the parsley, garlic, and chilli are pulverized, everything can go into the blender.

Cod dyed yellow from a supermarket will probably be saltier than the fresher, undyed version from a fishmonger who smokes his own: you will have to adjust the amount of salt you use accordingly. You will similarly have to use your discretion over the chilli, since some have almost no heat at all whereas others are blistering. As a general rule, larger ones tend to be milder, but this by no means always applies: a safer guide is to bite a small piece (cautiously) before proceeding. If it is very hot, use half; if mild, use two.

Allow 12-18 minutes for cooking the cod.

Serve with strips of green pepper, which perfectly complement the sharp flavour, and hot, thin brown toast, crusty bread, or rusks.

FOR 4-6

400 g/ 14 oz smoked cod
Pepper
Small bunch parsley (enough for 2 tablespoonsful when chopped)
2 smallish/ medium cloves garlic
1 green chilli
50 g/ 2 oz shallot
1 small lemon
2 tablespoonsful oil
2 tablespoonsful double cream
Salt

Set the oven to 200 C, 400 F, Gas Mark 6. Skin the cod: pull firmly from the thickest corner and ease the skin from the flesh with a sharp knife. Wash, season moderately with pepper, and wrap in a parcel of cooking foil. Place on a baking tray and bake for 12-18 minutes, until the flesh is opaque all the way through and can be flaked with a fork.

Trim the ends of the parsley stems if bought; wash, dry, and chop roughly. Peel and slice the garlic. Wash and dry the chilli: trim the stalk end, remove the inner membrane and all the seeds, and dice. As the chemical which gives it heat, capsaicin, may cause your skin to smart, wash your hands after handling it; if you have sensitive skin, wear polythene gloves. Crush the parsley, garlic, and chilli to a paste in a mortar. Peel and finely chop the shallot; squeeze 2 tablespoonsful lemon-juice. Drain off the liquor which will have run from the fish, put all the ingredients, including just a pinch of salt, into the blender, and blend thoroughly. Taste, and add more seasoning if necessary.

ARBROATH SMOKIE PATÉ WITH SMOKED GARLIC AND WHISKY

Arbroath smokies are hot-smoked haddock and almost as different from the usual cold-smoked haddock as kippers from the original herring. The smoking process, which is carried out over oak logs, is a small-scale, cottage-type industry virtually unique (at the moment) to Arbroath, on the east coast of Scotland. Only haddock of a certain size (about 225 g/ 8 oz) are chosen for smokies: after cleaning, they are tied in pairs by the tail, lightly salted, left to dry, and smoked for 40-60 minutes (cold-smoking takes up to 24 hours). The finished product is brown-skinned with an autumnal golden sheen and tastes more of oak-smoke than salt. The traditional way to eat it is simply to grill it with a knob of butter for just long enough to heat it through; however, if you want to add a vegetable, accompany it with boiled Pink Fir Apple potatoes. You can also use it for chowder (see page 49) or the following, which is much subtler than the usual smoked fish paté and leaves a gentle aftertaste of smoke and whisky.

In the south, smokies can be bought from major food halls and a few good fishmongers; otherwise, you can order them direct from

Arbroath (they will keep for 7-10 days without refrigeration; mine were in perfect condition after a week wrapped in newspaper in the back of the car).

Smoked garlic, which could be called a peculiarly British equivalent to roast garlic, is now available at some supermarkets, but if you cannot obtain it, omit it: do not substitute fresh (raw) garlic.

The paté takes minutes to prepare but must be made within a few hours of serving, since it loses its flavour fairly quickly. Some smokies weigh slightly less than 225 g/ 8 oz: as the amount of liquid in the paté is calculated on the basis of 450 g/1 lb, it is important to use the full weight.

Serve with brown bread or rusks (see page 18).

FOR 4-5

40 g/ 1½ oz (½ small) onion
2 medium-sized (not large) cloves smoked garlic
450 g/ 1 lb (1 pair, or 3 if necessary) smokies
Pepper
2 teaspoonsful lemon juice
1 tablespoonful whisky
142 ml/ ¼ pint double cream

Peel and finely chop the onion; peel and slice the garlic. Pull the smokies apart down the middle and lay out flat, skin-side down. Lift off the backbones and pick the flesh from the skin with your fingers (you can use a fork if you prefer, but it is easier to detect bones with your fingers). Be very careful to remove all the small bones, which may not be pulverized in the blender. Add the flesh to the onion and garlic and season with a generous grinding of black pepper. Squeeze and add the lemon juice. Add the whisky and cream and blend. Chill until needed.

PORK AND PIG'S LIVER PATÉ WITH PISTACHIO NUTS AND GIN

This is the most popular version of pig's liver paté that I have ever made, no doubt because of the gin, which subtly mellows and unifies the flavours. The recipe is also easy on the cook: all the ingredients except the pistachio nuts are minced, so that only preliminary chopping is needed.

Apart from a little streaky bacon to moisten it, the pork and bacon used should be lean; if much fat is included, the paté will shrink slightly in the dish and run surplus juice as it cooks: this jellifies when chilled and does not affect the taste, but makes it look less attractive.

It can be made up to 2 days in advance; cooking-time is 1¾ hours.

The quantities below are enough for 8-10 but can be halved, in which case cook for 1¼ hours.

Serve with hot toast.

150 g/ 5 oz (1 medium) onion
4 cloves garlic
5-6 sprigs thyme (enough for 2 teaspoonsful leaves)
Small lemon (zest only)
200 g/ 7 oz unsmoked lean back bacon
40 g/ 1½ oz unsmoked streaky bacon
350 g/ 12 oz lean pork escalopes
225 g/ 8 oz pig's liver
½ teaspoonful allspice
¼ teaspoonful salt
Generous grinding pepper
1 teaspoonful juniper berries
25 g/ 1 oz pistachio nuts
lard for greasing

1.5-litre/ 2½-pint soufflé-dish or similar ovenproof dish about 16 cm/ 6¼ inches across

Peel and roughly chop the onion and garlic. Wash, shake dry, and pull the leaves from the thyme (pull downwards: pick off top leaves or those growing on short stems individually). Scrub and dry the lemon: finely grate half the zest. Trim the rind from the bacon and any fat from round the pork; wash and dry the pork and liver and chop all the meat into chunks small enough to go through your mincer. Add the allspice, salt, pepper, and juniper berries (whole) and mince. Roughly crush the pistachio nuts, add, and mix thoroughly.

Set the oven to 150 C, 300 F, Gas Mark 2 and very lightly grease the ovenproof dish with lard. Pack the mixture into the dish, smooth the top, cover closely with cooking foil or a lid, and bake for 1¾ hours. Serve at room temperature.

POTTED HAM WITH NUTMEG

This is particularly useful, not in the sense that it is a way of giving new interest to left-over ham (although it is) but because you can serve it on almost any occasion: in my house, it is eaten for lunch, as a first course, on picnics, and even for breakfast. It is loosely based on a recipe given by Isabella Beeton, who similarly recommended it as 'A nice addition to the breakfast or luncheon table' [*Household Management*, 1861 edition, page 381].

On the assumption that you will make it when you have a fairly large surplus of ham, I have given amounts for 8-10: use half quantities if you prefer. Cooking time for the full amount is 1 hour 15 minutes, for half 55 minutes.

Serve with hot toast.

50 g/ 2 oz (½ smallish) onion
450 g/ 1 lb lean cooked smoked ham
50 g/ 2 oz butter (which must be unsalted or only lightly salted)
½ a nutmeg
1 scant teaspoonful hot chilli powder
2 level teaspoonsful mace
2 teaspoonsful Dijon mustard
2 size 2 eggs

Soufflé-dish or other ovenproof dish about 16 cm/ 6¼ inches across and 8 cm/ 3 inches deep, or for half quantities 12 cm/ 5 inches across and 6 cm/ 2½ inches deep

Peel and roughly chop the onion; remove any fat from the ham and chop into chunks small enough to go through your mincer. Mince very finely, twice if necessary.

Set the oven to 150 C, 300 F, Gas Mark 2. About three quarters melt the butter in a small saucepan over low heat; leave until the rest has melted and add and thoroughly beat in all the other ingredients. Lightly butter the dish; pack the mixture into it, smooth the top, and cover with either a lid or cooking foil. Bake for 1 hour 15 minutes or 55 minutes according to quantity. Serve cold (but not chilled).

FERGUS HENDERSON'S HAIRY TATTIES

Fergus Henderson recently opened a restaurant (St John, near Smithfield, London) with an aim very similar to mine: to revive British cooking by offering modern versions of traditional dishes. As well as classics such as grilled ribs of beef, and ham with caper sauce, the menu includes (to my joy) Welsh rarebit and the following, which consists very simply of salt ling or cod, mashed potato, and milk, enriched with nothing but a very little butter. The name is derived from the nature of the cod or ling, which when cooked flakes into long, hair-like filaments: after very brief pounding, however, the hairs disintegrate to give a surprisingly light, smooth, delicate *brandade* (I can think of no other word to describe it).

Ling may be obtainable in Scotland (it is a North Atlantic fish related to cod), but in London can only be bought at Billingsgate fish market; salt cod, however, is stocked at some supermarkets. It should be soaked for 24 hours before use and the water changed 4-5 times.

At the restaurant, the tatties are served with a boiled egg, but a poached egg would be equally suitable; alternatively, accompany it with a salad of cherry tomatoes and bitter leaves (although I suspect that Fergus, who is a purist, will disapprove of this suggestion).

FOR 2

225 g/ 8 oz salt cod, soaked for 24 hours
225 g/ 8 oz (1 medium) floury potato (see page 109)
About 40 g/ 1½ oz butter
6 tablespoonsful milk

Rinse and skin the cod; ease off the skin with a knife. Cover with unsalted water, bring to the boil, skim, and cook uncovered at a fast simmer for 18-25 minutes, until soft (how long it takes will depend on its thickness). Drain thoroughly and mash with a fork, removing all the bones (this is difficult because they look almost exactly like the fish). If the potatoes are not yet mashed, return to the warm saucepan and cover to keep warm.

As soon as you have set the fish to cook, peel the potato, cut into even-sized chunks, just cover with slightly salted water, and boil for 15-20 minutes, until soft. Drain very thoroughly, add 25 g/1 oz of the butter, and mash.

Set the oven to 200 C, 400 F, Gas Mark 6. Taking a third or half at a time, pound the cod and potato in a mortar until smooth; provided that the fish is still warm, this is very easy. Stir in the milk (do not add any seasoning). Very lightly butter an ovenproof dish, turn the (now unhairy) tatties into it, dot the top with the rest of the butter, and heat for 5-7 minutes: the *brandade* should be served hot but the top should not be allowed to brown.

BEETROOT AND TOMATO SOUP WITH GIN

The inspiration for this recipe came from the combination of seeing a delivery of fresh, muddy beetroot, with its long, deep green leaves, being carried into my local organic foodshop and the fact that it was a particularly depressing raw, wet day.

The soup is smooth, thick, and rich-tasting: one of its heartening properties is its colour, which, as the ingredients suggest, is a dark, dramatic red. Gin is optional but accentuates the taste of the beetroot while removing any hint of mawkishness.

Although fresh chicken stock is obviously preferable, the positive flavour of the other ingredients means that stock cubes are perfectly satisfactory: the stock is needed only to give depth to the taste.

Preparation is fairly quick but the beetroot (which must be raw) may take a good hour to cook; however, as the flavour of the soup is improved by keeping, it can advantageously be made a day ahead.

Serve very hot (it cools quickly) with a generous spoonful of yoghurt in the centre of each portion.

FOR 4-6

450 g/ 1lb ripe tomatoes
450 g/ 1 lb raw beetroot
75 g/ 3 oz (1 medium) carrot
175 g/ 6 oz (1 largish or 1½ medium) onions
2 cloves garlic
2-cm/ ¾-inch piece cinnamon stick
5 cloves
6 black peppercorns
900 ml/ 1½ pints chicken stock
1½ tablespoonsful oil
¾ teaspoonful salt
1 fairly flat dessertspoonful soft brown sugar
1½ tablespoonsful tomato purée
1 tablespoonful red-wine vinegar
3 tablespoonsful gin (optional)
150 g/ 5 oz natural, thick whole-milk yoghurt

Skin and chop the tomatoes. Peel and chop the beetroot into (about) 1.5-cm/ ½-inch squares; peel and slice the carrot. Peel and finely chop the onions and garlic. Bruise the cinnamon and crush the cloves and peppercorns in a mortar. Dissolve stock cubes if necessary according to the instructions on the packet.

Warm the oil in a large wok or saucepan with a lid and fry the onion over low heat, turning often, for 7-10 minutes or until soft but not brown. Add the garlic and fry for 3-4 minutes. Add the prepared spices and turn to coat in the oil. Add the tomatoes, season with the salt, and simmer for 7-10 minutes, pressing the flesh against the bottom of the pan until dissolved. Stir in the sugar, tomato purée, and vinegar; add the stock, carrot, and beetroot, and simmer for 1 hour or until the beetroot is tender. Blend until very smooth and stir in the gin. If you are making the soup in advance, allow to cool, cover, and store in the refrigerator. When needed, set over low heat and bring to just above simmering point, stirring gently from time to time. Simmer, covered, for 15-20 minutes. Serve before adding the yoghurt.

MUSHROOM SOUP WITH SAGE

The point of this soup is that it really tastes of the mushrooms: to make the most of the flavour, I have added the minimum of thickening necessary to take up the cooking oil (of which in turn as little as possible has been used). After liquidizing, the soup is nutty-textured and dark grey. The colour is lightened by cream, but you may like to relieve it with a little finely-chopped parsley strewn over each portion.

Ideally, use wild mushrooms, but otherwise choose very large ones, which usually have more flavour than smaller ones or buttons.

The soup can be prepared up to 24 hours in advance.

FOR 4

750 g/ 1½ lb large mushrooms
4 largish or 5 small cloves garlic
About 12 leaves of fresh sage (enough for 1 tablespoonful when chopped)
1 tablespoonful oil
25 g/ 1 oz butter
1½ teaspoonsful salt
Pepper
150 ml/ ¼ pint medium-dry or dry rosé wine
25 g/ 1 oz (1 slice) brown bread without crust
675 ml/ 1⅛ pints milk
Handful parsley
2 level teaspoonsful Dijon mustard
142 ml/ ¼ pint double cream

Trim the mushroom stalks fairly close to the gills; peel, wash, and dry the mushrooms and chop finely. Peel and finely chop the garlic. Wash the sage and blot or shake dry; chop fairly finely.

Warm the oil and butter over medium heat in a large saucepan or deep frying-pan; add the garlic and allow to fry until just showing signs of changing colour. Reduce the heat to very low; add the mushrooms, sage, salt, and a generous seasoning of pepper, and turn until the pan is dry. Continue to cook, turning frequently at the beginning, for 20-25 minutes or until the mushrooms have run quite a lot of juice. Raise the heat to medium, pour in the wine, and cook until the pan is again almost dry. Add the bread and 600 ml/ 1 pint milk; simmer 10-15 minutes. Allow to cool a little and liquidize until nubbly rather than completely smooth. If you are making the soup ahead of time, leave to cool and store in the refrigerator.

Unless the parsley is home-grown, trim the ends of the stems; wash, blot dry, and chop finely. Add 75 ml/ ⅛ pint more milk to the soup and bring slowly to the boil; stir constantly. Add the mustard and keep at a bare simmer 3-5 minutes, still stirring frequently; stir in the cream and thin with a little more milk if you wish. Taste, adjust the seasoning if necessary, and serve. Sprinkle the parsley over the individual portions.

BROAD BEAN SOUP WITH CHIVES AND MUSTARD SEED

Although a thick soup, this is light, summery, and in several senses undemanding, since the taste is gentle rather than bold and it is both economic and fairly quick to make: I reckon that you can have it on the table (hot) in 45 minutes flat. It can be served hot, warm, or chilled: considerations of weather aside, I prefer it hot, but only by a small margin.

Do not buy beans with black spots on the pods, as the beans inside will also be diseased. Suitable varieties of potato include King Edward and Marfona; others are listed on page 109.

The soup can be made a day ahead; simmering-time is 15-20 minutes.

Serve with warm, crusty rolls.

FOR 4

400-450 g/ 14 oz-1 lb broad beans (enough for 200 g/ 7 oz when
podded)
Salt
225 g/ 8 oz (2 smallish) onions
2 large or 3 small cloves garlic
200 g/ 7 oz (1 average) floury potato
Bunch chives (enough for 2½ tablespoonsful when chopped)
1 tablespoonful oil
15 g/ ½ oz butter
1 teaspoonful yellow mustard seeds
Pepper
150 ml/ ¼ pint milk or a little more
75 ml/ ⅛ pint double cream or a little more for serving cold

Pod and wash the beans, bring to the boil in 750 ml/ 1¼ pints slightly salted water, and boil 6-8 minutes or until tender. Drain and reserve the cooking liquor.

Peel and chop the onions and garlic fairly finely. Peel the potato and cut into smallish cubes. If you are making the soup in advance or wish to serve it chilled, wash, blot dry, and chop 1 tablespoonful of the chives; otherwise, prepare them all, chopping the remaining 1½ tablespoonsful into 5-mm/ ¼-inch lengths.

Put the oil and butter into a largish wok or saucepan with a lid and warm over low heat. Add the onion and fry very gently for 5-6 minutes, turning often. Add the garlic and fry 2-3 minutes more or until the onion is soft but not brown; turn constantly. Add the mustard seeds (whole), 1 teaspoonful of salt, a generous grinding of pepper, and the first tablespoonful of the chives; turn for about ¾ of a minute. Add the potato and stir to coat in the flavourings and oil. Pour in the bean liquor, bring to the boil, and simmer, covered, 15-20 minutes, until the potato is soft. Add the beans; liquidize until very smooth. Return the soup to the pan and bring just to the boil; add the milk and simmer for 2-3 minutes. To serve hot, stir in the cream, thin with a little more milk if necessary, and adjust the seasoning to taste. Sprinkle the remaining chives over the individual portions. For serving cold, chill; prepare the rest of the chives and stir in the cream, plus a couple of tablespoonsful extra if you wish, just before serving. Adjust the seasoning and sprinkle chives over the individual portions as before. If the soup is being made in advance, allow to cool after simmering with the milk and store (covered) in the refrigerator. When needed, prepare the chives; for serving hot, bring very gradually to the boil, stirring constantly, and simmer for 3-5 minutes (still stirring) before adding the cream; for serving cold, add cream to taste. Add seasoning and chives as above.

BAKED TOMATO SOUP

Everybody, myself included, complains about the tastelessness of British tomatoes. Lack of sun does not help, but the real problem is that flavour comes low on the growers' list of priorities: as with other types of produce in heavy demand, economic considerations such as yield and resistance to disease are put first. If this helps to keep down prices, one should perhaps not complain; however, the popularity of cherry tomatoes suggests that a larger equivalent which could be used for cooking as well as salads would find a market. In the meantime, unless you resort to canned tomatoes, which always seem to me to taste of the can, you can either bake the fresh ones, as here and on page 102, or use other ingredients to give them interest.

If the tomatoes are hard, unwrap any packaging and leave them at room temperature for a day or two: do not use them while unripe, since they will be tart and lack juice.

Baking time is 50-60 minutes.

FOR 4

900 g/ 2 lb ripe tomatoes
225 g/ 8 oz (2 smallish) onions
1 head garlic
Salt
Pepper
1 teaspoonful caster sugar
1 red pepper
1 tablespoonful virgin olive oil
100 ml/ 3 ½ fl oz double cream

Set the oven to 190 C, 375 F, Gas Mark 5. Peel and roughly chop the tomatoes (see page 16); remove the cores but reserve the juice. Peel and finely slice the onions; separate and peel (but there is no need to chop) the cloves of garlic. Put the onion, garlic, and tomatoes with their juice into a shallow baking tray, season with 1 teaspoonful of salt and a generous grinding of pepper, sprinkle with the sugar, and bake 50 minutes-1 hour, until soft and slightly charred. Put the pepper into the oven on a separate tray. Remove after 45 minutes, enclose in a sealed foodbag for 10-15 minutes, and peel. Halve over a bowl to catch the juice, discard the seeds (which are hot) and chop roughly. Transfer all the baked ingredients, including the juice from the pepper, to the blender and liquidize until very smooth.

Pour the soup, which at this stage will be very thick, into a saucepan. Add 300 ml/ ½ pint water and the oil, bring to the boil over low heat, stirring constantly, and simmer for 2-3 minutes, still stirring constantly. Stir in the cream. Taste, adjust the seasoning if necessary, and serve.

PEA AND ASPARAGUS SOUP

The Elizas Smith and Acton, who each gave a couple of recipes for pea soup without meat, used lettuces with either spinach or cucumbers as accompanying vegetables (one of Eliza Smith's recipes also called for marigolds). In my version, the sweetness of the peas is complemented by asparagus: obviously, the more flavour the asparagus has the better the soup will be, but it is not necessary to use the best British asparagus in season. It is, however, essential that the peas should be young: frozen ones are perfectly satisfactory.

Unlike the broth for Pea Soup with Smoked Ham and Mint (page 43), the stock takes only 30-40 minutes to simmer and does not involve much extra time, since you can prepare the other ingredients in the meanwhile. Apart from this, the soup takes about an hour to prepare and cook and is light on labour (in contrast to formerly, when any sort of smooth soup had to be pounded by hand and/or sieved). It can be prepared a day in advance, but in that case the asparagus tips should be boiled separately on the second day.

Serve hot, warm, or chilled, accompanied by freshly baked rusks (see page 18). For serving chilled, cream is definitely needed, but I think that the soup is as good, or almost as good without it when hot.

FOR 4-5 WITH CREAM, OR 4 WITHOUT

450 g/ 1 lb asparagus
Salt
450 g/ 1 lb unpodded peas or enough for 225 g/ 8 oz podded,
or 225 g/ 8 oz frozen
2 medium-sized leeks
1 large (outer) stick celery
225 g/ 8 oz (2 medium/ smallish) onions
75 g/ 3 oz (1 largish) carrot
2 bay leaves
1 sprig, or 10-12 leaves mint
½ tablespoonful oil
25 g/ 1 oz butter
½ teaspoonful caster sugar
Pepper
142 ml/ ¼ pint double cream (optional if the soup is to be served hot)

Wash the asparagus and cut off the tips. Put the stalks into a saucepan with 1.5 litres/ 2½ pints of slightly salted water, bring to the boil, cover, and simmer for 30-40 minutes. Strain, reserving the liquor; throw away the stalks. Unless you are making the soup in advance, cut thick tips across into 2 or 3 (thin ones can be left whole). Return the liquor to the pan, add the tips, and boil gently for 7-12 minutes or until just tender. Strain again; refresh the tips under the cold tap and set both tips and the liquor aside. If you do not plan to serve the soup until next day, store the uncut tips in the refrigerator.

While the stalks simmer, pod the peas if necessary. Trim the roots and leaves of the leeks; peel off the outer layer and slice fairly thinly. Wash and set on a plate lined with kitchen paper to dry (leeks should be washed after slicing to ensure that any mud or grit between the layers is removed). Trim the root-end and leaf from the celery; wash, dry, and dice. Peel and finely chop the onions; peel and dice the carrot. Wash the bay leaves. Wash and tear the mint leaves into pieces.

Warm the oil and butter over very low heat in a wok or large saucepan with a lid. Add the onion and celery and sweat for 5 minutes, turning often. Add the carrot, leeks, and bay leaves and continue to cook, turning constantly, for 7-10 minutes or until the onion is soft but not brown. Add the asparagus liquor, bring to the boil, and simmer, covered, 10-15 minutes or until the carrot is soft. Add the peas, mint, sugar, and 1 teaspoonful salt and continue to simmer for 2-3 minutes if the peas were frozen or 5-10, until soft, if fresh. Liquidize until completely smooth. If being made in advance for serving hot, allow to cool, cover, and store in the refrigerator; if made ahead of time for serving cold, simmer as below before allowing to cool and storing in the refrigerator.

Return the soup to the saucepan and bring to the boil over low heat, stirring constantly (as it is thick, it will spit if the heat is high). Add a generous sprinkling of pepper and simmer, covered, for 20-25 minutes. If made the day before, cut large tips across, just cover with slightly salted water, and boil briskly until tender; drain and refresh. For hot soup, add and simmer for another couple of minutes; for cold, allow to cool and add.

Soup to be eaten cold on the day it is made should be chilled for at least 3 hours. For serving either hot or cold, stir in the cream if you are using it just before serving; taste, and add a little more salt if necessary.

PEA SOUP WITH SMOKED HAM AND MINT

P ea soup is a long-established classic: Eliza Smith gave four recipes, one for dried peas and three for fresh, and Eliza Acton six. Miss Acton's remark about suitable fresh peas is worth repeating: 'the peas for these soups must not be *old*, as when they are so, their fine sweet flavour is entirely lost, and the dried ones would have almost as good an effect' [*Modern Cookery*, Longman, 1856 ed, page 40]. If fresh young ones are not available, use frozen.

The following is not much like any of the Elizas' versions, partly because an important element in the flavour is smoked ham and its cooking liquor, whereas, in those of their recipes which were not vegetarian, the Elizas used beef broth. The obvious time to make it is after simmering a ham (see page 45), when you have both the liquor and ham available, but stock can also be made specially (see below). With the stock below, I suggest simmering strips of raw gammon in the soup rather than adding ready-cooked ham at the end because it will add to the flavour; however, you can use cooked ham if you prefer.

Another important ingredient in my recipe is mint, of which there are many varieties: the kind usually sold for cooking, spearmint, or 'garden' mint, is perfectly satisfactory, but if you have the choice, apple or pineapple will give a much softer, subtler flavour.

The stock can be made up to 3 days and the soup up to 24 hours in advance. Allow 2 hours for simmering the stock and 20-30 for simmering the soup.

Serve with rusks (page 18) or warm, crusty brown rolls.

FOR 4

Stock
175 g/ 6 oz (1 largish) onion
175 g/ 6 oz (2 medium) carrots
225 g/ 8 oz smoked gammon, which can include rind
2 bay leaves
6 peppercorns
1 tablespoonful cider vinegar or red-wine vinegar

Soup
450 g/ 1 lb unpodded peas or enough for 225 g/ 8 oz podded,
or 225 g/ 8 oz frozen
100 g/ 3½ oz (1 largish) carrot
225 g/ 8 oz (2 smallish) onions
1 medium leek
2 good-sized stems, or about 24 leaves applemint or spearmint
100 g/ 3½ oz lean (cooked) smoked ham or (uncooked) smoked gammon
1 tablespoonful oil
15 g/ ½ oz butter
Pepper
Salt

Stock
Peel and roughly chop the onion and carrots; wash the gammon and bay leaves. Put into a largish saucepan with a lid and add the peppercorns, vinegar, and 1.5 litres/ 2½ pints water. Bring to the boil, cover, and simmer 2 hours. Strain, throwing away the vegetables and gammon (which by now will have lost all its flavour). If made ahead of time, allow to cool, cover, and store in the refrigerator.

Soup

Shell fresh peas; peel and fairly finely chop the carrot and onions. Trim the root and green leaves from the leek; peel off the outer layer, slice thinly, and wash. Wash and roughly tear the leaves from one stem of mint, or about 12 leaves (the rest is needed for serving). Trim any fat from the ham or gammon; dice cooked ham or cut uncooked gammon into strips 6 mm/ ¼ inch wide and about 2 cm/ ¾ inch long. Skim the fat from the surface of cold stock and add water if necessary to make up the quantity to 1.3 litres/ 2¼ pints.

Warm the oil and butter over very low heat in a large saucepan or wok with a lid. Add the onion and sweat for 5 minutes, turning often. Add the leek, carrot, and prepared mint and continue to cook over low heat for 7-10 minutes or until the onion is soft but not brown; turn constantly. Pour in the stock; add uncooked gammon. Bring to the boil, stir, cover, and simmer for 15-20 minutes or until the carrot is soft. Add the peas, return to the boil (frozen peas will considerably reduce the temperature of the liquor), and simmer frozen ones 2-3 minutes or fresh ones 5-10, until tender (the time fresh ones take to cook varies widely according to age and size). Add cooked ham and liquidize very thoroughly. If you are making the soup a day ahead, allow to become cold and store (covered) in the refrigerator.

Wash the remaining mint leaves and cut into strips. Set the soup over low heat: as it is thick, it will spit if heated quickly. Season fairly generously with pepper and bring to the boil, stirring constantly: taste before it becomes very hot and add a little salt if necessary. Simmer very gently, stirring frequently, for 5-7 minutes; add the strips of mint to the individual plates after serving.

SHAUN HILL'S NORTH SEA FISH SOUP

Shaun Hill, who is well known for his cooking at Gidleigh Park in Devon, has now started a restaurant on his own in Shropshire (Merchant House, Ludlow). A distinguishing mark of his cooking is his liking for clear, fresh flavours and his insistence on perfect ingredients. Of this soup he says: 'The fish are as important as the broth in which they are served. They must be well chosen, fresh and in top condition . . . The finished soup should taste fresh and natural.' The selection of fish given in the recipe is flexible: provided that it includes white fish and shell fish and at least as much variety, choose whichever is freshest, i.e. hardest, glossiest, and liveliest-eyed (if the eyes are sunk, the fish is stale).

The two essentials for the broth are not to overcook it and to be generous with its contents. I suggest that you ask the fishmonger to fillet the fish and to give you not only the heads, tails, and bones of the mullet and sole, but also the trimmings of a small haddock, or a plaice or whiting (the recipe calls for only a small piece of haddock) and a few extra prawn-shells as well. If this is impossible, Shaun suggests using chicken stock (page 52), which has more body than fish stock and will take on the taste of the fish in the soup.

Fish stock can be made in advance: (you can in fact keep it for up to two days, but in that case you will have to obtain the ingredients for it independently of the fish for the soup). The soup must be eaten directly, since if it is left the fish will continue to cook in the warm liquid and become tough.

The croûtons for the soup are fried in this recipe; if you prefer, you can bake them (see page 18).

As the egg yolk which is used for thickening is not heated until set, the egg must be very fresh.

Allow 20 minutes for poaching the stock and 5 minutes for simmering the soup.

FOR 4 AS A MAIN COURSE, OR 6 AS A FIRST COURSE

Stock

150 g/ 5 oz shallots
4-5 sprigs parsley
3-4 sprigs marjoram
2 bay leaves
65 g/ 2½ oz prawns in their shells
Heads, tails, and bones of a sole, red mullet, haddock or other white fish,
and extra prawn shells
25 g/ 1 oz butter, or a little more
8 peppercorns
300 ml/ ½ pint dry white wine

Soup

65 g/ 2½ oz shallots
About 125 g/ 4 oz (2) firm tomatoes
Small bunch parsley (enough for 2 tablespoonsful when chopped)
½ lemon
About 30 g/1¼ oz white bread (one slice from a large loaf),
weighed without crust
65 g/ 2½ oz prawns in their shells
150 g/ 5 oz (1) red mullet, skinned and filleted
450 g/ 1 lb (1) Dover sole, skinned and filleted
65 g/ 2½ oz haddock fillet
2 scallops
Salt
Pepper
1 litre/1¾ pints fish stock
1 large egg (yolk only)
1 tablespoonful double cream
About 25 g/1 oz butter

Stock

Peel and finely chop the shallots; wash the herbs. Peel the prawns: pull off the heads and tails and pick off the rest of the shells with your fingers. Set the prawns aside. Rinse the fish-trimmings. Melt the butter in a large wok or saucepan over low heat and sweat the shallots for 5-7 minutes or until soft, turning from time to time; add a little more butter if necessary. Add the trimmings and prawn-shells, herbs, peppercorns, and wine, with 900 ml/1½ pints water and bring to the boil. Skim, several times if necessary, lower the heat, and cook (uncovered) at just under a simmer for 20 minutes. Remove from the heat and strain. If made ahead of time, allow to cool, cover, and store in the refrigerator.

Soup

Peel and very finely chop the shallots and tomatoes (see page 16), discarding the tomato cores. Wash, dry, and finely chop the parsley. Squeeze 1 tablespoonful lemon juice; cut the bread into small squares for croûtons. Wash and chop all the fish (except the prawns) into 1-2-cm/½-inch squares; keep the haddock and scallops separate. Sprinkle a little of the lemon juice over the haddock; toss the sole and mullet in the rest. Season all the fish (again, except the prawns) fairly lightly with salt and pepper.

Bring the stock to the boil; while it heats, separate the egg. Beat the yolk smooth (the white is not needed) and stir into the cream. The fish should be added to the stock in order of cooking time, which in this selection means starting with the haddock and ending with the prawns and scallops. When the stock boils, reduce the heat to a bare simmer and add the haddock; cook 1 minute and add the sole and mullet. Cook until the flesh of both is just opaque; add the prawns and scallops, cook for a few seconds, and remove from the heat. Mix a tablespoonful of the hot broth with the egg yolk and cream; add and stir in.

Warm the butter over medium heat in a small frying-pan and fry the bread until golden. Add the parsley and tomato to the soup, taste, and adjust the seasoning. (Shaun is very emphatic about the importance of tasting, which, as he puts it, 'makes the difference between a bowlful of boiled milky fish and a delicate, elegant soup'. He also points out that to taste realistically, you need to try a soup spoon rather than a teaspoon, since this is how the soup will be eaten.) Scatter the croûtons over the soup and serve immediately.

SMOKIE CHOWDER WITH SMOKED SCALLOPS

As a lover of smoky flavours, I was really excited by this when I first made it and described it with a string of superlatives. It is ultrasmoky, not because of the combination of smokies and scallops but because the skins of the smokies, the part of the fish most exposed to the smoke and hence the most strongly imbued, are used for the stock.

Like Scottish lamb soup, it is sufficiently substantial to serve as a main course for lunch: accompany by crusty brown bread and follow with Old Scotland cheese, which is soft-tasting and mellow but robust enough to hold its own against the chowder.

Check the weight of the smokies when you buy them, since it varies considerably and the quantities below are calculated on 450 g/ 1 lb.

Cooking time is about 45 minutes, including simmering the stock.

FOR 4-5 AS A MAIN COURSE OR 5-6 AS A FIRST COURSE

450 g/ 1 lb (1 pair) Arbroath smokies
125 g/ 4 oz shallots
2 sticks celery (1 from the outside)
2 leeks
3-4 sprigs parsley
2 bay leaves
8 peppercorns
225 g/ 8 oz floury potato
½ tablespoonful oil
25 g/ 1 oz butter
20 g/ ¾ oz porridge oats
Pepper
4 smoked scallops
1 lemon
100 ml/ 3½ fl oz double cream

Wash the smokies, peel off the skin, and pick the flesh from the bones. Flake the flesh and set aside; put the skin and bones (including the tails) into a large saucepan. Peel and slice 25 g/ 1 oz of the shallots; wash and slice the outside stick of celery. Trim the leaves from one of the leeks, peel off the outer layer, slice, and wash. Trim the ends of bought parsley stems and wash the parsley and bay leaves. Add all the prepared ingredients to the smokie skins and bones with the peppercorns and 1.4 litre/ 2⅜ pints water. Bring to the boil, skim, and cook (uncovered) at a bare simmer for 20 minutes. Remove from the heat but leave in the pan.

Peel and very finely chop the rest of the shallots; trim the root and leaf-end of the remaining celery, wash, dry, and dice finely. Trim and peel the second leek; slice very finely and wash. Peel and quarter the potato; slice very thinly.

Warm the oil and butter over medium heat in a wok or large saucepan and fry the shallots for 2 minutes. Add the celery and fry 2-3 minutes more, or until the shallots are soft but not brown, turning constantly. Pour in the stock through a sieve; throw away the solid ingredients. Stir in the porridge oats. Add the leek, potato, and a generous seasoning of pepper and simmer, uncovered, for 15-20 minutes or until all the vegetables are soft.

Chop the scallops into 1-cm/ ⅓-inch squares. Add the smokie-flesh to the soup, stir, and simmer for about 1 minute. Squeeze 1 teaspoonful of lemon juice and add. Stir in the scallops and cream. Taste, add a little more pepper, lemon juice, or water if needed, and serve at once.

Puy Lentil and Mushroom Soup

For this, it is essential to use black Puy lentils, which have a sweetness and delicacy so like mushrooms that it almost seems unnecessary to add any; the lentils are also an obvious partner to chicken and fish. The soup is therefore a simple amalgam of sympathetic flavours; its only disadvantage (as with other mushroom soups) is its drab colour; to some extent, however, this is alleviated by cream.

Fresh lentils cook more quickly than those which have been kept for a long period: if fresh, cooking time is an hour. The soup can be made up to 24 hours in advance: either allow to cool and store in the refrigerator after blending or make entirely ahead of time.

FOR 4-6

275 g/ 10 oz medium-sized button mushrooms
225 g/ 8 oz (2 smallish) onions
4 cloves garlic
Small sprig rosemary (enough for 1 teaspoonful when chopped)
1 bay leaf
175 g/ 6 oz Puy lentils
125 g/ 4 oz unsmoked streaky bacon
2 tablespoonsful oil
Pepper
150 ml/ ¼ pint dry white wine
1.2 litres/ 2 pints chicken stock (see page 52)
½ lemon
Salt
3 tablespoonsful double cream

Trim the mushroom stalks close to the caps; wash, dry, and dice the mushrooms finely. Peel and finely chop the onion and garlic. Wash the rosemary, strip the leaves from the stems (drag downwards), and chop very finely. Wash a fresh bay leaf; rinse the lentils. Remove the rind from the bacon and dice finely.

Warm the oil in a large wok or saucepan with a lid over very low heat and sweat the onions and bacon for 5 minutes, turning occasionally.

Add the mushrooms and garlic, season with pepper (but no salt) and continue to cook, turning frequently, for 10 minutes or until the onion is soft but not brown. Add the wine and bring to the boil. Add the bay leaf, rosemary, lentils, and stock and return to the boil. Skim, boil briskly for 2 minutes, cover, and simmer for 35 minutes or until the lentils are soft. Thicken the soup by putting half of it through the blender and blending smooth, leaving the rest unblended to give textural interest. Return the blended soup to the pan. If made in advance, allow to cool, cover and store in the refrigerator.

Squeeze 2 teaspoonsful lemon juice. Add 1½ teaspoonsful of salt to the soup, bring just to the boil, and simmer 3-4 minutes. Add the lemon juice, stir in the cream, and taste: add more pepper and lemon juice if you wish. Serve immediately.

CHICKEN AND ALMOND SOUP WITH SHERRY

When I first made this I had at the back of my mind a soup which was fashionable in Victorian Britain, Soup à la Reine, a rich purée of pounded chicken and almonds with cream. My version retains the spirit of the original but contains relatively little cream; also, instead of being pulverized, the chicken is chopped into slivers and simmered very briefly at the last moment, as in Oriental cooking, which I think brings out the flavour far better.

It is a good idea to make the stock the previous day so that it can be chilled overnight and thoroughly skimmed of fat. Except for the final simmering, you can also make the soup in advance of the meal, but if you buy a whole chicken and use the carcass for stock and the breasts for the soup, it is preferable not to keep the breasts for more than a day. (Directions for cutting up a whole chicken are given below.)

Whether you use a whole bird or a cooked carcass plus ready-cut pieces, the chicken should be as fresh as possible.

Allow 3½-4 hours for simmering the stock and 25-30 minutes for simmering the soup, plus 15-20 minutes just before serving.

FOR 4-6

Stock

1 free-range chicken or 1 chicken carcass (preferably uncooked)
50 g/ 2 oz (½ small) onion
75 g/ 3 oz (1 largish) carrot
1 outside stick celery
6 peppercorns

Soup

125 g/ 4 oz (1 smallish) onion
3 cloves garlic
75 g/ 3 oz (1 largish) carrot
2 large sticks celery
75 g/ 3 oz smoked streaky bacon
1 tablespoonful oil
1.5 litres/ 2½ pints chicken stock
2 bay leaves
Salt
Pepper
100 g/ 3½ oz ground almonds
2 tablespoonsful medium-dry sherry (e.g. Amontillado)
225 g/ 8 oz chicken breasts
2 tablespoonsful double cream

To cut up a whole chicken, you will need a sharp, preferably thin-bladed knife. Thoroughly wash the chicken inside and out and place breast-side down on a chopping surface. Cut round the legs, twist the thigh-joint so that you can see where to cut, and sever the legs through the joints. Turn the chicken over and cut down each side of the breast-bone as far as the wings to release the breasts: cut as close to the bone as possible. Leave the wings on the carcass. If you wish, or if it seems easier, skin the breasts before cutting; otherwise, pull off the skin afterwards. Put the chicken pieces on a plate, cover with foodwrap, and place at once in the refrigerator. (The legs are not needed for this recipe: in fact, they have more flavour than the breasts but are difficult to cut tidily.)

Stock

Peel and finely chop the onion; peel and thinly slice the carrot. Cut the leaf-end from the celery, pare off any discoloured patches, and wash; slice finely. Put the carcass, the prepared vegetables, and the peppercorns into a large saucepan with a lid, add 1.75 litres/ 2¾ pints of water or enough to cover the breast-bone, and bring to the boil. Skim, cover, and simmer 3½ – 4 hours. Strain, allow to become cold, and leave (covered) in the refrigerator until next day. Thoroughly skim off the fat, which will have solidified.

Soup

Peel and thinly chop the onion and garlic; peel and thinly slice the carrot. Trim the leaf- and root-ends of the celery; remove any discoloured patches, wash, dry, and slice finely. Cut the rind from the bacon and dice. Warm the oil in a wok or deep frying-pan with a lid over low heat and sweat the onion, celery, and bacon for 5 minutes, turning often; add the carrot and garlic and sweat for another 5-7 minutes or until the onion is soft but not brown. Add 1.5 litres/ 2½ pints of the stock (which will be nearly all of it), bay leaves, 1 teaspoonful salt, a fairly generous seasoning of pepper, and the almonds, and bring just to the boil. Cover, simmer 25-30 minutes, remove the bay leaves and liquidize until very smooth. The soup can now be left until shortly before serving.

To serve, add the sherry, bring to the boil over low heat, stirring often, and simmer very gently, covered, for 15-20 minutes. Cut the chicken breasts into strips 6 mm/ ¼ inch wide and 2 cm/ ¾ inch long; season moderately with salt and pepper. Add, stir, return the soup to a moderate simmer, and cook for 3 minutes. Stir in the cream and serve.

SCOTTISH LAMB SOUP WITH PEARL BARLEY AND CLARET

Originally, this soup would have been made with the bone from boiled mutton and was probably served as a cheering prelude to a main course of the cold remains of the mutton. I suggest following it with Stilton and Walnut or Grilled Vegetable Salad or simply accompanied by crusty bread and a glass of good claret for lunch.

A knuckle (lower) half of a leg of lamb has more bone, which is needed for the stock, than an upper (fillet) half. Shoulder is cheaper but carries a higher proportion of fat; it is also relatively difficult to bone and the bone has to be chopped if it is to fit into a saucepan (the end of a knuckle half of leg is usually sold already broken). A butcher will prepare either a leg or shoulder for you, but directions for boning a knuckle end yourself are given below. Some of the meat is needed for the soup: the rest can be used for Lamb and Kidney Pie (page 166) or Lamb Sausages (page 168).

A vital point about the soup is that it must be left for 24 hours to allow the flavour to develop: if served as soon as it is made, it will be but the shadow of its future self. It is also desirable to make the stock in advance so that it can be thoroughly skimmed of fat (it can be kept for several days in the refrigerator). The stock takes 4-4½ hours and the soup 3 hours to simmer: if this sounds inconvenient, it is offset by the fact that relatively little work is needed and, since some of the lamb can be used for another dish, the soup is economic.

FOR 4

Stock
Bone of knuckle half of leg of lamb
125 g/ 4 oz (1 medium/ small) onion
75 g/ 3 oz (1 medium) carrot
2 or 3 sprigs parsley
2 bay leaves
4 or 5 sprigs thyme
6 peppercorns
Salt

Soup
225-275 g/ 8-10 oz lean lamb
Pepper
150 ml/ ¼ pint claret
50 g/ 2 oz pearl barley
2 medium leeks
1 largish stick celery
175 g/ 6 oz (2 medium) carrots
1 smallish turnip

Bone the lamb if necessary. Wash the leg in cold water and place it on a chopping board with the side carrying most of the meat uppermost. Using a sharp knife, cut 2 slices the thickness of steaks from the upper end. Detach the slices on a line with the bone, leaving the small amount of meat on the other side to flavour the stock. Remove the rest in one piece by cutting round the bone as closely as possible. Put the meat on a plate, cover, and place at once in the refrigerator.

Stock
Peel and slice the onion and carrot; wash the herbs. Put the bone, onion, carrot, herbs, peppercorns, 1 teaspoonful salt, and 1.7 litres/ 2¾ pints water into a large saucepan with a lid. Bring to the boil, reduce the heat, and skim thoroughly. Cover and simmer very gently for 4-4½ hours. Strain, throwing away the solid ingredients, cover with a plate, and allow to become cold. Chilling ensures that the fat solidifies firmly, which makes removing it easier, but the stock can be left at room temperature for up to 24 hours.

Soup
To prepare the soup, trim the meat rigorously of all visible fat, cut into (about) 1-cm/ ⅓-inch squares, and season fairly generously with salt and pepper. Skim the fat from the stock. Pour the claret into a large saucepan with a lid, set it over medium heat, and let it boil almost away. Add the stock and lamb and bring to the boil. Lower the heat and simmer, covered, for 30 minutes. Rinse the barley under the cold tap, add, and continue to simmer (covered) for 2 hours.

Cut the leaves and roots from the leeks; peel off the outer layer, slice finely, and wash. Trim the celery, pare off any discoloured patches, wash, and slice finely. Peel and finely slice the 2 carrots; peel the turnip and dice into 1-cm/ ⅓-inch squares. When the barley has cooked for 2 hours, add the prepared vegetables with 2 teaspoonsful salt (it is important that it should be sea-salt: see page 13) and simmer for another 20 minutes or until the vegetables are just tender. Cover and leave to stand at room temperature for 24 hours, or at least overnight. Before serving, pour in 300 ml/ ½ pint water (some of the liquid will have been absorbed by the barley) and bring to the boil, stirring often. Season with a generous grinding of pepper, simmer gently for 10 minutes, taste, and add a little more salt if necessary. Serve at once.

PHEASANT SOUP

This soup bears out the maxim: Never waste your carcass. It is clear and virtually fat-free, bulked out only by a little macaroni, but tastes rich, vinous, and gamey. Plan to serve it three or four days after the pheasant or pheasants: make the stock on the same day or the day after; the following day or the day after that make the soup; serve it on the next. Allow 3 hours for simmering the stock, 25 minutes for simmering the soup, and 30 minutes for cooking the macaroni (which sounds a long time for pasta but is because it is simmered rather than boiled).

Serve as a first course before a fairly plain dish such as steak.

FOR 4

Stock
75 g/ 3 oz (1 small) onion
50 g/ 2 oz (1 small) carrot
1 outside stick celery
3 or 4 sprigs thyme
3 or 4 sprigs parsley
2 bay leaves
75 g/ 3 oz unsmoked streaky bacon
1, or preferably 2, pheasant carcasses
20 g/ ¾ oz lard
4 cloves
6 peppercorns
1 scant teaspoonful fennel seeds

Soup

175 g/ 6 oz red onion
2 sticks celery (not outside)
125 g/ 4 oz chestnut, organically grown, or other button mushrooms
2 bay leaves
125 g/ 4 oz unsmoked lean back bacon
1 tablespoonful oil
Salt
Pepper
6 cloves
1 teaspoonful allspice
2 tablespoonsful red-wine vinegar
300 ml/ ½ pint claret
600 ml/ 1 pint pheasant stock
25 g/ 1 oz thick-cut macaroni
½ tablespoonful redcurrant jelly

Stock

Peel and dice the onion and carrot. Trim the leaves from the celery; wash, dry, and finely slice. Wash the herbs; dice the bacon (use scissors). Rinse the carcass(es) if necessary to remove any remains of stuffing or sauce. To reduce the amount of water needed to cover them, break into pieces.

Melt the lard over medium heat in a wok or largish saucepan with a lid and fry the bacon and vegetables for 7-8 minutes or until the onion is fairly brown; turn frequently. Add the cloves, peppercorns, and fennel seeds and turn; add the carcass(es) and 1 litre/ 1¾ pints water. Tie the parsley and thyme into a bunch with string, add with the bay leaves, and bring to the boil. Reduce the heat, cover, and simmer for about 3 hours. Strain and leave to cool; store (covered) in the refrigerator.

Soup

The next day, peel and finely chop the onion. Cut off the leaves and trim the root-end of the celery; remove any brownish streaks, wash, dry, and slice finely. Trim the mushroom stalks; wash, dry, and slice the mushrooms very finely. Rinse the bay leaves. Remove the rind from the bacon and dice.

Warm the oil in a wok or saucepan with a lid over medium heat and fry the onion and celery for 5 minutes, turning often. Add the bacon and turn; add the mushrooms, season generously with salt and pepper, and fry, turning constantly, for another 5 minutes or until the onions are deep brown. The mushrooms will absorb the fat so that the pan is dry but thereafter run juice; add more oil if necessary. Add the cloves and turn; add the allspice and turn. Add the vinegar, allow to boil, and pour in the claret and stock. Bring back to the boil, lower the heat, cover, and simmer gently for 25 minutes. Allow to cool, cover, and store in the refrigerator until the following day, by which time the flavour will have developed and mellowed considerably.

About 35 minutes before you wish to serve, skim off the fat which will have set over the surface of the soup like a skin, bring slowly to the boil, and stir in the redcurrant jelly. Taste, and if the flavour seems too strong add up to 150 ml/ ¼ pint water. Add the macaroni, stir, and simmer, uncovered, 25-30 minutes or until the macaroni is just tender. Serve immediately: if left to stand, the macaroni will swell and absorb the liquid.

EGG AND CHEESE
DISHES

EGGS ARNOLD BENNETT

I have included this recipe, named after the playwright Arnold Bennett, chiefly as a compliment to smoked haddock, which seems to me to be much underrated, perhaps because of its relative cheapness. A smallish fish, which has a finer texture than a large one, without added colouring, is a genuine delicacy which needs nothing except a little pepper and a gentle, creamy sauce to add moisture. Scrambled eggs form the ideal sauce: as such, you only need one per person. It is, however, essential that they should be very fresh, since they are not sufficiently cooked to kill bacteria; for this reason (sadly), I do not recommend this recipe for children.

Serve with potato cakes or hot toast.

FOR 2

175 g/ 6 oz smoked haddock
Pepper
150 ml/ ¼ pint milk
20 g/ ¾ oz butter
2 size 2 eggs
Salt
1 tablespoonful double cream

Skin the haddock if necessary: starting at the thickest corner, ease the skin from the flesh with a knife. Wash, check for bones, and season moderately with pepper. Put into a smallish saucepan with a lid and add the milk and a very little of the butter. Bring to the boil, reduce the heat to under a simmer, cover, and cook for 2-3 minutes. Turn gently and continue to cook for another 1-2 minutes, or until the fish is opaque all the way through and flakes with a fork but is still moist and juicy. Drain thoroughly; return to the warm saucepan and cover.

While the haddock cooks, lightly beat the eggs with a small pinch of salt and rather more pepper. Put half the remaining butter into a small, thick-bottomed frying-pan or saucepan and set over a low heat just until the butter has melted sufficiently to coat the bottom. Remove from the heat until the haddock is drained. When the fish is ready, pour the eggs into the buttered pan and stir over gentle heat

EGG AND CHEESE DISHES

until they start to set. Add the fish and continue to stir until all the egg is thick and there is no free liquid in the pan. Stir in the cream and remove from the heat. Serve at once.

LANCASHIRE CHEESE AND CHIVE SOUFFLÉ

Any number of flavourings can be used for soufflés, but cheese is always especially successful. In this one, the sharpness of the Lancashire sets off the taste of the chives; the Parmesan adds saltiness and a little extra edge.

As Parmesan quickly loses its flavour after grating, either grate it yourself or use ready-grated pecorino, which retains its sharpness rather better.

Soufflés are actually extremely easy to make: all you have to remember is that rising depends on whipping the egg whites to just the right point. It also helps to use a proper, straight-sided soufflé-dish which if possible should be slightly too small: to contain the risen soufflé, tie a collar of cooking foil round the top.

Alas, soufflés are at their best when still slightly molten and creamy in the middle; however, as this means that the eggs are not sufficiently cooked to kill bacteria, it is more prudent to bake them until they are completely set.

Cooking time is 25-30 minutes.

Serve as a first course or for lunch with a salad.

FOR 4-6 AS A FIRST COURSE OR 4 FOR LUNCH

1 large bunch or 2 packets chives
125 g/ 4 oz Lancashire cheese
25 g/ 1 oz Parmesan or pecorino
5 size 2 eggs
300 ml/ ½ pint milk minus 2 tablespoonful
15 g/ ½ oz butter
1 tablespoonful oil
25 g/ 1 oz flour
3 teaspoonful Dijon mustard

Pepper
Salt

16-cm/ 6¼-inch (1.5-litre/ 2½-pint) soufflé-dish

Trim the ends of the chives if bought; wash in cold water, blot dry with kitchen paper, and chop very finely. Finely grate the cheese or cheeses. Separate the eggs (see page 17), setting aside 2 of the yolks, which are not needed for this recipe: if possible, use them for custard, pastry-cream, or sweet pastry. Lightly butter the soufflé-dish: take a piece of cooking foil long enough to wrap all the way round it, fold it in half lengthways, and tie it round the top of the dish with string.

Heat but do not boil the milk. Melt the butter in the oil over low heat and add the flour; stir until it is completely amalgamated but take care not to let it brown. Pour in the milk by degrees, stirring continuously. Continue to stir until the sauce is thick. Add the mustard, a moderate dusting of pepper, and 1 teaspoonful of salt and simmer gently, still stirring continuously, for 3 minutes. Remove from the heat and allow to cool a little.

Set the oven to 200 C, 400 F, Gas Mark 6. Beat the egg yolks lightly with a fork and add: stir until thoroughly mixed. Add and stir in the cheeses and chives. Whip the egg whites until they are fine-textured, opaque, and stiff enough to hold their shape completely. They should not, however, be whipped to the stage at which liquid appears at the bottom of the bowl (I find it easier to judge when to stop with a hand whisk rather than electric whisk: if you use an electric one, watch carefully). Fold the whites into the sauce by degrees; to keep as much air in the mixture as possible, do not stir more than is necessary. Turn into the soufflé-dish and bake 25-30 minutes or until golden, well risen above the dish, and just firm: as with a cake, if the eggs are cooked until set, a skewer inserted in the middle will come out clean. Serve immediately.

BROWN-CAP MUSHROOM AND PORCINI SOUFFLÉ

This is a favourite non-cheese soufflé: it is distinctive but delicate and especially suitable as a light first course before a roast such as duck, chicken, or lamb.

Despite their names, porcini (or ceps) are no more Italian or French than British, since they grow wild in Wales, Scotland, and elsewhere: they are simply not marketed or dried in this country.

Allow 25-30 minutes for soaking the porcini and 30-35 minutes for baking.

FOR 6 AS A FIRST COURSE

5 g (1 small packet) porcini
175 g/ 6 oz brown-cap or other firm, closed mushrooms
50 g/ 2 oz shallots
4 cloves garlic
5 size 2 eggs
300 ml/ ½ pint milk
25 g/ 1 oz butter
1 tablespoonful oil
Salt
Pepper
75 ml/ 2½ fl oz dry white wine
25 g/ 1 oz flour
2 scant teaspoonsful Dijon mustard

16-cm/ 6¼-inch (1.5-litre/ 2½-pint) soufflé-dish

Soak the porcini in enough warm water to cover for 25-30 minutes. Dry and dice; keep the liquor. Trim the stalks of the fresh mushrooms fairly close to the caps; wash, dry, and dice very finely. Peel and very finely chop the shallots and garlic. Separate the eggs (see page 17), setting aside 2 of the yolks, which are not needed for this recipe (use if possible for pastry or ice-cream). Set the oven to 200 C, 400 F, Gas Mark 6; lightly butter the soufflé-dish and tie a collar of cooking foil round the top (see previous recipe).

Heat but take care not to boil the milk. Melt the butter in the oil over medium/low heat and fry the shallots and garlic, turning often, for about 2 minutes or until soft but not brown. Add the mushrooms and porcini, season with 1 teaspoonful salt and a generous sprinkling of pepper and fry until they have exuded and re-absorbed their juice. Pour in the wine and porcini liquor, raise the heat to high, and cook all the liquid away; do not proceed until the pan is quite dry. Lower the heat and stir in the flour (which will make it very dry). Add the milk by degrees, stirring continuously; stir until the sauce is thick and simmer 2-3 minutes, still stirring continuously. Add the mustard, stir again, and leave to cool. While the sauce cools, whip the egg whites, which should be stiff enough to stand in peaks when lifted on the whisk but not beaten to the point at which they start to run liquid. Beat and stir the egg yolks into the mushroom sauce; then fold in the whites very gently. Turn into the prepared dish and bake 30-35 minutes, until risen well above the top of the dish, browned, and firm: if the eggs are cooked until completely set, a skewer inserted into the middle will come out clean, as with a cake.

CHESHIRE CHEESE AND RED ONION TART

The sweetness of red onions was amply demonstrated the first time I made this, when I used too many and received the following (utterly deserved) protest: 'What on earth have you put into this? You won't like my saying so, but it tastes of Worcester Sauce.' In the present version, the onion is balanced by chives and the Cheshire cheese, which comes over as soft, smoky, and distinctive, especially if the tart is eaten warm or cold rather than hot. Obviously, the flavour is better if you use good farmhouse cheese.

Given its fairly positive character, I suggest serving the tart for lunch rather than as a first course, accompanied by green or tomato salad.

As tarts go, it is fairly quick: preparation, including frying the onions, takes about 35 minutes, and baking 30-35. Much depends on frying the onions to exactly the right point: they should be changing colour and just starting to become crisp but still sweet.

FOR 6-8

Shortcrust pastry (see page 19) made with:
175 g/ 6 oz plain white flour
Pinch salt
25 g/ 1 oz lard
50 g/ 2 oz butter

Bunch chives
185 g/ 6½ oz red onion
185 g/ 6½ oz shallots
4 cloves garlic
2 tablespoonsful oil
175 g/ 6 oz Cheshire cheese
1 teaspoonful hot chilli powder
2 size 2 free-range eggs
1 teaspoonful salt
Pepper
2 teaspoonsful Dijon mustard
142 ml/ ¼ pint double cream

22-cm/ 8½-inch tart tin

Heat the oven to 200 C, 400 F, Gas Mark 6. Roll out the pastry 3-4 mm/ ⅛ inch thick and line the tart tin. Cover all over with cooking foil, including the rim, taking care to press it closely to the pastry. Weigh down with baking beans if available and bake 10 minutes. Remove the foil and bake for another 5. Leave to cool.

Trim the cut ends of the chives if bought, wash, and leave to dry in a colander or on kitchen paper. Peel and finely slice the onions, shallots, and garlic; keep each separate.

Warm the oil over medium heat in a wok or frying-pan (for frying onions evenly, I recommend a wok, since any pieces which colour too quickly can be pushed up the sides). Add the red onion and fry 2-3 minutes, turning constantly; add the shallots and fry for another 2-3 minutes, still turning constantly. Add the garlic and fry 8-10 minutes or until the onion and shallot are reduced and starting to colour but not very brown; stir constantly, especially towards the end. Remove from the heat and continue to stir for a moment or two (cooking will continue as long as the oil is still hot). Leave to cool.

Re-heat the oven to 200 C, 400 F, Gas Mark 6. Finely grate the cheese and mix thoroughly with the chilli powder. Beat the eggs smooth with the salt and a generous grinding of pepper; stir in the mustard, add the cheese plus chilli powder, and mix to a rough, stiff paste. Finely chop the chives and stir in with the cream. Turn the onions and shallots into the cheese and egg paste and mix very thoroughly. Transfer to the pastry case and bake for 25-30 minutes or until firm and a deep golden brown.

LEEK AND DERBY SAGE TART

Derby sage cheese, which is mottled pale green with the herb and fairly strong when eaten *per se*, is not as widely sold as Cheshire and Lancashire (of which it is a cousin); however, you should be able to buy it at any cheese shop or counter with a reasonable selection of British cheeses.

If you have no fromage frais and do not mind about fat, 142 ml/ ¼ pint double cream gives an excellent taste, though a slightly less firm texture; with cream and farmhouse cheese, you can omit fresh sage if you prefer.

Serve with a green salad for lunch or with a garnish of salad leaves as a first course before something robust such as roast beef or venison sausages.

Shortcrust pastry (see page 19) made with:
125 g/ 4 oz plain white flour
50 g/ 2 oz plain wholemeal flour
Pinch salt
25 g/ 1 oz lard
50 g/ 2 oz unsalted or slightly salted butter

2 leeks
125 g/ 4 oz (1 smallish) onion
3 cloves garlic
9-10 sage leaves
1 tablespoonful oil
25 g/ 1 oz butter
185 g/ 6½ oz Derby sage cheese
40 g/ 1½ oz ungrated Parmesan or ready-grated pecorino Romano
About 400 g/ 14 oz firm tomatoes
1 size 2 egg
275 g/ 10 oz low-fat fromage frais
Salt
Pepper
A little caster sugar

22-cm/ 8½-inch tart tin

Heat the oven to 200 C, 400 F, Gas Mark 6. Roll out the pastry to a thickness of 3-4 mm/⅛ inch, cover with cooking foil, and blind-bake (see page 20). Leave to cool.

Trim the green leaves and root-ends of the leeks, peel off the outer layer, and slice very finely; wash and leave on kitchen paper to dry. Peel and slice the onion into thin rings; peel and finely chop the garlic. Wash, dry, and chop the sage into fine strips.

Warm the oil and butter in a wok or frying-pan and fry the onion over medium heat for 2 minutes. Add the garlic and stir-fry for 1 minute. Add the leeks and fry for 4 minutes, turning constantly; add the sage and fry 1-2 minutes more, still turning constantly, until the onions and leeks are golden. Remove from the heat.

Re-heat the oven if necessary to 200 C, 400 F, Gas Mark 6. Grate the cheese or cheeses and peel the tomatoes (see page 16). Beat the egg into the fromage frais, season with ⅓ teaspoonful of salt and a moderate grinding of pepper, and stir in the grated cheeses. Add the contents of the frying-pan and mix gently but thoroughly. Turn into the pastry-case.

Chop at least 1 cm/ ⅓ inch from the stalk-ends of the tomatoes, or slightly more if they are large and the cores hard, and slice the rest of the flesh fairly thickly. Arrange in slightly overlapping circles over the top of the tart. Season moderately with salt and pepper, add just the slightest sprinkling of sugar, and bake 30 minutes. Serve warm rather than hot.

LANCASHIRE PIZZA

As with a fruit tart, the tomatoes are arranged in layers over an egg filling (and after all, tomatoes are a fruit). This means that when baked their flavour is concentrated but much fresher than if they had been cooked with tomato purée; a further edge is given to the taste by slight charring. The charred tomatoes which are covered with a sprinkling of chopped garlic, make the tart look rather like a pizza (hence the name). I have used oatmeal pastry partly because it browns relatively slowly, which allows more time for the tomatoes to char, and partly because its soft, crumbly texture suits the cheese.

If you have no fresh thyme, substitute 1 teaspoonful dried oregano. Serve hot with a salad of bitter leaves.

FOR 6-8

Oatmeal pastry (see page 19) made with:
150 g/ 5 oz plain white flour
25 g/ 1 oz oatmeal
Pinch salt
25 g/ 1 oz lard
50 g/ 2 oz butter

900g/ 2 lb ripe tomatoes
small bunch thyme (enough for 1 tablespoon when stripped)
6 cloves of garlic
125 g/ 4 oz medium-fat soft cheese
Salt
Pepper
2 size 3 eggs
2 teaspoonsful Dijon mustard
150 g/ 5 oz Lancashire cheese, finely grated
A little caster sugar
Oil for drizzling (optional)

22-cm/ 8½-inch ovenproof tart dish (rather than tin)

Set the oven to 200 C, 400 F, Gas Mark 6. Roll out the pastry 3-4 mm/ ⅛ inch thick, line the tart dish, and cover all over with cooking foil. Blind-bake for 10 minutes; remove the foil and bake 7-8 minutes more or until the pastry is very slightly coloured, and leave to cool.

Peel the tomatoes (see page 16), chop at least 1 cm/ ⅓ inch from the stalk-end which will remove the hardest part of core, and cut into thick slices (3 per average tomato). Leave to drain while you prepare the rest of the ingredients.

Wash, blot dry, and strip the leaves from the thyme (grip the top of the stems between the thumb and forefinger and pull downwards; they will then come all together). Peel and very finely chop the garlic.

Mash the soft cheese with ⅓ teaspoonful of salt and a generous grinding of pepper, beat in the eggs one by one and continue to beat until the mixture is smooth. Thoroughly stir in the mustard. Finely grate and stir in the Lancashire and turn into the pastry case. Set the oven to 200 C, 400 F, Gas Mark 6. Arrange half the tomatoes over the egg and cheese mixture, season generously with uncrushed or barely crushed sea-salt and coarsely ground pepper, add a slight dusting of sugar and sprinkle with half the thyme. Cover with a second layer of tomatoes, season in the same way, and sprinkle with the rest of the thyme. Do not add the juice which will have run from the tomatoes since it will make the tart soggy. Scatter the garlic evenly over the top and bake for 50-55 minutes, until the garlic is brown and the tomatoes slightly charred. Drizzle a little olive oil over the top before serving if you wish.

SPINACH TART WITH SMOKED GARLIC AND PINE NUTS

If anyone were asked to identify the flavours in this tart, I very much doubt if they would recognize the garlic, which contributes a powerful smoky taste but has none of the pungency of raw or fried fresh garlic. A friend whose opinions on food I greatly value does not favour smoking it for this reason, feeling that the natural character of the garlic is destroyed; however, in this recipe the smokiness is the point.

You can buy smoked garlic at some supermarkets or order it direct from Scotland. It is essential for this recipe; do not substitute fresh garlic. It is also essential to use fresh, real spinach. Sometimes, beet-spinach, which has larger leaves and thicker stems, is sold instead: for some purposes, it is a satisfactory alternative, but as it does not have the same flavour I do not recommend it here.

If possible, char the pepper over a gas flame (see page 16), since the flesh will be firmer and easier to chop than when it is baked or grilled; with electric hobs, grill rather than bake.

Serve the tart hot, warm, or cold, alone or with a plain green salad.

FOR 6-8

Shortcrust pastry (see page 19) made with:
175 g/ 6 oz plain white flour
Pinch salt
25 g/ 1 oz lard
50 g/ 2 oz butter

1 large red pepper
275 g/10 oz spinach
Salt
1 head smoked garlic
125 g/4 oz shallots
25 g/ 1 oz butter
1 tablespoonful oil
50 g/ 2 oz pine nuts
175 g/ 6 oz medium-fat soft cheese

Pepper
2 teaspoonsful Dijon mustard
2 tablespoonsful double cream
75 g/ 3 oz freshly grated Parmesan or ready-grated pecorino or a mixture
2 size 2 eggs

22-cm/ 8½-inch tart tin

Set the oven to 200 C, 400 F, Gas Mark 6. Roll out the pastry to a thickness of 3-4 mm/⅛ inch; line the tart tin. Cover all over with cooking foil and blind-bake (see page 20).

Skin the pepper (see page 16); char it very black so that the flesh is darkened as well as the skin, since the charcoal taste adds to the smokiness of the tart. Quarter over a bowl to catch the juice from inside; reserve the juice. Discard the inner membranes and all the seeds and chop into strips about 5 mm/ ¼ inch wide and 5 cm/2 inches long.

Pick over and wash the spinach, twice if necessary; even ready-washed spinach should be rinsed because the water clinging to the leaves is needed for cooking. Put it into a saucepan with a lid, add ½ teaspoonful of salt, cover, and set over medium heat for 4 minutes; stir and cook for 1-2 minutes more or until it is tender and submerged in liquid. Drain through a sieve and press out as much moisture as you can with the back of a spoon. Chop finely.

Peel and roughly chop the garlic; crush to a paste in a mortar. Peel and finely slice the shallots. Melt the butter in the oil over medium heat and fry the shallots for 3 minutes or until soft but not brown, turning continuously; add the nuts and stir-fry for 30 seconds. Remove from the heat and thoroughly stir in the spinach, crushed garlic, and strips of pepper plus their juice.

Heat the oven to 200 C, 400 F, Gas Mark 6. Mix together the soft cheese, ½ teaspoonful of salt, a generous grinding of pepper, the mustard, and the cream; stir in the Parmesan. Thoroughly beat in the eggs one by one. Add and very thoroughly stir in the spinach mixture. Turn the filling into the pastry case and bake for 25-30 minutes or until firm and slightly browned.

FERGUS HENDERSON'S
WELSH RAREBIT

O ne variation of Welsh rarebit or another (depending on the sort of cheese I happen to have) is my favourite late-night pick-me-up; however, until I had it at St John (Fergus's restaurant near Smithfield, London), it was a long time since I had found it in a restaurant. It arrived piled in an impressive hillock on the toast, striped with brown from a very hot grill. I cannot reproduce the stripes with my grill, but in other respects the following is identical.

The only satisfactory way to make toast for Welsh rarebit is to bake it in the oven, which dries it out and ensures that it will be crisp: if made under the grill or in a toaster, it becomes soggy.

FOR 2

2 rounds of brown bread from a small loaf
Butter
200 g/ 7 oz farmhouse (strong) Cheddar cheese
4 teaspoonful white flour
½ teaspoonful dry English mustard
⅔ teaspoonful hot chilli powder
4 tablespoonful Guinness
½ teaspoonful salt
A few drops Worcestershire sauce

Set the oven to 200 C, 400 F, Gas Mark 6. Cut the crusts from the bread, butter thinly, and bake 7-10 minutes, until light brown. Coarsely grate the cheese. Sift together the flour, mustard, and chilli powder.

Set the grill to high. Melt 15 g/ ½ oz butter in a wok or smallish saucepan over low heat. Add the flour mixture off the heat and stir until thoroughly amalgamated: it will be brown, extremely stiff, and collect in lumps. Add the Guinness, salt, and sauce, return to the heat, and stir until very thick. Remove from the heat and stir in the cheese to form a stiff, rough mass. It is essential that the cheese should not melt or it will form strings; however, it is also essential to mix it with the sauce while the sauce is hot, since if it cools it will become too thick to mix. Pile the cheese on to the pieces of toast, making sure that all the toast is covered (any parts which remain exposed will burn). Grill for 1-1½ minutes or until golden.

SALADS
AND VEGETABLE
SIDE DISHES

STILTON SALAD WITH PARMESAN AND WALNUTS

The idea of this comes from the decorative extras often served with the cheese course at restaurants: with first-class cheese which deserves to be enjoyed *per se*, I tend to regard them as merely a distraction, but they work extremely well when deliberately designed as a salad.

The use of walnut rather than olive oil for the dressing is an important detail, since olive oil and Stilton definitely do not flatter each other. The amount of dressing given is the minimum needed: you may prefer to increase it to 6 tablespoonsful of oil and 1½ of vinegar.

The avocados should give slightly to the touch without being soft. If they are hard when bought, leave them to ripen for a day or two at room temperature.

Serve as a main course for lunch, accompanied by crusty brown bread.

FOR 4.

Bunch watercress (40-50 g/ 1½-2 oz)
4 largish (but not outside) sticks celery
50 g/ 2 oz walnuts (shelled)
4 tablespoonsful walnut oil
1 tablespoonful red-wine vinegar
Salt
Pepper
2 largish avocado pears
2 Cox apples
175 g/ 6 oz Stilton
75 g/ 3 oz Parmesan (ungrated)

Set the oven to 200 C, 400 F, Gas Mark 6. Pick over the watercress, trim the ends of the stems, and wash; leave in a colander or on a plate lined with kitchen paper to dry. Trim the celery; pare off any discoloured patches, wash, dry, and chop into 1-cm/ ⅓-inch slices. Toast the nuts in the oven for 6-8 minutes; allow to cool a little and roughly chop or crush. Beat together the oil, vinegar, and a moderate seasoning of salt and pepper.

Halve and peel the avocados; cut out any black patches and chop into 1.5-cm/ ½-¾ -inch squares. Wash and dry the apples (or peel them if you prefer): quarter and cut into squares of about the same size and mix with the avocado and celery, taking care not to break the pieces of avocado. Beat the dressing again, pour it over them, and toss gently (the apple and avocado should be dressed as soon as they are cut because they discolour when exposed to the air). Place the dressed ingredients in the centre of the serving plates. Crumble or chop the Stilton and arrange on top. Pare the Parmesan into very thin slices; cut into small oblongs and add. Sprinkle with the walnuts and surround with the watercress. Serve promptly.

DAN EVANS'S WARM JERUSALEM ARTICHOKE SALAD WITH SPINACH AND POACHED EGG

I recently read a remarkably funny article by a young man who applied for a job with Albert Roux, of Le Gavroche, and was turned down (kindly) because he did not know how to poach an egg. Instead of setting into a smooth, round dome, his egg frothed and sent out furious tentacles in every direction. The reason was that he cooked it in vigorously boiling water, whereas for an egg with a neat white and runny yolk, which is more than usually important here, the water should not even simmer.

Dan (who founded the Fire Station restaurant, London SE1) describes this salad as 'luxurious'; my word for it is masterly. Each component balances another and the total adds up to something else again. As Dan also says, it is a little different: this applies in particular to the dressing, which is made with the oil used for frying the artichokes and thickened with the egg yolks as you eat them.

Truffle oil can be bought at good grocers or delicatessens: it is expensive, as you would expect, but only a very little is needed.

As the eggs are not heated enough to kill bacteria, they must be very fresh; do not serve the salad to children or anyone vulnerable.

Serve as a first course.

FOR 6

225 g/ 8 oz baby spinach
450 g/ 1 lb Jerusalem artichokes
1 lemon
Salt
6 size 2 eggs
3 slices moderately fresh white bread cut 1.5 cm/ ½ inch thick
About 3 tablespoonsful groundnut oil
1 tablespoonful balsamic or sherry vinegar
Coarsely ground or crushed pepper
Truffle oil for drizzling

Carefully pick over the spinach, discarding any weeds or damaged leaves. Wash, twice if necessary, and leave in a colander or on kitchen paper to dry.

Scrub or peel the artichokes and cut into 6-mm/ ¼-inch slices. Squeeze the lemon. Set a pan of lightly salted water over high heat; add the lemon juice, bring to a 'vicious' boil (Dan's word) and add the artichokes. Return to the boil and simmer for 5 minutes; drain.

Poach the eggs. If possible, use a pan 10-12 cm/ 4-5 inches deep; three-quarters fill it with water (unsalted) and bring to a brisk boil. Place a bowl or another pan of cold water to hand in which to put the eggs when they are cooked. Break three of the eggs into the boiling water and reduce the heat until it is not quite simmering: the surface should scarcely move. Cook for 4 minutes: lift on a perforated spoon, check that the whites are firm, and transfer to the cold water. Repeat with the remaining eggs.

Remove the crusts from the bread and cut into small squares. Line a plate with kitchen paper and set conveniently to hand. Warm about half the oil in a frying-pan over medium heat, fry the bread until golden, and set on the paper to drain.

Arrange the dry spinach on the serving plates: remove the eggs from the cold water and place on a second plate lined with kitchen paper to dry. Wash or wipe the frying-pan clean, just cover the bottom with fresh oil, and place over high heat until smoke rises. Add the artichokes and fry light brown on both sides: this takes only a few seconds. Distribute the artichokes over the spinach, which will wilt slightly (this is intentional). Add the vinegar to the pan, stir, bring just to the boil, and sprinkle a little over each serving. Put an egg on top, season with the pepper, and scatter with croûtons. Add salt, drizzle with the truffle oil, and serve immediately.

SEAN AND BENEDICT'S FIG AND ROSY GRAPEFRUIT SALAD

This is a light, refreshing salad which makes an ideal first course before game in particular. As always, it stands (rather than falls) by the dressing, in this case walnut oil and juice from the grapefruit laced with sherry. In scaling down the quantities from restaurant proportions, I have perhaps been more generous with it than necessary: there is just, but only just enough for 6 if you use 2 tablespoonsful each of oil, juice, and sherry.

Before Sean and Benedict started at 15 North Parade, Oxford, they worked under Sonia Blech at Mijanou (London SW1) and, when I said that I would like to publish this recipe, stressed that I should credit it to her – as I now am, with many thanks for the pleasure it will and has already given.

Wash the salad leaves well in advance so that they have time to dry. Serve with brown, seed, or walnut bread.

FOR 6

About 125 g/ 4 oz mixed bitter salad leaves, e.g. three or
four of the following; chicory, curly endive, lamb's lettuce,
oakleaf lettuce, radiccio, rocket
75 g/ 3 oz walnuts
6-9 fresh figs
2 pink grapefruit
3 tablespoonsful walnut oil
3 tablespoonsful sweet or medium dry (not dry) sherry
1 teaspoonful redcurrant jelly
Salt

Pick over the salad leaves, wash, and dry in a colander or on kitchen paper (if used while still wet, they will make the dressing watery). Set the oven to 200 C, 400 F, Gas Mark 6; when heated, toast the walnuts for 5-6 minutes. Allow to cool a little and chop coarsely. Wash, dry, and chop the figs into pieces. Using a very sharp knife, peel the grapefruit, removing all traces of pith. Cut into 6-mm/ ¼-inch slices; reserve the juice which escapes. Divide into segments, discarding the inner membranes and tough centres. Strain 3 tablespoonsful of the juice and beat into the oil. Add and beat in the sherry. Melt the redcurrant jelly in 3 teaspoonsful water: stir over low heat until dissolved. Pour into a cup through a strainer if necessary and add another teaspoonful of cold water. Stir and add 1 teaspoonful to the dressing with a pinch of salt. Taste and add more if you wish (how much is needed depends on the sweetness of the grapefruit and sherry).

Just before serving, transfer the salad leaves to a bowl; beat the dressing again, pour it over them, and toss thoroughly but lightly. Drain and distribute the grapefruit between the serving plates; add the leaves and arrange the figs on top. Sprinkle with the walnuts and serve.

GRILLED VEGETABLE SALAD WITH PARSLEY AND WALNUT PESTO

Lots of restaurants offer something like this, but my original model was a platter of colourful, carefully arranged vegetables served at Joe's Restaurant/Bar at Harvey Nichols, London. Apart from its appearance, the charm of the salad is that all the vegetables are freshly cooked and still warm. At Joe's, they were served with a simple French dressing; however, another possibility is pesto, of which I suggest an anglicized version made with parsley and walnuts (I have chosen walnuts because they go well with aubergine and tomatoes, but almonds, which give a lighter, more delicate sauce, can also be used).

Aubergine, tomatoes, and red peppers are essential for flavour, but the other ingredients can be varied according to preference and availability.

The pesto sauce can be made up to a day in advance.

Serve for lunch with walnut bread (to complement the sauce).

FOR 4

275-350 g/ 10-12 oz aubergine
Salt, some of which should be finely ground
4 largish tomatoes
1 large or 2 smaller red peppers
5-6 tablespoonsful virgin olive oil
225 g/ 8 oz button mushrooms
Pepper
175-185 g/ 6-6½ oz asparagus tips or thin asparagus
175 g/ 6 oz green haricot beans or 150 g/ 5 oz French or Kenya beans
450 g/ 1 lb Pink Fir Apple or other small, waxy potatoes (see page 99)
Caster sugar

Wash and slice the aubergine into 6-mm/ ¼-inch rounds. Sprinkle with fine salt and leave in a colander or on a plate to sweat for 45-60 minutes, or while you prepare the rest of the ingredients. Rinse under the cold tap and squeeze as dry as possible with kitchen paper.

Skin the tomatoes (see page 16), remove the cores, and turn upside-down to drain. Skin the pepper(s), if possible over a gas flame, since this does not cook the flesh (see page 16). Wipe off any charred bits of skin which stick to the surface and paint with oil. (Do not pierce or cut them.) Trim the mushroom stalks in line with the cups; wash and dry the mushrooms, season with salt and pepper, and moisten with 1-2 tablespoonsful of the oil. Trim the asparagus; top and tail the beans.

Scrub or wash the potatoes, just cover with slightly salted water, and boil 15-20 minutes, until tender. Drain, and leave until cool enough to handle. Skin if you wish (personally, I prefer them unskinned).

Set the grill to high and cover a large baking sheet with cooking foil. Turn the tomatoes cutside-up, season moderately with salt and pepper, and sprinkle with a little sugar. Place on the baking sheet. Add the mushrooms, aubergine, and pepper (still whole) and grill for 6-7 minutes or until the aubergine and pepper are beginning to brown. Turn (with the exception of the tomatoes) and grill for another 3-5 minutes, until the second side of the aubergine is pale brown.

While the vegetables grill, just cover the beans and asparagus with slightly salted water and boil 5-8 minutes or until tender. Drain and refresh very briefly under the cold tap.

Cut the tops from the peppers, discarding the juice inside, quarter, and remove the inner membranes and seeds. Cut into strips and put on the serving-plates; add the beans and asparagus (one way to arrange them is to set them fanning outwards towards the edges). Place the tomato opposite the pepper, add the other vegetables (leave the potatoes whole), and drizzle with oil. Serve at once with the pesto.

PARSLEY AND WALNUT PESTO

Small bunch parsley (enough for 2 tablespoonsful when chopped)
1½ largish or 2 medium/ small cloves garlic
4½ tablespoonsful virgin olive oil
65 g/ 2½ oz walnuts or walnut pieces
40 g/ 1½ oz freshly grated Parmesan or ready-grated pecorino

Trim the ends of the parsley stems if bought; wash and thoroughly blot the parsley dry with kitchen paper and chop finely. Peel, slice, and crush the garlic in a mortar. Add the parsley and a little of the oil and pound to a rough paste. Add and pound the walnuts, leaving some pieces a little coarser than others to give textural interest to the sauce. Add the cheese and the rest of the oil and stir to a purée. (If you use almonds instead of walnuts, toast them for 10-12 minutes at 200 C, 400 F, Gas Mark 6 before pounding.)

SALMON SALAD WITH BLANCHED LEEKS AND DILL

The idea of this (but not the recipe) comes from a visit to Antony Worrall-Thompson's restaurant in Soho, London, dell'Ugo, where blanched leeks dressed with sour cream and dill were served with smoked salmon and potato pancakes as a first course. Since I happen to think that the leeks go better with fresh than smoked salmon, I have transposed it into a main-course dish with fresh salmon and, partly for the sake of simplicity, plain new potatoes.

Blanching the leeks removes their sharpness but means that they retain their body and crispness. To give them time to absorb the dressing, which will thicken to the consistency of a fairly thick sauce, they should be prepared about two hours before the meal.

Allow 15-20 minutes for cooking the salmon and potatoes.

FOR 4

Handful dill (enough for 1 tablespoonful when chopped)
4 medium-sized leeks
Salt
2 tablespoonsful virgin olive oil
1 tablespoonful red-wine vinegar
284 ml/ 1/2 pint sour cream
Pepper
900 g/2 lb Pink Fir Apple or other waxy new potatoes (see page 99)
Watercress for serving (about 50 g)
4 steaks or 625-750 g/1 1/4-1 1/2 lb farmed salmon

Trim the ends of the dill-stems; wash, blot dry, and chop very finely. Trim the roots and leaves from the leeks, peel off the outer layer, and chop into diagonal 12-mm/1/2-inch slices. Wash and just cover with slightly salted water. Bring briskly to the boil, boil 1 minute, drain, and refresh under the cold tap. Drain again and leave in a sieve to dry. Make the dressing: beat the oil and vinegar into the cream with a moderate seasoning of salt and a generous grinding of pepper. Toss with the leeks as soon as they are completely dry (it is desirable that they should still be warm).

Scrub or peel (preferably scrub) the potatoes. Just cover with salted water and boil 15-20 minutes, until tender; drain. Pick over the watercress, removing any limp, discoloured, or damaged leaves; trim the stems fairly close to the tops, pulling off lower leaves, and wash. Leave to dry in a colander lined with a double layer of kitchen paper.

Set the oven to 200 C, 400 F, Gas Mark 6. Wash and dry the salmon, season lightly with salt and pepper, and wrap into a parcel with cooking foil; do not add oil or butter. Bake 10-14 minutes, until the flesh flakes easily with a fork and is opaque all through, but for no longer, since it is important that it should only be very lightly cooked. Leave wrapped for a few minutes or until you are ready to serve.

Unwrap, thoroughly drain off the cooking liquor, and flake, removing the skin and all the bones. Surround with the leeks and arrange the potatoes (whole) round the edge. Decorate with the watercress and serve.

DAN EVANS'S SMOKED EEL AND WATERCRESS SALAD WITH BEETROOT CHIPS

This is the kind of recipe which everyone who likes cooking constantly tries to invent but all too seldom with success. It is simple, foolproof and quick to prepare – and totally delicious because each ingredient balances the others: the watercress and horseradish offset the richness of the eel, while the crispness of the chips adds tone and textural interest. I served it as a first course before the turkey on Christmas Day and it lent distinction to the entire meal.

A variation on Dan's recipe, which alters the balance but is still excellent, is to boil and shallow-fry the beetroot in slightly thicker slices: this gives a less crisp result but emphasizes its sweetness, which contrasts in a very satisfying way with the eel and horseradish.

Fresh horseradish root is difficult to buy: Dan would probably disapprove, but if you cannot find it, use plain ready-grated, which comes in jars or air-tight packets (do not, however, use it if preserved in vinegar).

Serve with thin slices of rye or wholemeal bread.

FOR 6

6 small (tangerine-sized) raw beetroots
2 or 3 bunches watercress, depending on size and condition
125 g/ 4 oz smoked eel fillet
1½ tablespoonsful red-wine vinegar
6 tablespoonsful virgin olive oil
Salt
Pepper
Groundnut oil for deep-frying or 3 tablespoonsful olive oil
for shallow-frying
A little stale bread or a sugar thermometer if the beetroot
is to be deep-fried
5-cm/ 2-inch piece fresh horseradish

If you wish to boil and shallow-fry the beetroot, peel it, cover with slightly salted water, and boil 30-40 minutes or until tender. Allow to cool and cut into 6-mm/ ¼-inch slices.

Carefully pick over the watercress, rejecting any dull, damaged, or limp leaves; pull off those growing lower down so that only the upper part of the stem is included in the salad. Wash and leave in a colander lined with a double layer of kitchen paper to dry. Flake the eel (as chilling impairs the flavour, it should not be served straight from the refrigerator). Make the dressing: beat the vinegar into the oil with a moderate seasoning of salt and pepper.

If you wish to serve the beetroot as chips, peel and slice it very thinly, as for potato crisps. Use a smallish saucepan or wok for deep-frying; make sure that it is perfectly dry before pouring in the oil or it may spit. As a precaution against accidents, it is also advisable to set a saucepan with the handle facing away from you (hot oil is inflammable). Pour in the oil to a depth of 2 cm/ ¾ inch and set over medium/high heat until it has reached 190 C / 375 F. If you have no thermometer, leave it to heat for 2 minutes and cut the bread into small squares. Lower one of them into the oil at frequent intervals (lower gently to avoid splashing): when it turns golden in 40 seconds, the oil has reached the required temperature. Reduce the heat to medium and set a large plate lined with kitchen paper to hand by the cooker. Lower the slices of beetroot into the oil a few at a time and fry for a few seconds; turn and continue to fry until the edges curl. Place on the paper-lined plate to drain off surplus fat. When all are fried, leave the oil in the pan to cool for at least 10-15 minutes (it can be reused at least twice).

To shallow-fry the beetroot, place a paper-lined plate by the cooker as above, warm the olive oil in a wok or frying-pan over medium/high heat, and fry the slices until fairly crisp and with a golden tinge; drain on the plate as before.

Peel the horseradish; transfer the watercress to a bowl and beat the dressing with a fork. Pour it over the cress, toss lightly, and arrange the cress on the serving plates. Scatter with the eel and distribute the beetroot on top. Finely grate just enough horseradish to make your eyes water as you grate; sprinkle a little over the top of each portion and serve at once (the flavour of horseradish diminishes rapidly on exposure to air).

PEAR AND WARM CHICKEN SALAD WITH CONCENTRATED YOGHURT DRESSING

Concentrated yoghurt is simply yoghurt drained in a cloth or jelly-bag to a stiff cream. It has a tart, slightly cheese-like rather than sharp flavour; the longer it is drained, the stiffer and cheesier it becomes. It can be used in various ways, notably instead of cream with sweet dishes or as the basis of a thick, mayonnaise-type salad dressing; it also makes a distinctive sauce for pancakes and fritters. Here, its tartness accentuates the taste of the chicken and offsets the sweetness of the pear – which, unless you like very sweet flavours with meat, should be slightly under-ripe.

The avocado pears, on the other hand, must be ripe: when at the right stage, they give slightly to the touch all over. Avoid any which are very soft, since the flesh will be fibrous and streaked with black; if hard, leave at room temperature for a day or two.

The chicken can be part of a whole one or pieces, but if you use skinned breasts, they should be poached rather than baked.

I should perhaps stress that, although it may look healthy, this is not a dish for the calorie-conscious, since avocado pears are over 20 per cent fat and the dressing contains a high proportion of oil. It can be made with low-fat yoghurt, but the result will be sharper and more yoghurt will be needed (at least 150 g/5 oz).

Allow 4-6 hours for draining the yoghurt, 1½ hours for roasting a chicken, or 20-40 minutes for cooking chicken pieces. (The yoghurt can be drained the previous day.)

FOR 4 AS A MAIN COURSE OR 6-8, WITHOUT POTATOES,

AS A FIRST COURSE

450 g/1 lb mild, whole-milk yoghurt
1 small free-range chicken or 4 pieces, on the bone (legs have more
flavour than breasts, but breasts have a smoother texture)
A very little butter
Salt
Pepper
2 Little Gem lettuces
Small bunch of chives (enough for 1 tablespoonful when chopped)
About 9 cm/ 3½ inches cucumber
625-750 g/1¼-1½ lb waxy new potatoes, e.g. Jersey Royal
6 tablespoonsful olive oil
⅔ teaspoonsful hot chilli powder
1½ tablespoonsful red-wine vinegar
2 small, firm (i.e. under-ripe) Conference pears
2 medium-sized avocado pears

New sterilized cleaning-cloth or cheesecloth or a jelly-bag

Drain the yoghurt. A new sterilized cleaning-cloth can be used directly, but cheesecloth or a jelly-bag should be boiled before use. Turn the yoghurt into the bag or a sieve lined with the cloth; set over a bowl at room temperature for 4-6 hours, until very thick. When drained, store in the refrigerator.

To roast a whole chicken, wash inside and out, dry, rub with a little butter, and season lightly inside with salt, and outside with salt and pepper. Roast at 200 C, 400 F, Gas Mark 6 for 18 minutes per 450 g/1 lb plus 15-20 minutes; when ready, it should be crisp, brown, and tender, and exude no pink liquid when the breast and thighs are pierced to the bone. To bake, wash, season, place on a lightly greased tray and bake at the same heat for 25-40 minutes, until very tender.

Wash the lettuces and leave in a colander to dry; trim the ends of the chives if bought, wash, and leave to dry on a plate lined with kitchen paper. Wash the cucumber. Scrub or peel the potatoes, just cover with slightly salted water, and boil 15-20 minutes, until tender; drain.

Make the dressing; beat the oil into the yoghurt until smooth, add the chilli powder and ½ teaspoonful salt, and stir in the vinegar.

When the chicken is cooked but still warm, quarter and peel the pears; halve and peel the avocados. Chop the cucumber, both sorts of pear, and the chicken into 12-mm/½-inch squares, removing the skin from the chicken if you wish.

Mix with the dressing and pile in the centre of the serving plates. Very finely chop the chives and sprinkle over the top. Arrange lettuce leaves and potatoes round the edge of the plate and serve.

BROAD BEAN AND BACON SALAD WITH LEMON DRESSING

Part of the appeal of this salad is the contrast of the smooth beans, prawns and potato with the crisp bacon, croûtons, and radishes. In terms of taste, it is brought to life by a vigorous, rather peppery lemon dressing: with an ordinary French dressing, it loses its edge and character.

The prawns should be fresh, i.e. chilled, rather than frozen; unshelled ones have a better texture and more flavour than ready-shelled ones.

Young, small beans are preferable to large, old ones. Large ones have tough skins which wrinkle when cooked and if possible should be peeled off before serving. Do not buy (or pick) beans with black spots on the pods: the beans inside will also be affected.

Ideally, use organic radishes and Jersey Royal potatoes: for other suitable varieties of potato, see page 99.

2 Little Gem or 1 small Cos lettuce
Bunch radishes
225 g/ 8 oz unshelled or 125 g/ 4 oz shelled prawns
450-500 g/ 1-1¼ lb broad beans, or enough to give
225 g/ 8 oz when podded
Salt
750 g/ 1½ lb waxy new potatoes
1 small or ½ large lemon
4½ tablespoonsful oil
Pepper
225 g/ 8 oz streaky, unsmoked bacon
50 g/ 2 oz (2 slices) brown bread, weighed without crust

Strip the lettuces (or lettuce), halving or quartering the hearts; wash and leave in a colander to drain. Trim and wash the radishes. Shell the prawns if necessary; wash and leave on kitchen paper to dry.

Pod the beans; just cover with slightly salted water and boil 6-8 minutes or until tender. Leave to cool.

Scrub the potatoes, cover with salted water, and boil 12-15 minutes or until just tender. While they cook, make the dressing. Squeeze the lemon and beat 2 tablespoonsful of the juice with the oil. Stir in a moderate seasoning of salt and a grinding of pepper equal to about ¼ of a teaspoonful. As soon as the potatoes are cool enough to handle, peel them if you wish and slice fairly thickly. Beat the dressing again, sprinkle half of it over them, and toss gently.

Set the oven to 200 C, 400 F, Gas Mark 6. Trim the rind from the bacon and crust from the bread, cut both into 8-mm/ ⅓-inch squares, and bake for 8 minutes; turn, not only to ensure even cooking but so that both sides of the croûtons are moistened with bacon fat, and bake 2-4 minutes more or until the bacon is crisp and the bread an even gold.

While the bacon and croûtons are in the oven, arrange the lettuce round the sides of the serving plates; set the dressed potato in the middle. Slice the radishes into 3 or 4 and distribute on top of the lettuce; place the beans over the potato and the prawns over the beans. Scatter the bacon and croûtons over the top as soon as they are cooked, sprinkle with the rest of the dressing, and serve at once.

WARM SLIVERS OF BEEF WITH ROCKET AND GREEN HARICOT BEANS

The point of this salad is to make the very best of first-class beef. The meat is cut into strips, marinated briefly in oil, and stir-fried for just long enough to sear the outside but still be juicy and retain all its flavour. The other ingredients are designed simply to point it up: the fact that the yellow peppers and purple onion also make a particularly successful colour combination is incidental.

Kenya or French beans can be substituted for haricots when necessary, but the larger size and slightly more robust texture of haricot (sometimes called 'round') beans suits the salad better; however, they must be young and very fresh, since if old they may be tough or woody.

FOR 4 AS A LIGHT LUNCH OR 6-8 AS A FIRST COURSE

300-375 g/ 11-13 oz fillet steak
Salt
Pepper
About 5 tablespoonsful virgin olive oil
300-375 g/ 11-13 oz green haricot or 275-300 g/ 10-10½ oz Kenya or French beans
40 g/ 1½ oz rocket
2 yellow peppers
2 small or 1 large red onion
1 clove garlic
1½ teaspoonsful Dijon mustard
¾ teaspoonful caster sugar
¾ tablespoonful red-wine vinegar

Wash and dry the beef, trim off any visible fat, and cut against the grain into strips 6 mm/ ¼ inch wide and 2 cm/ ¾ inch long; then slice each piece, which will be the thickness of the steak, into two.

Season moderately with salt and pepper, toss in about 1½ tablespoonsful of the olive oil, and leave while you prepare the rest of the ingredients.

Top and tail and wash the beans, just cover with slightly salted water, and boil briskly 5-8 minutes or until tender. Drain, refresh under the cold tap, and leave to dry.

Pick over the rocket, discarding any bruised or broken leaves; wash and leave in a colander or on kitchen paper to dry. Wash and dry the peppers; cut off both ends, remove the core, seeds, and pale inner flesh, and slice into fine rings. Peel and slice the onion(s) into very fine rings; peel and slice the garlic. Make the dressing: mix the mustard, sugar, and a moderate seasoning of salt and pepper with the vinegar and beat in 2½ tablespoonsful of olive oil.

Arrange the beans in the bottom of the serving plates. Heat 1 tablespoonful of oil in a wok or frying-pan over high heat and add the garlic. Allow to fry for 20-30 seconds or until changing colour: if using a wok, push it up the sides to stop it from cooking further; with a frying-pan, remove it with a perforated spoon. Add the beef to the pan and fry, turning continuously, until brown and opaque on all sides: this will take only a few seconds. Remove from the heat and distribute over the beans with any oil or meat juices left in the pan. Place the rings of pepper over the meat. Set the onion on top, beat and add the dressing, and garnish with the rocket. Serve immediately.

MUSHROOM SALAD WITH GARLIC CROÛTONS

This is a very simple salad which goes particularly well with lamb sausages or burgers (see page 168) or grilled pork or lamb chops, and can also be served on its own as a first course. Be warned: it contains a lot of garlic.

I suggest using large closed, button-type mushrooms because they tend to have more flavour than small button ones but are firmer and closer-textured than open ones. If they are really fresh, they will be plump and hard almost to the point of snappiness all over.

If served as a first course, accompany with bread to mop up the juices.

FOR 4-6, OR 4 IF SERVED ALONE

750 g/ 1½ lb very fresh, large button-type mushrooms
6 largish and 1 small clove garlic
French dressing made with 4 tablespoonsful oil (see page 98)
3 tablespoonsful oil
Salt
Pepper
40 g/ 1½ oz (1½ slices) brown or white bread, weighed without crust
20 g/ ¾ oz butter

Trim the mushroom stems fairly close to the caps. If the skin comes away easily, peel the mushrooms; whether peeled or not, wash and blot them dry with kitchen paper. Slice fairly thickly. Peel and finely chop the 6 large cloves of garlic. Make the French dressing.

Warm the oil over medium heat in a frying-pan or wok and fry the chopped garlic 30-40 seconds or until pale gold; turn if necessary to ensure even cooking. Take the pan from the heat and remove the garlic quickly (it will continue to cook in the hot oil): use a perforated spoon so that the oil is left in the pan. Set the garlic aside. Fish out any browned remains of it in the oil and return the pan to very low heat. Add the mushrooms, season fairly generously with salt and pepper, and turn constantly until they have absorbed all the oil and begun to exude juice. Continue to cook over very low heat, turning from time to time, for 15-20 minutes or until a substantial amount of juice has run. Turn up the heat to medium and cook until it is reduced by about half. Remove from the heat. Transfer to the serving plates and sprinkle with the French dressing while still warm.

Set the oven to 200 C, 400 F, Gas Mark 6. Peel, roughly chop, and crush the remaining clove of garlic in a mortar. Chop and add the butter. Season moderately with salt and pepper and pound until soft and thoroughly mixed. Spread over the bottom of a small baking dish. Cut the bread into 6-mm/ ¼-inch squares and place on top of the butter. Bake for 8 minutes; turn and bake for another 2-4 minutes or until golden brown. Allow to cool a little. Distribute the browned garlic over the top of the mushrooms, add the croûtons, and serve.

ROCKET SALAD

It may have taken the Italians to reintroduce us to rocket, but it is in fact native to Britain and grows as readily as mint or parsley. Its slightly sharp, distinctive taste means that to make an interesting salad, you need no more than one or two other kinds of leaf, which should be bitter, and perhaps a few cherry tomatoes: their sweetness complements the rocket wonderfully, but they can be omitted if a plain green salad suits your menu better. Without the tomatoes, put it into one large bowl (here, I have suggested serving individual portions).

The fresher the rocket is, the more flavour it will have; also, like mint and basil, it wilts quickly. It is therefore especially worthwhile to grow your own, which has recently been made easier by the fact that some supermarkets are, very sensibly, selling herbs in pots rather than cut.

Wash the salad leaves ½-1 hour before serving to give them time to dry (but no more, or not too much more, or the rocket may wilt).

FOR 4

1 small oakleaf lettuce, or a batavia, or curly endive
2 heads chicory, white with oakleaf or, if possible, red with endive or
batavia
About 30 g/ 1¼ oz rocket
20-24 cherry tomatoes
French dressing (see below)

Pull apart the lettuce and chicory, discarding the roots and outermost leaves; leave the chicory hearts whole (if cut in advance, they may brown on exposure to the air). Remove any discoloured patches and wash. If the rocket was bought cut, trim the ends of the stems; discard any damaged leaves and wash. Put the salad into a colander and leave ½-1 hour. Wash the tomatoes and leave in a sieve or on a plate lined with kitchen paper to dry. Make the dressing.

Directly before serving, cut the chicory hearts into halves or quarters and arrange the chicory round the serving plates. Tear the lettuce into convenient-sized pieces and mix with some of the rocket, leaving enough large leaves to decorate each portion. Beat up the dressing, pour over the lettuce and rocket, and toss gently. Add to the serving bowls. Stud with the tomatoes and arrange the rest of the rocket on top.

FRENCH DRESSING

Like mayonnaise, the dressing can be made up to 2 days in advance.

4 tablespoonsful virgin olive oil
1 tablespoonful red-wine vinegar
Salt
Pepper

Add the oil to the vinegar, season moderately with salt and pepper, and beat together very thoroughly with a fork. As the oil and vinegar will not emulsify, beat again before use.

POTATO SALAD

Potato salad is deservedly a classic; however, it is essential to use waxy potatoes with plenty of flavour. Easily the best are Jersey Royal, Belle de Fontenay, Charlotte, and Pink Fir Apple; the last is my favourite but difficult to find.

One could fill a book with variations on potato salad: like the other dishes in this chapter, however, the ones below are intended as accompaniments and are therefore plain, with the addition of only a chilli or herbs.

FOR 4

Salad
450 g/ 1 lb waxy new potatoes
Salt
Bunch chives or dill (enough for 1½-2 tablespoonsful when chopped)

Mayonnaise
1 size 2 egg (yolk only)
1 tablespoonful red-wine vinegar
Salt
Pepper
About 225 ml/ 8 fl oz oil

Sour Cream
2½ tablespoonsful oil
142 ml/ ¼ pint sour cream
¾ tablespoonful red-wine vinegar

Salad
Scrub the potatoes, cover with slightly salted water, and boil for 15 minutes or until just tender. While they boil, trim the cut ends of bought herbs; wash, blot dry, and chop finely. Drain the potatoes and leave until cool enough to handle; peel if you wish. Cut into 6-7-mm/ ¼-inch slices and mix gently with the dressing; they should be dressed while still warm. Sprinkle with the herbs.

With Mayonnaise

There is no problem about making mayonnaise provided that the egg is at room temperature (rather than straight out of the refrigerator, where there is no need to keep it anyway) and that you add the oil slowly, especially at first.

You can make it up to 2 days ahead of time: store (covered) in the refrigerator.

As the egg is used raw, it must be very fresh, the more if the mayonnaise is made in advance. Do not serve uncooked eggs to children.

Separate the egg (see page 17); set aside or discard the white, which is not needed. Whisk the yolk with ½ a tablespoonful of the vinegar and a moderate seasoning of salt and pepper until pale, thick, and frothy. Add one or two drops of oil and whisk for a moment or two; repeat. Add 3 or 4 drops of oil, whisk, and repeat; then 6 or 7, and by degrees larger quantities, whisking in each addition before adding the next, until 150 ml/ ¼ pint of the oil is amalgamated. Stir in the remaining ½ tablespoonful of vinegar; then gradually add as much extra oil as is needed to bring the mayonnaise to the consistency of very thick cream: it should stand when lifted on the whisk. Either serve or store in the refrigerator.

With Sour Cream

I do not like this as much as the salad with mayonnaise, but it is pleasant and does not contain raw egg yolk. Dill will give it more zest than chives.

If the cream is thin when bought, keep it for a day or two (staying within its dates).

Beat the oil into the cream; when thoroughly mixed, stir in the vinegar.

With French Dressing

This is quite as good in a different way as the salad with mayonnaise. You can add either chives or chopped green chilli. The chilli should be only moderately hot: large ones tend to be milder than small ones, but it is wise to taste a tiny piece before chopping. If it turns out to be very hot, use only a little.

With a thin dressing, you will probably want slightly more potato.

625 g/ 1¼ lb waxy potatoes
Salt
Bunch chives (enough for 1½-2 tablespoonsful when chopped) or 1 mild
to medium-hot green chilli
French dressing (see page 98)

Proceed as for the salad with mayonnaise or sour cream but (unless it is already made) mix the dressing as well as preparing chives or a chilli while the potatoes cook. If using a chilli, wash, trim the stalk end, and slit; remove the seeds and white inner flesh and chop as finely as possible. As it may make your skin smart, do not touch your eyes while handling it and wash your hands immediately afterwards; alternatively, wear disposable polythene gloves. Slice and dress the potatoes as quickly as possible, while still really warm.

DAVID EYRE'S BAKED TOMATOES

The point of this recipe is that baking concentrates the flavour of the tomatoes, which is further intensified by draining beforehand. It is based on a recipe for *crostini* which was given to me some time ago by David Eyre, chef and co-proprietor of The Eagle, London EC1, and which is so effective that I have used it ever since instead of grilling tomatoes.

Allow about 45 minutes for draining the tomatoes and 35-45 minutes for baking.

Serve with lamb-steaks, chops, or other grilled dishes.

FOR 4

8 (about 450 g/ 1 lb) fairly ripe tomatoes
¾ teaspoonful caster sugar
Salt
Pepper
3 or 4 sprigs thyme or 1 rounded teaspoonful dried oregano
A little oil

Skin the tomatoes (see page 16). Cut off the tops fairly generously and remove the cores. Sprinkle with the sugar and a moderate seasoning of salt and pepper and turn upside-down to drain for ¾ of an hour or longer.

Set the oven to 200 C, 400 F, Gas Mark 6. Wash, dry, and pull the leaves from the thyme if you are using it (pull the leaves downwards: pick off top leaves individually). Line a baking tray with lightly greased cooking foil and place the tomatoes on it the right way up. Sprinkle with the thyme or oregano, drizzle with just a little oil, and bake 35-45 minutes, until charred. If you want to use the grill in a combined grill and oven, bake the tomatoes until beginning to char and leave in the centre of the oven while other items are grilling. Remove from the foil carefully to ensure that they do not collapse.

RATATOUILLE

You may argue that this is patently, indisputably French – but then, so were (and still are) soufflés, omelettes (referred to as 'amulets' by Eliza Smith), patés, French dressing, and puff pastry. Ratatouille goes perfectly with roast lamb in particular, but also with roast beef, grilled lamb steaks, and any number of other relatively plain British dishes: if the ingredients had been available in earlier times, it would have been nationalized long ago.

The texture of the vegetables is firmer on the day it is made, but the flavour develops if it is kept overnight: on balance, it is probably better if made a day in advance.

If possible, use small courgettes, which have a firmer texture than large ones; brown markings round the seeds of aubergines, by the way, are not a sign of staleness (but wrinkles and flabbiness are).

Allow ½-1 hour for the aubergine(s) to sweat; cooking time is 1½-1¾ hours.

FOR 4-6

450-625 g/ 1-1¼ lb (1 largish or 2 small) aubergines
Finely ground or crushed salt
1 red, 1 yellow, and 1 green, black, or white pepper
About 350 g/ 12 oz courgettes
185 g/ 6½ oz (1 large or 2 small) onions
4 cloves garlic
2 tablespoonsful virgin olive oil
Salt
Pepper
450 g/ 1 lb ripe tomatoes

Wash the aubergine or aubergines, trim off the ends, and cut into 7-8-mm/ ⅓-inch slices. Sprinkle with fine salt and leave in a colander to sweat for ½-1 hour. Rinse and leave to drain.

Wash, dry, and halve the peppers; remove the seeds and white inner flesh and chop into strips of about the same thickness. Wash, dry, and trim the ends of the courgettes; pare off any discoloured patches of skin and slice fairly thickly. Peel and finely chop the onions and garlic.

Warm the oil in a large, heavy-bottomed casserole over low heat and sweat the onion for 8-10 minutes, turning often; add the garlic and sweat for another 5 minutes or until the onion is soft but not brown, turning constantly. Add the other prepared vegetables, season very lightly with salt and moderately with pepper, and turn to mix. Cover and cook over the lowest possible heat for 45 minutes, turning very gently once or twice.

Meanwhile, skin and chop the tomatoes, discarding the cores (see page 16). Add when the vegetables have stewed for 45 minutes and continue to cook, covered, for another 15 minutes. Turn gently and leave over the heat for a further 15-20 minutes or until the aubergines are soft and cooked (taste a slice). Either serve or store overnight, covered, in the refrigerator. Re-heat (covered) over very low heat.

BRAISED CELERY

B raising is a very good method of cooking not only celery but also red or green cabbage: I originally meant to give a recipe for red cabbage, but have replaced it with this because the cabbage does not go with any of the dishes which I finally decided to include.

I do not really like celery except when it is stir-fried or braised because of the slightly fibrous texture of all but the inner stems; braising, however, gives it an almost velvety tenderness. The only drawback to the recipe is that you need a little stock of a kind suitable for the dish with which it is to be served (when available, use ham-liquor or the stock you are making for gravy).

Cooking time is 7-11 minutes.

Serve with simmered ham or roast chicken, pigeons, or pheasant.

FOR 4

4 large sticks celery
15 g/ ½ oz butter
½ tablespoonful oil
3 tablespoonsful stock

Trim the ends of the celery; pare off any brownish streaks, wash, dry thoroughly, and cut into 6-7-mm/ ¼-inch or slightly thicker slices. Warm the butter and oil over medium/high heat and stir-fry for 1 minute. Add the stock, allow to boil, cover, and simmer over very low heat for 6-10 minutes, until just tender; if any liquid is left, boil it away. Serve at once.

CREAMED CELERIAC

Celeriac is an underused vegetable: served raw, cut into fine strips or grated, it is delicious in salads, and (rather like beetroot) it can also be fried as chips. This recipe is unhealthy because of the cream but so popular, and in particular so excellent with venison sausages, that I felt that it could not be omitted.

Allow 20-25 minutes for baking.

FOR 2

350 g/ 12 oz celeriac
Salt
6 tablespoonsful double cream

Peel the celeriac, taking care to remove the bits of skin which are twisted under the surface. Chop into fairly small pieces, just cover with slightly salted water, and boil for 6-8 minutes, until tender; drain. Set the oven to 225 C, 425 F, Gas Mark 7. Mash the celeriac (like carrots, it will not mash completely smooth). Mix with most of the cream and add the rest to the top. Bake until just beginning to brown.

SPICED SPINACH

I n this, the spices are sufficiently evident to be interesting but not so potent as to overwhelm either the taste of the spinach itself or plain or delicately flavoured accompaniments: in particular, I recommend it with grilled lamb chops or steaks, grilled or baked salmon, or salmon fish-cakes (both flavours).

It is really not worth making without real spinach. When proper spinach is unobtainable, a variant known as beet-spinach, which has larger leaves and thick white stems, may be sold instead. Although suitable for some purposes, it does not have the same flavour as proper spinach and demands slightly different treatment, partly because the stalks take longer to cook than the leaves. Organically grown spinach tends to have more flavour than that grown by conventional methods; spinach on the root is generally in better condition than single leaves (unless ready-washed).

As in other recipes, I have left the spices whole, which not only saves time but adds a nutty texture to the dish.

The spinach can be boiled up to 24 hours in advance; allow 6-7 minutes for cooking and adding the spices.

FOR 3-4

400 g/ 14 oz spinach
Salt
75 g/ 3 oz shallots
4 fair-sized cloves garlic
2-cm/ ¾-inch knob root ginger
½ lemon
25 g/ 1 oz butter
1 tablespoonful oil
1 teaspoonful cumin seeds
2 teaspoonsful coriander seeds
Pepper

Pick over and wash the spinach, twice if necessary (even ready-washed spinach must be washed, since the water clinging to the leaves is needed for cooking). Pack into a saucepan with a lid and add 1 teaspoonful salt (but no water: added water will leach flavour). Set over medium heat for 4 minutes, stir, and cook 1-2 minutes more, until tender and submerged in liquid. Drain over a bowl and press out surplus moisture with the back of a spoon. Set aside the liquor; roughly chop the spinach. If you are boiling it in advance, allow to cool and store, covered, in the refrigerator.

Peel and finely slice the shallots; peel and finely chop the garlic and ginger, discarding any tough, fibrous patches on the ginger. Squeeze the lemon. Melt the butter in the oil over a medium heat and fry the shallots for 2 minutes, turning often. Add the garlic and ginger and fry 2-3 minutes more or until the shallots are starting to change colour; turn constantly. Add the seeds and fry for 30-40 seconds, turning continuously. Add 1 tablespoonful lemon juice, reduce the heat to low, and stir in the spinach with 1 tablespoonful of the spinach-water. Season moderately with pepper and turn for 1-2 minutes, until the spinach is thoroughly heated through and mixed with the flavourings. Serve at once.

ROAST POTATOES

Just as roast meat is probably more popular in Britain than anywhere else, so no other nation roasts potatoes, or at least not in quite the same way as the British. Compared to roast meat, however, they are a recent invention, since they could not be roasted with the meat when cooking was carried out over an open fire. Nor, in higher social circles, would there have been occasion for them because potatoes were not customarily served with the meat, but accompanied fish at the first course.

The perfect roast potato, like perfect roast beef, is crisp on the outside and meltingly tender within. There has been some discussion lately on how best to achieve this: the kind of potato and the fat used are important, but the chief issue is whether or not to boil the potatoes beforehand. I am sorry to have to report (sorry because it means another pan to wash up) that a series of tests has convinced me that boiling for just two minutes really makes a difference: it not only ensures an evenly creamy centre but improves flavour because of the salt in the boiling-water. At a lower oven heat (180 C, 350 F, Gas Mark 4), the difference is less evident, but at the high heat needed for beef, the improvement is very noticeable.

The kind of potato used should be floury; waxy ones will be soggy and tough. Particularly recommended for roasting are Maris Piper and King Edward; other good choices are Kerr's Pink and Golden Wonder. The last may be difficult to find but has excellent flavour.

In general, the fat you use will be dripping from the meat you are cooking, which from the point of view of overall taste is usually the best, but taken *per se*, the ideal fat is duck or goose fat. Failing these or dripping, use lard. A little olive oil added to moisten the potatoes before the fat has run from the meat will produce very good results provided that they are afterwards basted with dripping; olive oil alone, however, tends to produce leatheriness rather than crispness. You do not need much fat or oil: the potatoes need only to be painted or rolled in it and basted at intervals; if they are cooked in a tray, a thin coating over the bottom for rolling and to prevent them from sticking is enough.

Season fairly generously; do not crowd them, but leave space between them for air to circulate. Turn at intervals, but not too often, remembering that those on a tray will colour at the bottom as well as the top. Depending on the kind of meat you are roasting, cooking times for the potatoes are about one hour at 180 C, 350 F, Gas Mark 4, 45-60 minutes at 200 C, 400 F, Gas Mark 6, or 40-50 minutes at 225 C, 425 F, Gas Mark 7.

BAKED POTATOES

A recipe for baked potatoes (as opposed to stuffed baked potatoes) is unnecessary beyond a few remarks, but much might be said about the potatoes themselves. As one would expect, growers put yield and other economic factors beyond taste, with the result that a number of the potatoes with distinctive flavour are difficult to buy; also, as Dr Jeremy Cherfas (of the Henry Doubleday Research Association) has pointed out, the fact that this has led to concentration on relatively few varieties is short-sighted because of the risk of blight (which cannot necessarily be controlled by fungicides). However, of the 15 or so easily obtainable varieties, Estima (August-March) and Cara, Marfona, and King Edward (September-May) are probably the best for baking. Harder to find, but worth the search is Kerr's Pink, which is not only full of flavour but exceptionally dry and floury; others which are particularly recommended are Aran Victory, Golden Wonder, and British Queen. (It does no harm to ask for potatoes which are not stocked: as I have said before, demand begets supply.)

Points about cooking them are: that any green patches where chlorophyll has formed should be cut out (which will not spoil the result, since a crust will form over the cut); that they should be pricked to prevent them from bursting; and that to promote a crisp skin, they should be rubbed with oil before baking. You can cook them at any heat between 180 C, 350 F, Gas Mark 4 and 225 C, 425 F, Gas Mark 7, but at the lower heat even smallish ones (185-225 g/6½-8 oz) will take about 1½ hours; at 200 C, 400 F, Gas Mark 6, a 225 g/ 8 oz potato will take an hour or a little more, or a large one (450 g/1 lb) 1¼-1½ hours. Above this, you will save only about 5 minutes' cooking time with small ones, 10 minutes with large ones, but the higher heat will promote the all-important (to me) crisp skin. They are ready when soft all through; if overcooked, they will be crisper-skinned but with less flavour.

Stuffed potatoes are a separate subject: to serve as part of a meal, I can find only two worthy substitutes for simply serving them with butter, one of which is to mash and brown them (see below), and the other to replace the butter with concentrated yoghurt, which is both healthy and delicious but suitable only with certain dishes, notably chicken (it is also a very good stuffing for baked potatoes served alone). Use it plain, without oil or seasoning, but if you like add just a suspicion of salt to the potato.

BAKED POTATO CUPS

These may not be an ultra-refined dinner-party dish but they look very tempting nevertheless. They can be stuffed with a proportion of cheese (I particularly recommend Gorgonzola and nutmeg) but as an accompaniment are usually better served plain.

For preference, use potatoes small enough for each person to have two or three halves, about 175-225 g/6-8 oz each; also, for the result to look like cups, the potatoes should be round rather than oblong. If oblong, you can make them cup-shaped by cutting them across the narrow side, but in that case they may not stand up unless you have a baking dish in which they fit closely.

Like mashed potatoes, they can be prepared in advance. Allow about an hour for baking the potatoes and 35-40 minutes for browning the cups.

Serve with chops, lamb-steaks, or baked or grilled chicken.

FOR 4

750-875 g/1½-1¾ lb small baking potatoes
50 g/2 oz butter or a little more
Salt
Pepper
2½ teaspoonsful Dijon mustard
2 tablespoonsful milk

Set the oven to 200 C, 400 F, Gas Mark 6. Scrub, prick, and rub the potatoes with oil and bake 1 hour or until soft all through. Leave until cool enough to handle and cut in half to make two cups, using a sharp knife so that the skin does not tear. Hollow out the halves, leaving a margin of flesh of about 5 mm/ less than ¼ inch. Mash the potato with 40 g/1½ oz butter and a moderate seasoning of salt and pepper; beat in the mustard and milk, pile back into the skins, and put a small knob of butter on each. Arrange in a baking dish. If made in advance, cover and store until the next day in the refrigerator. Bake at 200 C, 400 F, Gas Mark 6 for 35-40 minutes, until light brown and bubbling: if you are using the grill in a combined oven and grill, leave the potatoes to finish browning in the middle of the oven while the grill is in use.

OVEN-CHIP POTATOES

These are an alternative to real chips and are crisper, do not involve deep-frying and its accompanying smell, and need relatively little oil (they are merely turned in it, as with roast potatoes). They need relatively little attention: I know that they will be evenly cooked and browned if I turn them once and time them accurately. Their one drawback is that the slices of potato must be spread out on a baking tray, which means that to bake them for more than three or four takes up an inconvenient amount of oven space.

The chips look better if you use small floury potatoes which can be sliced whole.

Cooking time is 25-30 minutes.

Serve with chicken, chops, steaks, sausages, and game instead of fried game chips.

FOR 4

450-500 g/1-1¼ lb floury potatoes
2-3 tablespoonsful oil
Salt
Pepper

Shallow baking tray 30-36 cm/12-14½ inches square: 450 g/1 lb potatoes will just fit the 30 cm/12 inch size

Depending on what else you are cooking, set the oven to 200 C, 400 F, Gas Mark 6 or 225 C, 425 F, Gas Mark 7: the cooler heat is preferable, but only marginally. Line the baking tray with cooking foil, shiny side-up, and spread with the oil. Scrub or peel the potatoes, removing any green patches, chop into two or four if necessary, and cut into even 4-5-mm/ less than ¼-inch slices, discarding the ends. Arrange in a single layer on the tray, turning each slice as you place it so that both sides are coated with oil. Season with salt and pepper and bake until the tops are pale gold. Turn (the undersides will be darker) and continue to cook until deep gold or mid-brown. Do not try to turn the chips until they are coloured or they may stick, and on no account remove them from the oven until they are ready: if allowed to cool, they will lose their crispness. Serve immediately.

SLICED POTATOES BAKED WITH ONIONS

In effect, these are an alternative to fried or sautéed potatoes. In culinary terms, they are an extension of oven-chips, although the result is rather different; however, if you bake them until they are brown they become the same except for the onions and the fact that the potatoes have a slightly softer, chewier texture.

FOR 2

About 200 g/ 7 oz (2 small) onions
225-275 g/ 8-10 oz floury potatoes
2 tablespoonsful oil
Salt
Pepper

Shallow 18 x 36 cm/7 x 14 inch baking tray

Set the oven to 200 C, 400 F, Gas Mark 6 and line the baking tray with cooking foil. Peel and finely slice the onions; scrub or peel the potatoes (for this recipe I prefer them unpeeled) and cut into 4-5-mm/less than ¼-inch slices, discarding the ends. Mix the oil with 4 tablespoonsful water, pour into the tray, and distribute the slices of onion over the bottom. Cover with the potatoes in a single layer, season moderately with salt and pepper, and bake 20-25 minutes, until the potatoes are just beginning to colour. Turn and bake for another 10 minutes. Both the potatoes and the onions at this stage should be slightly tinged with gold but not brown; the water will have evaporated. Serve, or if you like, cook for a little longer.

CRISP MASHED POTATOES

Just as roast potatoes are disobliging in that they benefit from boiling before roasting, so mashed ones are decidedly lighter and richer if baked rather than boiled: as they take 40-50 minutes to crisp and brown, this means that altogether they need 2 hours in the oven. I admit that this is extravagant if you are not using the oven for anything else and do not suggest that it is always worth it; however, I have given three variations using baked potatoes here. Since they are intended as straight potato dishes, none of them is strongly flavoured: in one, I have used fromage frais, which hardly tastes at all, and in another (partly to cut down on the butter) olive oil, which is more noticeable but suits certain dishes, for example plain chicken, or lamb with ratatouille. If you prefer to boil rather than bake the potatoes, use the recipe for the top of the cottage pie on page 159.

The same potatoes should be used as for baking, i.e. floury ones; particularly recommended are Kerr's Pink, Golden Wonder, and Aran Victory.

The potatoes can be prepared a day ahead, but it is essential to mash them while they are still hot.

FOR 4

Mashed Potatoes with Butter
750 g/ 1½ lb floury potatoes
50 g/ 2 oz butter
Salt
Pepper
3 teaspoonsful Dijon mustard
3 tablespoonsful milk

Set the oven to 200 C, 400 F, Gas Mark 6. Scrub the potatoes, removing the eyes and any green patches where chlorophyll has formed, prick, and bake for 1-1½ hours depending on size. Leave until cool enough to handle; peel, removing the tough layer underneath as well as the skin, and mash until smooth with 40 g/1½ oz of the butter and a moderate seasoning of salt and pepper. Gently but thoroughly beat in the mustard and milk. Lightly butter an ovenproof dish; turn the potato into it, rough the top with a fork, and dot with the remaining butter. If prepared in advance, allow to cool and store, covered, in the refrigerator. Bake for 40-50 minutes, until deep golden brown.

Mashed Potatoes with Fromage Frais
750 g/ 1½ lb floury potatoes
150 g/ 5 oz fromage frais
Salt
Pepper
3 teaspoonsful Dijon mustard
3 tablespoonsful double cream
15 g/ ½ oz butter

As above, but mash with the fromage frais, salt, and pepper; stir in the mustard and cream.

Mashed Potatoes with Olive Oil
750 g/ 1½ lb floury potatoes
15 g/ ½ oz butter
Salt
Pepper
3 teaspoonsful Dijon mustard
3 tablespoonsful milk
2 tablespoonsful olive oil

As before, but mash the potatoes with the butter, salt, pepper, and some of the milk. Gently beat in the mustard and the rest of the milk; stir in the oil last.

FISH DISHES

ROWLEY LEIGH'S GRIDDLED SCALLOPS WITH PEA PURÉE AND MINT VINAIGRETTE

When I tried this at Kensington Place, where Rowley is chef and co-owner, the very first mouthful was enough to tell me that no book on the best of British cooking could be complete without it. Another day, I had the same reaction to a chicken and goat's-cheese mousse, but was assured that it was unsuitable for (so to speak) domestic reproduction. The recipe below, however, although two sauces are involved, is perfectly straightforward and very convenient, since both sauces can be made ahead of time and the scallops take only 2 minutes to cook.

As the scallops are heated through and no more, it is essential that they should be absolutely fresh; it is also important that they should be thick enough to be juicy. Choose large, hard, fat ones: do not buy them if they show any sign of sagging, and use them on the same day. On the other hand, to ensure that the peas for the purée are tender and sweet, Rowley specifies frozen rather than fresh.

Serve either for lunch or as a first course: with large scallops, 3 or 4 each are enough for lunch, 2 or 3 as a first course.

FOR 4

Mint vinaigrette
About 10 g/ ⅓ oz (5-6 average sprigs) applemint or spearmint
3 teaspoonful caster sugar
3 tablespoonful white-wine vinegar
1½ tablespoonful groundnut oil

Pea purée
5 Cos or 10 large Little Gem lettuce leaves
3 leaves applemint or spearmint
2 sorrel leaves
5 spring onions
25 g/ 1 oz butter
225 g/ 8 oz frozen peas
Salt

Pepper
3 tablespoonsful white wine
160 ml/ generous ¼ pint double cream

Scallops
25-40 g butter
8-16 large scallops
Salt
Pepper

Vinaigrette

You should start making this first. Wash and blot the mint dry; pull off the leaves, tear into small pieces, and crush with the sugar to a rough paste. (Crushing extracts the juices and hence flavour: chopping or mincing does not have the same effect. The leaves pulverize easily: crushing does not take long.) Add 3 tablespoonsful boiling water and leave while you make the pea purée or for about half an hour. Then stir in the vinegar, add the oil, and whisk until smoothly mixed. Without the oil, the vinaigrette would be mint sauce: the oil, however, has an almost magical effect in lightening and mellowing the flavour.

Purée

Wash the lettuce, mint, and sorrel and blot or thoroughly shake dry; shred finely. Remove the roots and green part of the onions, peel off the outer layer, and chop into very fine rings. Warm the butter over low heat in a wok or saucepan with a lid and add the prepared vegetables. Stir gently for 5-6 minutes or until the lettuce has collapsed and is soft. Add the peas, season moderately with salt and pepper, and turn until thawed. Add the wine, cover, and cook, still over low heat, for 30-40 minutes, until soft. Pour in the cream and reduce over high heat for a few seconds, until the cream is slightly, but only slightly thickened and reduced (if reduced too much, the purée will be very thick). Remove from the heat and blend until very smooth. Before starting to cook the scallops, set the purée to heat over a very low flame; stir frequently.

Scallops

Shortly before you wish to serve, about three-quarters melt the butter over low heat; remove and allow to melt completely. Wash and thoroughly dry the scallops, season fairly generously on both sides with salt and pepper, and paint or roll in the butter; if you roll them, shake off the surplus. If possible, cook them in a griddle-pan; otherwise, use a heavy frying-pan.

Put the empty pan over the highest possible heat until just smoking (do not add fat). Add the scallops and leave without turning or moving for 1 minute. Turn and cook on the other side for another minute: when ready, the outsides should be brown and charred.

Place a generous portion of purée in the centre of each serving plate, distribute the scallops outside it, and dribble half a tablespoonful of vinaigrette round the edge. Serve the rest of the vinaigrette separately.

GRILLED MACKEREL WITH FENNEL SEEDS AND LIME JUICE

There are few more delicious fish, and certainly none cheaper, than absolutely fresh, hard, shining mackerel. At one time, when staying in the family cottage on the coast of Wales, I used to take the boat out and catch them in time for breakfast: they were eaten within an hour of being caught, and memorable. We simply grilled or fried them perfectly plainly, and until I discovered the following recipe I could think of no better way of cooking them. The combination of lime juice and fennel, however, offsets their richness and intensifies without cloaking their flavour; the fennel seeds, which are used whole, also add texture.

The only preparation needed, apart from washing the fish and gutting it if necessary, is rubbing it with a little butter and flour and squeezing a lime. As it is so quick, it seems an ideal dish for one: I have therefore given quantities per person.

The smell of mackerel tends to cling; for this reason, you may prefer to cook it on foil in the grill-pan rather than using the rack.

Cooking time is 6-7 minutes.

Serve either alone (which really suits it best) or with green haricot beans or broccoli and a baked potato.

FOR 1

1 mackerel
About 15 g/ ½ oz butter
Flour
Salt
Pepper
¾ – 1 scant teaspoonful fennel seeds
½ lime

Clean the fish if necessary. Using a sharp knife, cut off the head just behind the gills; slit the underside from the head end to about two thirds of the way to the tail and pull out the gut. Thoroughly rinse the inside and scrape off any remaining dark spots; rinse again. If the fish is already cleaned, you should still rinse the inside and check for specks of dark matter.

Wash and dry the outside. Make 3 or 4 diagonal slits about 2 cm/ ¾ inch deep across both sides to ensure even cooking. Rub all over, first with a little butter, then with a thin coating of flour, and season moderately with salt and pepper.

Set the grill to fairly high. Line the tray of the grill-pan with foil, spread with a little more butter, and either put the fish into it or above it on a rack. Grill for 2 minutes; baste and grill for another minute or until well browned or slightly charred and crisp. Turn and grill the second side for about 1½ minutes; baste and grill for another minute or until browned. Test to see if the fish is ready by inserting a knife to the back-bone: the flesh should be pale and opaque all the way through.

While the fish grills, spread the fennel seeds over a small baking dish and grill for about 40 – 60 seconds, until very faintly coloured and the smell is evident. Remove from the heat. When the fish is just cooked, sprinkle with the toasted seeds, baste, and return to the grill for 20 – 30 seconds. Squeeze a little lime juice over it and add the rest to the juice in the pan. Pour the juice onto the serving plate; set the fish on top.

BAKED RAINBOW TROUT WITH HORSERADISH AND CREAM

In terms of saturated fats, there is no defence for this recipe: use less cream by all means, but do not replace it with single cream, which will give a thin, unsatisfactory sauce.

You can either bake the trout whole or serve it filleted, skinned, and curled into rollmops: it tastes better whole but rollmops are more elegant and convenient to eat. If you serve it whole or buy it from a fishmonger, who will fillet and skin it for you, the dish is almost as quick to prepare as the mackerel on page 120. It will take a little longer with fillets from a supermarket because they will not be skinned (as the flesh of trout is soft, skinned fillets tend to fall apart when cooked: hence the rollmops).

Horseradish loses its flavour quickly after grating: do not prepare it until the trout is in the oven. As the root is difficult to buy, you may have to use ready-grated, which is satisfactory provided that it is plain rather than bottled in vinegar.

Cooking time is 7-14 minutes depending on the size of fish and whether it is filleted.

Serve with new potatoes and broccoli or baked courgettes.

FOR 2

2 trout
Salt
Pepper
Butter for greasing
½ small lemon
¼ teaspoonful sugar
142 ml / ¼ pint double cream
About 1 tablespoonful grated horseradish

Clean, fillet, and skin the trout if necessary. As the flesh is soft but the skin tough (and also slippery), it is essential to use a very sharp knife. To clean it, cut off the head just behind the gills, slit the underside from the head to about two thirds of the way to the tail, and pull out the gut. Scrape off further dark matter with a knife and rinse; if not completely clean, scrape and rinse again. To fillet the fish, extend the slit in the underside to the tail, cut off the tail, and lay the carcass out flat, skin-side down. Slide the knife under the ribs on each side of the backbone; then ease out the bone. The easiest way to cut the skin to make two fillets is to fold the fish back to its original shape and slit down the uncut side. Skinning needs care: ease off the skin very gently to avoid breaking the flesh.

Set the oven to 225 C, 425 F, Gas Mark 7. Wash ready-prepared fish or fillets: with a cleaned whole fish, check that no dark spots remain on the inside. Dry and season moderately with salt and pepper. Lightly butter a baking dish which fits whole fish or a small soufflé-dish for fillets. Lay whole fish in the dish; roll up fillets skin-side out, starting with the narrower tail-end. Place them in the soufflé-dish on their sides with the loose end at the bottom. Squeeze 1 tablespoonful of lemon juice, mix with the sugar, and sprinkle over them. Do not pour the cream over them until just before putting them into the oven. Bake until the flesh is just firm and opaque all the way through and the cream bubbling; with larger whole fish, it may begin to brown. Do not disturb it as it cooks, since if it is mixed with the lemon juice it may curdle. Peel and finely grate the horseradish if necessary. Sprinkle some of it over the fish; add more to taste.

HUGO ARNOLD'S BAKED GREY MULLET WITH LEMON AND PESTO

Many people will recognise Hugo's name from his daily cookery column in the London *Evening Standard*; it is less well known that his writing is informed by his experience as a working chef. As he points out, grey mullet (like smoked haddock) is underrated: 'Grey mullet is one of the cheapest fish available and yet its flesh resembles that of sea bass, without perhaps the latter's subtlety or delicacy of flavour.'

The recipe is quick and simple; the pesto can be made in advance. Allow 10 minutes for cooking.

Serve with new potatoes and/or French, Kenya or green haricot beans.

FOR 4

Pesto
25 g/1 oz pine nuts
30 g/1¼ oz (about 24) basil leaves
40 g/1½ oz freshly grated Parmesan or ready-grated pecorino
4-5 tablespoonsful virgin olive oil

Fish
3 lemons
4 grey mullet
Salt
Pepper
Maize flour or plain white flour for coating
2-3 tablespoonsful oil

Pesto
Toast the pine nuts in a dry frying-pan until golden, or in the oven at 200 C, 400 F, Gas Mark 6 for about 5 minutes (if you are not making the pesto in advance, you will have turned on the oven anyway) and follow the method for pesto on page 86, using the basil instead of parsley.

Fish

Set the oven to 200 C, 400 F, Gas Mark 6 and lightly oil an ovenproof dish large enough for the fish. Scrub two of the lemons and cut each into 6 slices, discarding the ends. Halve each slice, remove the pips, and set conveniently to hand. If the fish is not already cleaned, follow the directions on page 121. Wash and dry them inside and out; make three fairly deep slashes on both sides, season moderately with salt and pepper, and dust with flour. Warm the oil in a frying-pan over moderate/high heat and sear very quickly; they may open out a little, but this does not matter. Remove from the heat and stuff a half slice of lemon into each slit, skin inwards.

Transfer to the ovenproof dish and bake 10 minutes or just until the flesh is opaque all the way through and flakes easily with a fork. Dribble a strip of pesto over the top of each and serve with the remaining lemon cut into quarters.

SALMON PASTY WITH LEMON SAUCE AND SORREL

Farmed salmon is never going to match the texture and flavour of the best wild salmon, but if carefully fed can nevertheless be very good. This is an ideal way to cook it, since the pastry seals in the juices, thus maximizing flavour and keeping the flesh succulent but compact; even if the edges are not brilliantly tidy, it also looks very impressive. The quantities can be increased for a party: as well as looking attractive, the dish is convenient in that the pastry can be made up to 2 days, and the pasty assembled some hours, in advance.

The fishmonger will clean and bone the fish for you, but it is very easy to do it yourself (see below). If a fishmonger prepares it, remember to take the bone and head (if available) to make stock for the sauce.

Serve with Pink Fir Apple, Jersey Royal, or other new potatoes (see page 99), either accompanied by asparagus or followed by a rocket or green salad.

FOR 5-6

Puff pastry (see page 21) made with:
225 g/ 8 oz plain white flour
Pinch salt
50 g/ 2 oz lard
175 g/ 6 oz butter

1 kg /2.2 lb salmon, cut in 1 piece, preferably from the head end of a
largish fish
65-75 g/ 2½-3 oz shallots
1 outside stick celery
2 or 3 sprigs each parsley and marjoram
6 peppercorns
Salt
8-10 sorrel leaves
20 g/ ¾ oz butter
½ tablespoonful oil
150 ml/ ¼ pint dry white wine
3 size 2 eggs (yolks only)
½ lemon
Pepper
½ teaspoonful caster sugar
200 ml/ ⅓ pint double cream plus a little extra
25 g/ 1 oz flour

Make and chill the pastry (it is essential that it should be chilled before use). Prepare the fish if necessary: for this, you will need a sharp, preferably thin-bladed knife (fishmongers use long, slim knives with springy blades). Cut off the head behind the fin and gills and set aside. Slit the fish down the middle of the back: then slide the knife down each side of the back-bone, cutting to about three-quarters of the depth of the fish. Lift out the bone: the gut will come away with it. Keep the bone; check that no so-called 'pin-bones' are left in the flesh. Wash thoroughly in running cold water, taking care to remove any remaining traces of gut, and pat dry. If it is whole, cut off and reserve the tail. Turn it skin-side up and skin: slide the knife under the skin at the tail-end and pull the skin gently but firmly towards the head. Do not throw away the skin. Keep the fish covered while you prepare the sauce and stuffing.

Put the skin, bone, head, and, if available, the tail of the salmon into a largish saucepan. Peel and finely slice one of the shallots and add. Trim the leaves from the celery; wash, slice, and add. Wash the parsley and marjoram and add with the peppercorns and a fair pinch of salt. Barely cover with water, bring just to the boil, skim, and simmer for 20 minutes. Strain the stock over a bowl; throw away the solid ingredients.

Peel and very finely chop the rest of the shallots. Wash, blot dry, and slice the sorrel leaves into very fine strips. Melt the butter in the oil over fairly low heat and fry the shallots for 3 minutes, turning constantly; add the sorrel and continue to fry, still turning constantly, for 2-3 minutes more or until the shallots are soft but not brown. Transfer the sorrel and shallots to a plate; leave any remaining oil in the pan. Add the wine to the pan, turn up the heat to high, and cook it almost away. Add 300 ml/ ½ pint of the stock, stir thoroughly, and remove from the heat. (There will be some stock left over: use if possible. It will keep for 2 days in the refrigerator.)

Separate the eggs (see page 17); squeeze the lemon. Add ½ tablespoonful of the juice, a generous grinding of pepper, a moderate seasoning of salt, and the sugar to the yolks. Whisk or beat with a fork until smooth. Stir in the cream, fold in the flour, and beat until perfectly homogenous. Add the stock gradually, stirring continuously. Pour into a smallish saucepan, set over low heat, and bring just to the boil, still stirring continuously. Reduce the heat and simmer for 3½ minutes; continue to stir constantly. Leave to become cold.

Roll out the pastry to a rectangle about 12-13 cm/ 5 inches longer than the salmon and 8 cm/ 3 inches wider. Flatten out the salmon; season moderately with salt and fairly generously with pepper on both sides and sprinkle the inside surface with a little lemon juice. Spread one side with the sorrel and shallots and fold back to its original shape. Sprinkle a very little lemon juice over the top and cover with about a quarter of the cold sauce. Place, sauce downwards, on one side of the pastry, leaving equal margins at the top and bottom and 4 cm/ 1½ inches at the near side. Sprinkle the remaining surface with lemon juice and cover with another quarter or more of the sauce. Damp the edges of the pastry and fold it over to cover the fish; seal the edges, stamp with a fork, and make 4 or 5 diagonal slashes in the top.

If you have prepared the pasty in advance, cover and put in the refrigerator until needed. (As a whole fish may be difficult to pick up, I suggest storing it placed ready on a baking sheet.) To bake, heat the oven to 225 C, 425 F, Gas Mark 7, place the pasty in the centre of a baking-sheet lined with lightly greased cooking foil and bake 30 minutes or until lightly browned.

After taking it from the oven, stir 2 or 3 extra tablespoonsful of cream into the rest of the sauce, heat over low heat, stirring constantly, and serve separately.

CURRIED SALMON WITH SPINACH

Like kedgeree, salmon curry has a long history in this country. Apart from using curry powder rather than fresh spices, Mrs Beeton gave a very passable recipe for it.

I have included it because it is one of my favourite recipes rather than as a way of using up remains or of making 450 g/ 1 lb salmon stretch to 4 or 6 servings. The curry is not very hot, but just potent enough to point up the flavour of the fish: if you like, you can make it hotter by adding an extra chilli.

As with fish-cakes, the salmon should have been cooked until it is only just opaque, so that it remains tender and succulent. Real spinach is essential: avoid beet-spinach, which has larger leaves and thick white stems.

Cooking time, is 12-14 minutes.

Serve with plain rice, preferably Basmati, and wedges of lemon.

FOR 4-5

275 – 375g/ 10-13 oz Basmati rice
225 g/ 8 oz spinach
Salt
Bunch coriander leaves or parsley (enough for 2 tablespoonsful
when chopped)
450 g/ 1 lb lightly cooked salmon
1½ lemons
About 150 g/ 5 oz (2 medium) ripe tomatoes

> *150 g/ 5 oz shallots*
> *2 cloves garlic*
> *2.5-cm/ 1-inch knob root ginger*
> *1 hot or 2 milder green chillies (see page 28)*
> *¾ teaspoonful black peppercorns*
> *1 teaspoonful caster sugar*
> *2 tablespoonsful clarified butter or ghee*
> *1 teaspoonful cumin seeds*
> *2 teaspoonsful coriander seeds*

Set the rice to cook (see page 22). Pick over and wash the spinach, twice if necessary (rinse it even if it is ready-washed, since the water which clings to the leaves is needed for cooking). Put it into a saucepan with a lid, add ½ teaspoonful salt (but no more water), cover, and cook over medium heat for 4 minutes. Stir and cook for another 1-2 minutes, until just tender and submerged in juice. Strain over a bowl, pressing out as much liquid as you can with the back of a spoon; chop finely. Reserve the liquor.

Trim the ends of the coriander or parsley stems if bought; wash and leave to drain. Flake the salmon; keep any juices. Squeeze the ½ lemon. Skin and chop the tomatoes (see page 16); peel and finely slice the shallots. Peel and chop the garlic and ginger: discard and replace any tough, fibrous patches on the ginger. Wash and dry the chilli(es), cut off the stalk end, and dice (keep the seeds): either wear gloves while handling them or wash your hands directly afterwards. Crush the peppercorns in a mortar. Add the garlic, ginger, chilli, sugar, and one teaspoonful salt and crush to a paste.

Do not start cooking the curry until the rice is tender and resting. Heat the butter or ghee in a wok or frying-pan over medium heat and fry the shallots 3-4 minutes or until they start to change colour, turning constantly. Add the cumin and coriander seeds (whole) and fry for 30 seconds; add the paste from the mortar and fry for another 30 seconds, turning continuously. Add the tomatoes and fry 3-4 minutes, pressing the flesh against the bottom of the pan until dissolved. Reduce the heat to fairly low and add 1 tablespoonful lemon juice and the spinach. Turn to mix for about 1 minute; add 3 tablespoonsful of the spinach water and continue to cook, stirring constantly, for 1½-2 minutes. Gently stir in the salmon and juice and cook for a further 2 minutes; if the pan seems dry, add a little more spinach water. Serve immediately with the rice and the whole lemon cut into quarters or sixths.

COD FISH-CAKES WITH LIME AND PARSLEY SAUCE

These are light, fresh-tasting and suitably economic: 350 g/ 12 oz fish will serve 4. The sauce, which includes garlic, is very sharp, adding zest in much the same way as a hot chutney.

The flavour of the cakes improves very perceptibly if you mix them a day in advance.

As with salmon fish-cakes, I suggest baking both the fish and the potato; the fish should be cooked very lightly and carefully drained of cooking-liquor before being mashed.

Serve alone or with new potatoes and peas or broccoli.

MAKES 8-9 CAKES

275 g/ 10 oz (1 medium) floury potato (see page 109)
225 g/ 8 oz filleted smoked cod
125 g/ 4 oz filleted fresh cod
Salt
Pepper
Bunch parsley (enough for 2 tablespoonsful when chopped)
75 g/ 3 oz onion
½ teaspoonful black peppercorns
½ lime
60 g/ generous 2 oz stale brown or white bread, weighed without crust
3 tablespoonsful oil
20 g/ ¾ oz plain white flour
1 size 2 egg

Set the oven to 200 C, 400 F, Gas Mark 6. Wash the potato and bake 60-70 minutes, until soft; leave until cool enough to skin, peel, and thoroughly mash.

If necessary, skin the cod: starting at the thickest corner, pull the skin gently and ease it off with a sharp knife (as a general rule, the fresher the fish, the harder it is to skin). Season the smoked cod fairly generously with pepper and the fresh cod lightly with salt and moderately with pepper. Wrap both together in a parcel of cooking foil and bake while the potato is in the oven for 10-12 minutes or until the fish flakes easily with a fork and is just, but only just, pale and opaque all through.

Trim the ends of bought parsley stems; wash and very thoroughly blot the parsley dry and chop as finely as you can. Peel and chop the onion as finely as possible; coarsely crush the peppercorns. Squeeze 2 teaspoonsful of lime juice.

Mix the parsley, onion, crushed pepper, and ¾ teaspoonful of salt with the potato. Drain the fish, flake, and add to the potato with the lime juice; mash in gently. Form the mixture into flat cakes; if you are making them in advance, cover and store in the refrigerator.

Finely grate the bread, discarding any outsize pieces. Set the grill to medium/high, line a shallow baking tray with cooking foil, and spread with the oil. Sprinkle the flour over a plate; season moderately with salt and pepper. Break the egg into a bowl or saucer, beat until homogenous, and season similarly. Spread the breadcrumbs over another plate. Coat the cakes first with flour, then with egg, then crumbs, making sure that each is completely covered and shaking off any surplus. Place on the baking tray, turn so that each side is coated with oil, and grill 5-6 minutes or until the upper side is pale brown; turn and grill for another 2 minutes or until the second side is brown. Serve at once.

LIME AND PARSLEY SAUCE

This takes only a few minutes to prepare, although the parsley needs fairly energetic crushing. It can be made some hours in advance but preferably not the previous day.

Large bunch parsley (enough for 4 tablespoonsful when chopped)
1 medium (not large) clove garlic
½ lime
Pinch sugar
Generous grinding pepper
Salt
2 tablespoonsful virgin olive oil

Trim the ends of bought parsley stems; wash and very thoroughly blot the parsley dry (it is essential that it should be really dry). Chop finely. Peel, slice, and crush the garlic in a mortar. Add the parsley and pound to a fine, dark green paste. Squeeze 2 teaspoonsful of lime juice and add with the sugar, pepper, ¼ teaspoonful salt, and the oil; mix thoroughly.

SALMON FISH-CAKES WITH LIME-ZEST OR LEMON-GRASS

emon-grass flatters the salmon but is barely detectable *per se*; the lime is more distinctive. I cannot decide which I prefer and so leave the choice to you.

For cakes which are blended sufficiently to be light and smooth but at the same time retain the juiciness of the salmon, the fish must be cooked until it is only just opaque and gently flaked rather than beaten and bullied into the potato. In order to ensure maximum flavour, I recommend baking it; the potato should also be baked, since it is important to keep it as dry as possible.

You will need stale bread for breadcrumbs: fresh bread tends to form doughy lumps when grated (if, like me, you never have any, dry out the bread in a very low oven.

The cakes can be made a day in advance (in fact, I have sometimes kept them for 2 days, although this is not recommended).

Serve alone or with coriander butter (see below) and/or spiced spinach (see page 106).

MAKES 8-9 CAKES

275 g/ 10 oz (1 medium) floury potato
300 g/ 11 oz filleted salmon
Salt
Bunch coriander leaves (enough for 2 tablespoonsful when chopped)
30 g/ 1¼ oz shallot
16 peppercorns
Either 1 stick lemon-grass and ½ small lemon
or 2 limes
60 g/ generous 2 oz stale brown bread (not stone-ground), weighed
without crust
3-4 tablespoonsful oil
20 g/ ¾ oz white flour
Pepper
1 size 2 egg

Pre-heat the oven 200 C, 400 F, Gas Mark 6. Wash the potato and bake 60-70 minutes, until just soft all the way through (do not overcook). Leave until it is cool enough to handle and peel, removing both the outer and fine underlayer of skin. Mash thoroughly with a fork.

Wash the fish and skin if necessary: ease the skin off gently with a sharp knife. Check for bones. Season fairly generously with salt (which it is important should be sea salt) and enclose in cooking foil. Bake while the potato is in the oven for 10-13 minutes, until it can be flaked easily with a fork and is just, but only just, opaque all the way through.

Trim the ends of the coriander stems if bought; wash and thoroughly blot the coriander dry, and chop as finely as possible. Peel and very finely chop the shallot. Crush the peppercorns coarsely. If you are using lemon-grass, trim the root, peel off the outer layer, and dice very finely; squeeze 2 teaspoonsful of lemon juice. With limes, scrub in cold water, dry, and finely grate the zest of 1½. Squeeze 2 teaspoonsful of juice from one of them (use the other promptly, since without the zest it may go mouldy).

Mix the coriander, shallot, lime-zest or lemon-grass, pepper, and 1 very slightly rounded teaspoonful of salt with the potato. Thoroughly drain the cooking liquor from the salmon; flake and fold in the fish with the lime juice. Mash gently with a fork until thoroughly mixed. Mould into 8 or 9 flat cakes. If you are making them ahead of time, cover and store in the refrigerator.

Finely grate the bread, rejecting any oversized crumbs (the cakes will not brown evenly unless the crumbs are fine and regular). Set the grill to medium/high and line a shallow baking tray with cooking foil, shiny side up. Spread with 3 tablespoonsful of oil. Sprinkle the flour over a plate and season moderately with salt and pepper. Break the egg into a shallow bowl, beat with a fork until homogenous, and season similarly. Spread the crumbs over a third plate. Roll each cake first in the flour, then in the egg, and then in the breadcrumbs: make sure that it is coated all over and shake off any surplus. Place the coated cakes on the baking tray and turn so that both sides are moistened with oil; add a little more oil if needed. Grill 5-6 minutes or until the upper sides are pale brown; turn and grill 2 minutes more or until the second side is brown (do not turn the cakes before they are coloured or they may break). Serve at once with coriander butter or spiced spinach.

CORIANDER BUTTER

Like the fish-cakes, this can be prepared a day ahead.

FOR 4

Bunch coriander leaves (enough for 2 tablespoonsful when chopped)
1 medium clove garlic
50 g/ 2 oz butter
Salt
Pepper

Trim the ends of the coriander stems if bought; wash, blot very thoroughly dry, and finely chop. Peel and chop the garlic; roughly chop the butter. Crush the garlic in a mortar; add the coriander and pound to a paste. Add the butter, season very lightly with salt and moderately with pepper, crush to soften, and mix. Keep chilled until needed. To serve, place a blob on top of each fish-cake.

HOT-SMOKED HALIBUT STEAKS WITH SORREL AND LEMON BUTTER

I was in two minds about whether to include this because you will almost certainly have to go to a major food hall for the smoked halibut; on the other hand, demand stimulates supply. When I asked for it at my local fishmonger, where the proprietor does his own smoking, he thought for a moment and then said, 'I'll smoke some myself', which he did. Since then, he has found it worthwhile to maintain a regular supply in his shop. (The same applied to smokies: at first he ordered some, which immediately sold out, and he now smokes his own in large numbers.)

The taste of the halibut is subtler and less salty than that of most cold-smoked fish. Like smokies, it is cooked and can be served hot or cold; if sold in thin slices, serve cold as part of a salad.

The only actual cooking involved in this recipe is to heat 4 small steaks per person under a medium grill for 1-2 minutes; serve with a knob of sorrel and lemon butter on top and accompany with asparagus and tiny new potatoes.

FOR 3-4

Sorrel and lemon butter
5-6 leaves sorrel or a bunch of parsley (enough for 2 tablespoonsful when chopped)
40 g/1½ oz butter
Salt
Pepper
½ lemon

Wash, thoroughly blot dry, and finely chop the sorrel or parsley. Pound to a paste in a mortar, adding a little of the butter if it makes pounding easier. Chop up the rest of the butter, add with a little salt and a moderate seasoning of pepper and pound to a cream. Squeeze 2 teaspoonsful lemon juice and pound it in gradually.

FISH STEW WITH SAFFRON AND OYSTERS

I had originally meant this to be a recipe for a straightforward oyster stew such as was given by Eliza Acton and Isabella Beeton; however, in view of the cost of even the cheaper rock oysters, the following seems more practical. I have chosen monkfish and halibut as the other main ingredients because, although both are fairly expensive, they are firm-fleshed and give the stew body.

Rock, or Pacific oysters are oval rather than round, like natives, and available all the year round (though better in the winter); the ones I generally buy come from Whitstable, but those reared in Ireland and Scotland also have very good flavour. When buying them, choose heavy ones with shells which are either firmly shut or shut promptly when tapped. Although it is preferable to use them directly, they can be kept for at least 3 days wrapped in a damp cloth in the refrigerator. (If you are worried about the healthiness of oysters, it may help to know that unless reared in 'Grade A' water, they are kept in sterile tanks before being sold.)

If possible, use unshelled prawns.

Apart from shelling prawns and opening oysters (see page 17), the stew is fairly quick to make, since the only vegetable to prepare is shallots and cooking time is about 9 minutes. As their liquor is needed for the sauce, however, do not try to save time by asking the fishmonger to open the oysters.

Accompany with either waxy new potatoes or floury old ones to mop up the sauce (see page 109 for varieties of potato). Serve other vegetables separately.

FOR 4

12 British-reared rock oysters
75 ml/ 2½ fl oz double cream
3 g (¾ small packet) saffron threads
125 g/ 4 oz shallots
1 lemon
225 g/ 8 oz unshelled prawns or 125 g/ 4 oz shelled

350 g/ 12 oz monkfish
350 g/ 12 oz halibut
Pepper
1 size 1 or 2 egg (yolk only)
15 g/ ½ oz butter
½ tablespoonful oil
150 ml/ ¼ pint dry white wine

Open the oysters (see page 17), holding them over a bowl to catch the liquor. Rinse the flesh carefully in the liquor; pick off any remaining fragments of shell. Strain the liquor through a jelly-bag or very fine sieve. Set both the flesh and liquor aside.

Heat but do not boil the cream in a small saucepan. Shake in the saffron threads and leave to cool, stirring from time to time. Peel and finely chop the shallots; halve the lemon. Shell or rinse the prawns: if rinsed, leave them in a sieve or on kitchen paper to drain. Skin the monkfish and halibut. Really fresh halibut is particularly difficult to skin: use a sharp knife. Wash and chop into pieces about 3 cm/ 1¼ inches square; remove all bones and season lightly with pepper.

Separate the egg (see page 17): beat the yolk smooth and mix with 1 tablespoonful of the saffron and cream. Warm a casserole or other heatproof dish from which you can serve the stew (pour boiling water into it). Fry the shallots over medium heat in a wok for 3-4 minutes or until an even gold; turn constantly. Add the wine and cook about half of it away. Add the oyster liquor, monkfish, and halibut and bring to the boil. Reduce the heat to just under a simmer and poach the fish for 1 minute. Add the cream and saffron (without egg) and stir; add the oysters and prawns, bring back just to the boil, and boil gently for about 30 seconds or until the monkfish and halibut are opaque all the way through. Transfer the fish to the warm casserole with a perforated spoon and cover, leaving the sauce in the wok. Reduce the sauce for 3-4 minutes over high heat; stir a little of it into the egg yolk and cream and mix thoroughly. Remove the pan from the heat, add the egg yolk mixture, and stir until it thickens; set over low heat for a moment or two if necessary but do not let it boil. Pour over the fish, sprinkle with a few drops of lemon juice, and serve with wedges of lemon.

KEDGEREE

The original, Indian version of kedgeree contains neither fish nor eggs, but is a simple dish based on lentils. The idea was presumably imported by employees of the East India Company: by the middle of the last century, the familiar British adaptation (which was necessitated by the fact that lentils were not generally available) was becoming an increasingly popular breakfast or supper dish.

As fresh ginger was also unobtainable, a common flavouring was curry powder; however, I have used fresh ginger and garlic.

If you prefer, you can use only 450 g/ 1 lb of haddock: this gives an acceptable result but the taste of the dish is decidedly improved if you use more.

Preparation and cooking time together are about 45 minutes.

FOR 4-5 AS A MAIN COURSE FOR DINNER OR 6-8 FOR BREAKFAST
OR SUPPER

200 g/ 7 oz Basmati, Patna, or other long-grain rice
(preferably Basmati)
750 g/ 1½ lb smoked haddock
40 g/ 1½ oz butter
2 medium onions
3 medium cloves garlic
2-cm/ ¾-inch knob fresh ginger
5 black peppercorns
1 tablespoonful oil
⅔ teaspoonful sea salt
1 teaspoonful hot chilli powder
4 size 1 eggs

Rinse the rice under the cold tap until the water runs clear and leave to drain in a sieve. Prepare the fish. Rather than boiling or baking it uncovered, I suggest baking it wrapped in foil, which ensures that it stays moist and retains all its flavour: if boiled, it loses flavour which is not regained by using the boiling liquor to cook the rice. Set the oven to 200 C, 400 F, Gas Mark 6. Skin the fish (pull the skin sharply from the thickest corner), remove any bones, and wash in cold water.

Place a piece of cooking foil large enough to enclose it on a baking dish. Lay the fish on it, dot the top with 15 g/ ½ oz of the butter (chopped), and wrap in a parcel. Bake for 15-20 minutes or until it breaks easily when prodded with a fork. Flake, check again for bones, and drain the cooking liquor into a measuring jug or mug. Re-wrap the fish to keep it warm.

While the fish cooks, peel and finely slice the onions. Peel and roughly chop the garlic and ginger, removing any fibrous patches from the ginger; crush with the peppercorns in a mortar. Put the oil and the rest of the butter into a large wok or saucepan with a fitted lid. Melt the butter over medium heat, add the onions, and fry 6-7 minutes or until an even brown, turning constantly, particularly towards the end. Lower the heat or lift the pan for a moment to cool it, and add the salt, chilli powder, and crushed garlic, ginger, and peppercorns. Turn thoroughly to mix; add and stir-fry the rice until all the grains are coated with oil. Add 300 ml/ ½ pint of water and bring to the boil. Stir thoroughly, lower the heat, cover, and simmer. When the fish has been drained, make up the fish liquor to 75 ml/ 2½ fl oz with water and add. Cook Basmati rice for 18 minutes or other types of long-grain white rice for 20 minutes; brown rice will need about 30 minutes. Look at it towards the end of cooking and add a little more water if necessary.

Set the eggs to boil; boil for 12 minutes. Immerse in cold water, shell, and chop. Add to the wrapped fish.

Gently but quickly stir the eggs and fish into the cooked rice, still over low heat. Remove from the heat, cover, and leave to settle 10 minutes before serving.

MEAT
POULTRY AND
GAME DISHES

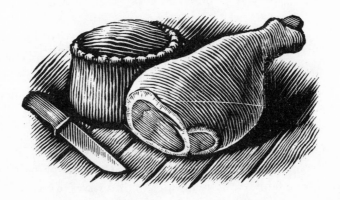

SIMMERED GAMMON WITH CAPER SAUCE

Pigs are omnivorous and, as is well known, will eat anything from truffles to potato-peelings. Their natural diet is a mixture of nuts and greenstuff, but their ability to thrive without access to open land is the reason for the relative cheapness (and lack of snob-appeal) of pork and its products over the centuries. In the 19th century, milk-fed pork was considered to have the most delicate flavour; in the 18th century, however, the superiority of meat from pigs who foraged for themselves was recognized. The breeder Ann Petch, whose pigs are all free-range, gives them oats, barley, and bran, with soya protein for piglets, to which the pigs add grass, clover, and whatever else they can find. This, plus breed (Ann specializes in old breeds) and the fact that they are relatively mature, produces pork and ham with real flavour and individuality.

Among other variables which affect the taste of ham are distribution of fat, curing, and whether or not it is smoked. As the flavour of food is transmitted by fat, marbled ham, like beef, will have more taste than lean; smoking gives strength and an added dimension to flavour. Curing can be dry or wet; dry-cured hams, such as York, are saltier. The subject of curing brings up the issue of so-called 'tumbling', which means treating the meat with phosphates. These are used as preservatives, to improve colour, and also to tenderize or 'moisturize' it by increasing liquid-retention, which in turn serves to add weight. A 10 per cent moisture- or water-content added by this process is permitted without being stated on the label; above this, it is marked, but only by the excess, so that a declared 10 per cent is in fact 20 per cent. A high moisture-content obviously means less actual meat for the weight; however, a high content is more likely at the lower than the upper end of the market and is almost certainly irrelevant in the case of free-range products.

At present (i.e. the time of going to press), true free-range gammon is not available from the major retailers, but non-intensively reared meat, which means that the pigs have had reasonable freedom, is sold at leading food halls and at least one supermarket chain. When possible, buy it on the bone; as mild cures are more popular than strong, buy smoked if you like a positive flavour. Further shopping advice, which comes from Ann, is that gammon should be freshly cut and when held to the light have an iridescent sheen; this is not evident when it is cut along the grain but can be seen where it is cross-cut.

Simmering the gammon is perfectly straightforward, but it must be gently simmered rather than boiled, i.e. the surface of the water should only just move; in my experience, this makes far more difference to tenderness than any amount of cosmetic moisturizing. Flavour is also improved if it is not leached by a large quantity of water: a pan which leaves room for only 1-1.5 litres/2-2½ pints will produce both full-flavoured gammon and rich stock.

Dry-cured gammon needs 24 hours' soaking before cooking; wet-cured, 8 hours or less (mild, 'moisturized' gammon may need only 1-2). Up to 2.5 kg/ 5 lb, cooking time is 30 minutes per 450 g/ 1 lb plus 15 minutes; 2.5-5 kg/ 5-10 lb, 20 minutes per 450 g/ 1 lb plus 20 minutes; 5.5-7.5 kg/ 11-15 lb, 16-20 minutes per 450 g/ 1 lb.

On the assumption that you will want to serve the remains cold, I have included breadcrumbs for the outside with the ingredients. Accompany with crisp mashed potatoes (see page 113) or boiled potatoes and green haricot beans, broccoli, carrots, or braised celery (page 104), or with gooseberry and elderflower jelly, which can also be served with it hot instead of caper sauce.

FOR 4

*1.75-2.25 kg/ 3¾-5 lb soaked gammon, preferably smoked (this
quantity allows for some to serve cold)
125-150 g/ 4-5 oz (1 small/medium) onion
175 g/ 6 oz (2 medium) carrots
1 outside stick celery
2 bay leaves
2 cloves
6 peppercorns
1 tablespoonful cider vinegar or red-wine vinegar
40-60 g/ 1½ -2 oz stale white bread, weighed without crust
Caper sauce (see below)*

Take the gammon from the soaking-water, rinse, and just cover with fresh water in a saucepan which fits it plus a little to spare. Bring to the boil, skim, and simmer uncovered for 15 minutes. Meanwhile, peel and finely chop the onion. Peel and finely slice the carrots. Trim the leaves from the celery, pare off any discoloured streaks, wash, and slice finely. Rinse the bay leaves.

After 15 minutes, taste the water in which the gammon is simmering and if very salty, change it. Add the prepared vegetables plus the bay leaves, cloves, peppercorns, and vinegar, bring back to the boil if necessary, cover, and simmer 1¾-2¼ hours, until tender but still firm (the initial 15 minutes must be counted in the cooking time). While it simmers, set the oven to 200 C, 400 F, Gas Mark 6; finely grate the bread, spread it over a baking tray and bake 7-10 minutes, shaking or turning several times, until an even gold. Set aside. Start making the sauce about 15 minutes before the ham is ready.

To serve, lift the gammon from the cooking liquor but leave the liquid in the pan, covered. After serving, return it at once to the liquor, cover, and allow to cool until lukewarm: this ensures that it will stay moist when cold. Remove from the pan, ease off the skin, using a knife if necessary, and trim the fat to a layer of about 6 mm/ ¼ inch. Rub the crumbs evenly over the fat and leave to become cold.

CAPER SAUCE

FOR 4

35 g/ 1¼ oz butter
15 g/ ½ oz flour
300 ml/ ¼ pint ham stock
1 size 2 egg (yolk only)
Pepper
1 teaspoonful Dijon mustard
2 tablespoonsful double cream
1 tablespoonful capers

Put 20 g/ ¾ oz of the butter into a small saucepan and set it over a low heat until three-quarters melted; remove from the heat and leave for a minute or two to cool and melt completely. Pour it into a basin, add the flour, and mix until perfectly smooth. Draw off the stock from the ham as it simmers. Separate the egg and beat the yolk until perfectly smooth; season moderately with pepper. Slowly pour about 1 tablespoonful of the hot stock into the egg, beating continuously. Gradually pour in more, still beating continuously, until all the stock is added. Add the thickened stock to the flour, stir until thoroughly incorporated, and transfer to the saucepan. Bring to the boil, again stirring continuously, add the mustard, and simmer for 6-8 minutes; stir constantly. When you are ready to serve, stir in the cream and add the capers. Finally, stir in the remaining 15 g/ ½ oz butter; remove from the heat. The finished sauce should be very smooth and just thick enough to coat the back of a spoon.

GOOSEBERRY AND ELDERFLOWER JELLY

For this, it really is worth going to find some elderflowers: they add an almost Oriental fragrance to the gooseberries. The gooseberries should be very fresh and slightly under- rather than over-ripe.

It is an enormous advantage in making jams and jellies to have a sugar-thermometer so that you know exactly when setting-point is reached; however, this can be judged by other methods (see below).

Allow 1¼ hours for simmering the fruit and 4 to 24 for straining the pulp (but no longer).

The jelly will keep for up to a year provided that you sterilize the jar and top. There is no need to use new jars: an empty one with a screw-top is perfectly adequate.

MAKES 300-350 G/ 10½-12 OZ

900 g/ 2 lb green gooseberries
4 good-sized heads elderflower
275 g/ 10 oz granulated sugar

Jelly-bag for straining
350-g/ 12-oz jam-jar

Carefully pick over and wash the gooseberries; rinse the flowers. Shake off surplus water in a colander, put into a saucepan with 300 ml/ ½ pint fresh water, and set over very low heat, stirring from time to time, for 1¼ hours or until the fruit has become pulp (long simmering extracts the pectin, a natural setting-agent). Scald the jelly-bag and spread it over a pudding-basin. Turn the pulp into it, suspend it over the basin, and leave for 4 hours or until next day.

Before making the jelly, sterilize the jar and top: wash both in detergent, rinse thoroughly, and immerse in a saucepan of water. Place a tablespoon inside the jar with the handle resting on the edge of the pan. Bring to the boil and boil for 10 minutes. Set the oven to 150 C, 300 F, Gas Mark 2; line a small baking tray with cooking foil. Remove the pan from the heat; do not drain it, but lift and turn the jar upside-down on the spoon and place it, still upside-down, on the tray (the handle of the spoon may be hot: use an oven-cloth). The outside of the jar does not matter, but if it is to remain sterile, nothing except the spoon must touch the inside. Use the spoon to fish out the top and place right-side-up on the cooking foil. Set the jar and top to dry in the oven; return the spoon to the water in the pan. Leave the jar in the oven until the foil on which it is placed is quite dry.

Pour the fruit juice into a largish saucepan, add a thermometer if you have one, and bring to the boil. To register accurately, the thermometer should not touch the bottom of the pan: unless it clips to the side of the saucepan, you will have to hold it while the jelly boils (only the bulb needs to be immersed). If the juice looks thin rather than sticky, simmer to reduce and thicken it for 3-5 minutes. Add the sugar and continue to simmer until it has melted. Then turn up the heat to high and boil fast for 3-4 minutes or until gel-point (105 C, 220 F) is reached. The juice will rise as it heats: hence the need for a large saucepan. Without a thermometer, boil for 3 minutes, remove the pan from the heat, and dip the sterilized spoon into it: if the drips are stiff and partly set as they drop, the jelly is ready. Skim with the spoon and pour at once into the jar: pour slowly, to one side, to prevent air-bubbles from entering. Seal and leave to cool.

ROAST SIRLOIN OR FORE-RIB OF BEEF
WITH PARSNIPS
AND YORKSHIRE PUDDING

To enjoy roast beef which is crisp on the outside but smooth and tender within, juicy, full of flavour, and altogether worthy not merely of writing home about but of coming to Britain to taste – then you must rationalize your feelings about fat and cholesterol. My butcher tells me with tears in his voice if not his eyes that all his customers are demanding lean meat. I am among them – but not when it comes to beef for roasting. If beef is to be tender and distinctively flavoured, it must be marbled with fat throughout. In effect, the fat in the lean bastes it from within: it also carries the flavour contributed by food. The amount of fat in question, however, is relatively small; all red meat (except, for practical purposes, venison) contains a little and the difference between the lean and liberally marbled, excluding the visible fat which you can cut off on your plate, is probably represented by only 25 to 40 calories per 100 g/ 3½ oz.

As the taste of the animal's food is transmitted via the fat, another essential of good flavour is that it should have been favourably fed, which means on grass and its accompanying plants. This points to free-range meat: if it has also been organically reared, its diet is guaranteed free of chemical additives and animal by-products.

A third factor which is crucial both to taste and tenderness is hanging: like game, beef needs to be kept for a certain period or it will be extremely tough; during this period, flavour also develops. The development of flavour continues for as long as the meat can be protected from the wrong sort of bacteria; in suitable conditions, it would continue to improve for months. The accepted time, however, is two weeks, although some butchers extend it to three or four. One of the disadvantages of supermarket shopping is that hanging is expensive and meat is frequently packaged under-hung, after which, without the free circulation of air, it has to be consumed fairly quickly.

As well as fore-rib and sirloin (which come from adjacent parts), topside, at only about half the price, is generally labelled as suitable for roasting. Do not be tempted: even a full two-week hanging time is no compensation for its lack of marbling. Despite being cooked with all possible care, a piece of topside from good Scottish cattle but bought packaged from a supermarket and visibly lean might as well have been a log of wood. No human teeth could broach it; the dog managed, but then she also eats pieces of wood. Another, hung for the due two weeks and generously barded all round with fat, ran superb gravy and was penetrable but still too tough to be eaten with comfort.

One of the best pieces of roast beef that I can remember was served by some friends for Sunday lunch accompanied simply by ratatouille; new potatoes with parsley butter followed, succeeded by salad. I had a notable dish of grilled rib, daringly rare and triumphantly crisp, at Fergus Henderson's restaurant, St John, near Smithfield, London, where it was accompanied by very mild, creamy horseradish sauce and Brussels-sprout tops. At the Camden Brasserie, in north London, grilled ribs are served with garlic butter. Here, however, I have given the traditional accompaniments of Yorkshire pudding, roast potatoes and parsnips, and horseradish sauce; with this, serve a plain green vegetable such as cabbage, Brussels sprouts (from September to November), or, as at St John, Brussels-sprout tops.

With Yorkshire pudding, plenty of gravy is essential. The simplest way to make it is simply with the vegetable-water added to the pan juices; richer versions, however, call for beef stock. As almost nobody has fresh beef stock to hand, I have added a recipe which may seem slightly extravagant but will do justice to the meat.

The cooking time for very rare beef, which is how I like it, is 15 minutes per 450 g/ 1 lb; if you prefer it less rare, allow 15 minutes per 450 g/ 1 lb plus 5-15 minutes.

FOR 4-6

Stock for gravy (simmer while the beef roasts: see below)
Yorkshire pudding (make in advance: see below)
750 g-1 kg/ 1½-2 lb floury potatoes (see page 109)
750 g-1 kg/ 1½-2 lb parsnips
Salt
1.25 – 1.5 kg/ 2½-3 lb piece sirloin or fore-rib, preferably on the bone
Pepper
Oil
Flour
Horseradish sauce (see below)

Beef, Roast Potatoes and Parsnips

Set the oven to heat to 230 C, 450 F, Gas Mark 8. Peel and cut the potatoes and parsnips into even-sized chunks. The potatoes will be perceptibly better if boiled before roasting: just cover with slightly salted water, bring to the boil, and boil briskly for 2 minutes; drain.

Wash, dry, and lightly paint the lean surfaces of the meat with olive oil and season generously with salt and pepper. Spread a little more olive oil over the bottom of a small roasting tray with a rack. Put the meat on the rack fat-side up and set to roast. Roast the potatoes and parsnips in the tray with the meat if you have no fan (a tray on another shelf may interfere with heat circulation); otherwise, use a separate tray in which there is no danger of their becoming soggy in the meat dripping and juices. Spread the tray with a film of oil and turn each piece in it to coat both sides; season boiled potatoes lightly with salt only but season unboiled ones and the parsnips moderately with both salt and pepper. Calculate your timing and put vegetables into the oven; turn and baste with meat dripping when you start cooking the pudding, and turn again when you remove the meat.

At 230 C, 450 F, Gas Mark 8, the potatoes and parsnips will take 40-45 minutes; this will make them very brown and crisp on the outside. In timing them, however, you should allow for at least an extra 5 minutes' cooking time after you take the meat from the oven while you make the gravy. This means starting to roast them at the same time as the meat if it weighs only 1.25 kg/ 2½ lb and you want it very rare. If it is to be cooked for longer, add them later.

If the vegetables are cooking with the meat, have a second roasting tray ready when you take it out so that they can be returned to the oven and served as hot as possible. Place the meat on a serving dish and leave somewhere warm; it will retain its heat for some minutes and is easier to carve if left to rest. Drain surplus dripping from the roasting tray and pour the stock for the gravy into it through a sieve. Thoroughly mix with the pan juices and either set the tray over a ring or pour the gravy into a saucepan. Season lightly with salt and reduce over high heat for 1-2 minutes. Serve the meat and gravy. Take the pudding and vegetables out of the oven while the meat is being carved.

Stock for gravy
125 g/4 oz (1 smallish) onion
1 outside stick celery
1 carrot
50 g/ 2 oz unsmoked streaky bacon
15 g/ ½ oz butter
1 tablespoonful oil
5 peppercorns
125-175 g/ 4-6 oz lean minced beef
Salt

Peel and finely slice the onion; trim the ends of the celery, wash, dry, and slice finely. Peel and finely slice the carrot; dice the bacon. Melt the butter in the oil and fry the prepared ingredients over medium heat 6-7 minutes or until the onion and carrot are beginning to brown. Add the peppercorns and turn in the oil; add 2-3 tablespoonsful of water and the beef. Press the meat against the bottom of the pan until separated, sprinkle lightly with salt, and add 450 ml/ ¾ pint more water. Bring to the boil, skim, and simmer while the beef cooks.

Yorkshire pudding
The proportions below will make a pudding which will be soft in the middle but have a deep brown, crisp crust. You can make it with plain or self-raising flour; it will rise with either, but more dramatically with self-raising. Its potential height must be allowed for in the oven: do not put it on a narrow top shelf. As it sinks even more promptly than a soufflé, take it straight from the oven to the table. Allow 30 minutes or more for the batter to stand and 30 minutes for cooking.

FOR 4-6

100 g/ 3½ oz plain or self-raising flour
Salt
2 size 2 eggs
300 ml/ ½ pint milk
Butter for greasing

16-cm/ 6¼-inch (2½ pint) soufflé-dish

Blend the flour with a generous pinch of salt, make a well in the middle, and break in the eggs. Stir the flour into them gently and gradually, starting in the middle and working outwards. Continue to stir until you have a stiff paste. Add a little of the milk and stir until smooth, pressing out lumps on the side of the bowl if necessary. Stir in the rest of the milk by degrees and leave to stand.

Butter the soufflé-dish. After standing, the batter will have thickened: stir it again, pour it into the dish, and put at once into the oven. If the oven has no fan, set it on a rack above the meat and vegetables but with the dish over the vegetables rather than the meat in case it slows down cooking. As lowering temperature will impede rising, do not open the oven door while it cooks except to remove the meat a few minutes before it is ready.

HORSERADISH SAUCE

This is a very mild sauce: with memories of my father, who cherished his horseradish plants as others might their asparagus or roses, and himself made them into a sauce of fervent intensity, I have never been able to face it except in its creamiest, gentlest form. To strengthen it, add more horseradish to taste or 1 (scant) teaspoonful Dijon mustard.

Use either unprepared or plain ready-grated horseradish, which is sold in bottles or air-tight packages: avoid bottles of it preserved in vinegar.

You can whip the cream and add the seasoning some hours in advance, but do not grate or add the horseradish until shortly before serving, since it loses pungency very quickly.

½ lemon
142 ml/ ¼ pint whipping cream
Generous pinch salt
Fairly generous grinding of pepper
Pinch sugar
1½ tablespoonsful finely grated horseradish

Squeeze 1 tablespoonful lemon juice. Add the cream and whip to the consistency of fairly thick sauce. Stir in the seasoning. Just before serving, peel and grate the horseradish if necessary and add; mix thoroughly.

STEAK, KIDNEY AND OYSTER PIE

Traditionally, oysters were used to give zest not only to fish but a wide variety of meat and poultry dishes. Turkeys, chickens, and mutton were stuffed with them, or they were slipped under the skin as one might insert garlic or spices today; fried oysters were served as a garnish to ragouts or stews, and, as well as being added as a flavouring, they were made into pies in their own right. In Isabella Beeton's day, they cost fourpence per half-dozen; wherever they were easily available, i.e. on the coast or in ports (including London), they were sold in oyster bars, which were the contemporary equivalent of fish and chip shops. Even today, when considered singly, the price of rock or Pacific oysters (about 60p each) does not seem exorbitant; however, it adds up, as I have found very much to my cost. I have therefore not given any other meat dish which includes them; here, however, they contribute a full-bodied richness which I feel is a bargain at the price.

The pastry can be made up to 2 days ahead and the meat cooked a day in advance; the oysters can be kept (see page 137) but will be better if bought and added on the day the pie is baked. Allow 1¾ hours for cooking the meat and 20-25 minutes for baking the pie.

I have given enough pastry to cover a standard oval 900 ml/1½ pint pie-dish; if you use a wider dish, you may need more.

Serve with boiled or mashed potatoes and green haricot beans or Brussels sprouts before, Brussels-sprout tops after Christmas.

FOR 4-6

150 g/5 oz shallots
4 cloves garlic
750 g/1½ lb lean stewing steak
250 g/9 oz ox kidney
Salt
Pepper
25 g/1 oz plain white flour
1 tablespoonful oil
25 g/1 oz butter
300 ml/½ pint dry red wine
3 or 4 sprigs thyme

3 or 4 sprigs parsley
2 or 3 sprigs marjoram
10 British-reared rock oysters
Egg or milk for glazing

Flaky pastry made with:
175 g/6 oz plain white flour
Salt
40 g/1½ oz lard
75 g/3 oz butter

Peel and finely slice the shallots; peel and finely chop the garlic. Wash and blot the steak and kidney dry, trim off all the visible fat, and cut into 2 cm/¾ inch squares. Season fairly generously with salt and pepper and roll thinly in the flour.

Set the oven to 150 C, 300 F, Gas Mark 2. Warm the oil and butter in a wok or frying-pan over medium heat and add the shallots. Fry 2-3 minutes, turning often; add the garlic and fry for another 2-3 minutes or until starting to change colour; turn constantly. Add the steak and kidney and sear on all sides. Pour in 150 ml/¼ pint of the wine, raise the heat, and boil until most of it has cooked away, leaving only a thick sauce. Add the rest of the wine, remove from the heat, and transfer to a casserole. Wash the herbs, tie in a bunch with string, and bury under the top layer of meat. Cover and cook for 1¾ hours or until the meat is tender but still firm: it must not be falling apart. As it is cooking in relatively little liquid, turn at intervals to prevent the layer on top from becoming dry. Leave to become cold. If you have cooked it in advance, store (covered) in the refrigerator.

Open the oysters (see page 17), holding them over a bowl to catch the liquor. Wash them in the liquor, being very careful to check for pieces of shell. Strain the liquor through a jelly-bag or very fine sieve, twice if necessary. Mix both the oysters and their liquor with the cold steak in the casserole and transfer all but 75 ml/2½ fl oz of the liquid to the pie-dish. The addition of the oyster liquor means that there is slightly too much gravy for a dish of this size: as the gravy in pies always tends to run short, I suggest heating it separately just before the meal and adding it after the first portions have been served.

Set the oven to 225 C, 425 F, Gas Mark 7. Roll out the pastry to a thickness of 4-5 mm/ less than ¼ inch. Cut a strip to line the rim of the dish, moistening both sides with water, and cover the pie. Trim underneath the rim, make an air-hole in the middle, and brush with egg or milk. Bake 20-25 minutes, until lightly coloured.

ALASTAIR LITTLE'S BEEF BRAISED WITH GUINNESS

This is an outstanding example of the principle expressed by the title of Alastair Little's cookery book, *Keep it Simple*: it is difficult to believe that the deep, rich flavour of the sauce could be achieved with so few ingredients. The only point about making it which needs comment is that it is important to cook the beef to just the right degree of tenderness.

Altogether, cooking time is three hours, but the dish can be made in advance: in fact, I found that it tasted even better on the second day, when the flavours had had time to develop.

Serve in shallow bowls with mashed potato.

FOR 4-6

1.25 kg/ 2½ lb skirt steak, cut to a thickness of 2 cm/ ¾ inch
Salt
Pepper
40-50 g/ 1½-2 oz plain white flour
4½ tablespoonsful or a little more sunflower oil
1.25 kg/ 2½ lb large Spanish onions
600 ml/ 1 pint Guinness
1 bay leaf
1 tablespoonful balsamic, sherry, or red-wine vinegar
1 teaspoonful Demerara sugar

Rigorously trim the steak of all visible fat. Wash it in cold water and dry with kitchen paper. Cut into 5-6 cm/ 2-2½ inch squares. Season generously with salt and pepper and roll in the flour. Using a large pan, brown it in 3 tablespoonsful of the oil (you will have to do this in two or more sessions). Transfer the meat to a colander to drain off surplus fat; do not wash up the pan.

Peel and finely slice the onions. Spread the remaining 1½ tablespoonsful of oil over the base of an iron-bottomed casserole. Add two-thirds of the onions and arrange the drained meat on top. Cover and place over very low heat until the onions are reduced and softened and there is quite a lot of liquid in the casserole: this will take about 20 minutes.

Meanwhile, fry the remaining onions over low heat in the pan in which the meat was browned. Turn constantly until they are a deep, even gold; add more oil if necessary.

When the onions in the casserole are reduced, arrange the fried ones over the meat. Add the beer and bay leaf and simmer, covered, 1¼ hours. Stir in the vinegar and sugar and simmer for another 20-30 minutes, until the meat parts when speared with a fork; it should not, however, disintegrate. Take it out of the casserole and set aside. Simmer the sauce (still covered) for another hour, until it is dark, thickened, and slightly reduced: if it is still very liquid, uncover, raise the heat a little, and reduce by boiling gently. Return the meat to the casserole and cook at a very slow simmer for 5-10 minutes before serving.

If the dish is being made in advance, remove from the heat directly after returning the meat. Allow to cool and put the casserole into the refrigerator. With the thick sauce, it must be re-heated carefully. Set over a low flame: stir frequently but be careful not to break the pieces of meat. Bring barely to the boil and simmer gently for 10 minutes.

COTTAGE PIE

If you mention British food, it seems that the very first thing which comes to people's mind is cottage pie. However, there are cottage pies and cottage pies. The following is quite unlike any that you might buy and is so popular in my family that I made it at least once a week for many years. My only reservation about it so far as this book is concerned is that it is not wholly indigenous, since the filling owes more to Italian *ragu Bolognese* than to the British country tradition. Like *ragu*, it is made with wine and should be simmered very slowly for a long time: this may be a bore but ensures that it has the full, rich flavour which makes the pie distinctive. To give the flavour even more time to develop, it is an advantage if you cook the meat a day ahead. Once the pie is assembled, it similarly needs a fairly long baking time so that the potato on top is thoroughly browned and crisp: when ready, the top should have a crust almost like *crème brulée*. Allow 3½-3¾ hours for simmering the meat and 40-45 minutes for baking the pie.

Use good quality, lean beef: if you like, trim off all visible fat and mince it yourself. The potatoes should be floury (see page 109): particularly recommended are Wilja (August-March) and Desirée (September-May).

Rather than serving vegetables at the same time as the pie, follow with rocket or any other green salad.

FOR 4

450 g/ 1 lb lean, finely minced beef
175 g/ 6 oz unsmoked streaky bacon
225 g/ 8 oz (3 medium) ripe tomatoes
1 stick celery
125 g/ 4 oz (2 smallish) carrots
275 g/ 10 oz (2 medium) onions
4 cloves garlic
2 sprigs rosemary, or enough for 1 tablespoonful when chopped
Handful parsley plus a few sprigs marjoram (enough for 1 tablespoonful together when chopped)
2 bay leaves

2 tablespoonsful olive oil
50 g/ 2 oz butter
Salt
Pepper
150 ml/ ¼ pint dry red wine
2 teaspoonsful red-wine vinegar
1 tablespoonful tomato purée
1 teaspoonful soft brown sugar
750 g/ 1½ lb floury potatoes
50 g/ 2 oz medium Cheddar cheese
3 tablespoonsful milk
3 teaspoonsful Dijon mustard

Large, preferably non-stick frying-pan or wok with a lid
Ovenproof dish about 19 cm/ 7½ inches across or (if oval) the equivalent

If the beef is not already minced, trim and mince it finely. Remove the bacon rind and dice the bacon into 1 cm/ ⅓ inch squares (use scissors). Peel and chop the tomatoes, discarding the cores (see page 16). Trim the leaves and root-end of the celery; pare off any brownish streaks, wash, dry, and slice very finely. Peel and finely slice the carrots; peel and very finely chop the onions and garlic. Wash the herbs and shake or blot dry. Strip the leaves from the rosemary (grip the stem tightly between your thumb and forefinger and pull downwards: they will then come away together); trim the ends of the parsley and marjoram stems if they were bought. Chop all three very finely.

Warm the oil and 15 g/ ½ oz of the butter in the frying-pan or wok over very low heat and add the onions and bacon. Sweat for 5 minutes, turning from time to time. Add the celery, carrots, garlic, and herbs, including the bay leaves, and continue to simmer for 7-10 minutes or until the onion is soft and just beginning to change colour; turn often, especially towards the end. Add the beef, season lightly with salt and moderately with pepper, and turn, pressing the meat against the bottom of the pan, until all parts of it are pale brown and opaque. Pour in the wine, raise the heat to medium, and boil until most of it has cooked away. Reduce the heat to low and stir in the vinegar. Add the tomatoes, season with just a touch of salt and pepper, and continue to cook, pressing the flesh towards the bottom of the pan, for 5-7 minutes or until liquefied. Stir in the purée, 2 tablespoonsful of water, and the sugar. Cover and cook at a bare simmer for 3½-3¾ hours. Look at it every now and again to check that there is still liquid in the pan and add a little more water if necessary; if it is kept covered and at only a gentle simmer, however, the quantity of liquid will remain almost constant. At the end of the simmering time, raise the heat to medium and cook, stirring continuously, for 8-10 minutes or until the pan is dry (this is important, since if there is any juice left with the meat it will seep over the potato and the pie will be soggy). Transfer to the ovenproof dish; if being made in advance, allow to become cold, cover with foodwrap, and store in the refrigerator.

For the top, peel the potatoes, cut into moderate-sized pieces, and just cover with slightly salted water. Boil for 15-20 minutes or until tender; while they boil, grate the cheese. Drain the potatoes and add the cheese, milk, mustard, a moderate grinding of pepper, a little salt, and 25 g/ 1 oz of the butter. Mash thoroughly. Spread evenly over the meat and rough the top with a fork. If it is more convenient, the pie can now be left for several hours before baking. Heat the oven to 190 C, 375 F, Gas Mark 5, dot the top with the remaining 15 g/ ½ oz butter, and bake 40-45 minutes or until the top is a rich golden brown.

OX-TAIL BAKED IN BREADCRUMBS

Although ox-tail soup is now better known, ox-tail baked or broiled in breadcrumbs (broiling means grilling over an open fire) used to be at least as popular. I prefer it because the crisp coating of crumbs contrasts with the gelatinous quality of the meat, making a lighter, fresher dish than either soup or a straightforward stew; it also has the advantage that whereas a good soup demands stock or a larger proportion of meat, the stewing liquor supplies the basis of a rich gravy without any addition except the option of extra port.

The Victorian chef Charles Francatelli directed that the pieces of tail should be tidily trimmed before the breadcrumbs were added; to today's cook, the removal of any remaining fat is of more concern, but in fact, with a thick coating of crumbs, the pieces look more elegant than you might suppose possible from the appearance of the original meat.

The large amount of fat that the tail carries means that stewing it in advance is essential so that the liquor can be chilled and the fat skimmed off completely. Stewing, which should be as slow as possible, takes 4½-5½ hours; if you like, it can be carried out over 2 days. Allow 30 minutes before serving for baking with the crumbs and simmering the gravy.

The bread for the crumbs should be really stale and dry: if it is not, the coating will brown less evenly and you will need at least an extra 25 g/ 1 oz.

Ox-tails should be treated as offal and cooked within 24 hours of purchase.

Serve with boiled or mashed potatoes (see page 113) and grilled mushrooms, braised celery (page 104) or Brussels sprouts.

FOR 4-5

About 1 kg/ 2 lb (1 small) ox-tail
Salt
Pepper
150 g/ 5 oz lean smoked gammon
1 large leek
2 outer sticks celery

125 g/ 4 oz (1 large or 2 smallish) carrots
225 g/ 8 oz (2 smallish) onions
3-4 sprigs parsley
5-6 good-sized sprigs thyme
2 bay leaves
5-6 tablespoonsful oil
8 cloves
150 ml/ 1/4 pint port plus an optional 75 ml/ 1/8 pint
40-50 g/ 1 1/2 – 2 oz dry, stale white bread weighed without crust
1 size 2 egg
40 g/ 1 1/2 oz plain white flour

Wash, thoroughly dry, and season the pieces of ox-tail fairly generously with salt and pepper. Remove any rind, wash, and dice the gammon. Trim the leaves and root of the leek, peel off the outer layer, finely slice, and wash. Cut the leaves from the celery, pare off any discoloured patches, wash, and finely slice. Peel and thinly slice the carrot and onion (keep the onion separate). Trim the ends of the stems of bought parsley and thyme and wash; wash the bay leaves.

Warm 1 tablespoonful of the oil in a large frying-pan or wok over a high heat and lightly brown the pieces of ox-tail on all sides; remove the pan from the heat and put the meat into a large iron-bottomed casserole or saucepan with a lid. Pour off any remaining oil in the frying-pan, wash or wipe it clean, and warm 2 more tablespoonsful of oil over medium heat. Add the onion and fry for 8-10 minutes or until a rich brown; turn often, and constantly towards the end. Add the cloves and turn in the oil; add the port and cook about two-thirds of it away. Add 750 ml/ 1 1/4 pints water and the leek, celery, carrot, and gammon, bring just to the boil, and pour over the ox-tail. Season very lightly with a little more salt and pepper, lay the herbs on top, cover, and simmer 4 1/2 -5 1/2 hours or until the meat is very tender and leaves the bones easily when prodded with a fork, but is not yet falling apart. Take the pieces of tail from the liquor, put into a dish, and leave to cool; when cold, cover and store in the refrigerator. Pour the liquor through a sieve into a bowl; press out as much juice as you can with the back of a spoon. Throw away the solid ingredients, allow to cool, cover, and store in the refrigerator overnight.

Set the oven to 200 C, 400 F, Gas Mark 6; line a baking tray with cooking foil large enough for the pieces of tail to be laid on it without touching, and cover the tails with a film of oil. Grate the bread very finely and evenly, throwing away any irregularly sized pieces, and spread over a plate. Spread the flour over another plate and season generously with salt and pepper. Break the egg into a small bowl, beat until homogenous, and season moderately. Using a sharp knife, trim off any fat left on the meat. Coat each piece with flour, then egg, and then the breadcrumbs, shaking off any surplus but making sure that all the crevices on the larger pieces are covered and that the coating of crumbs is thick. Drizzle with oil and bake 20 minutes or until the tops of the pieces of tail are brown. Turn the pieces on to their sides and bake 5 more minutes; turn again and bake for another 5 or until they are brown all over.

As soon as the meat is in the oven, skim the layer of fat from the stewing liquor, which should have jellified. Put the jelly into a smallish saucepan with 75 ml/ ⅛ pint more port if you wish, bring just to the boil, and cook at a fast simmer until the tail is ready; if it is still copious and thin, boil at medium heat to the consistency of gravy before serving. Serve separately so that the meat remains crisp.

BAKED IRISH STEW

I was particularly anxious to include Irish stew in this book, not only because of its deservedly classic status but because if there ever was a convenient, cook-friendly dish, this is it. It is quick and easy to prepare, can be made a day ahead, and is forgiving over cooking time: if it is left in the oven for half an hour too long, it will probably be all the better.

The following is based on a recipe from Eliza Acton's *Modern Cookery* (1845). Eliza Acton is less well known today than Isabella Beeton or Alexis Soyer but, partly because her recipes formed the backbone of Mrs Beeton's book, can be said to have founded British traditional cookery as we know it today. Ironically, she learnt to cook in France and (like Elizabeth David, of whom she was in many ways reminiscent) was always especially interested in foreign cookery of all kinds.

My version differs from hers in that I have included garlic, which was virtually banished from middle-class Victorian cooking, and have given lamb as an alternative to mutton. In fact, as it is used for pies and other commercial purposes, mutton is not so difficult to find as you may think: a good butcher will probably be able to supply it provided that you order it well in advance.

It is drier and much fattier than lamb but will give the stew a more distinctive flavour. If you use it, you will need considerably more of it to allow for the weight of fat and bone (which does not mean that it is a dearer option, since it is cheaper lb for lb).

The usual cut recommended for stews is best end of neck; middle neck is leaner and more economic, but the bones tend to separate during cooking, which means that it has to be eaten with care. If you use best end of neck of mutton, have the chops (which are very long) cut across to make them easier to arrange in a casserole.

If possible, bake the stew in a 23-cm/ 9-inch diameter, 9-cm/ 3½-inch deep casserole: this will exactly fit the quantities and give two layers of meat and vegetables, which means that half the potatoes will be crisp.

Cooking time is about 3-3½ hours.

The stew needs no accompaniment, but if you want an extra vegetable, carrots or broad beans are especially suitable.

FOR 4

900 g/ 2 lb best end of neck of lamb or 1½-1¾ kg/ 3-3½ lb of mutton, cut into chops
900 g/ 2 lb fairly firm, medium-sized potatoes (e.g. Wilja, Marfona, or Desirée)
450 g/ 1 lb onions
3 cloves garlic
Salt
Pepper
15 g/ ½ oz butter

Either ask the butcher to trim the chops closely or remove as much fat from them as possible yourself. Wash the trimmed chops in cold water. Scrub or peel the potatoes and slice fairly thickly. Peel and thinly slice the onions; peel and finely chop the garlic.

Lay a layer of chops in the bottom of the casserole; season moderately with salt and pepper. Distribute half the onion on top and sprinkle with half the garlic. Add a layer of potatoes and season moderately again. Repeat, finishing with a closely laid layer of potato. Dot the top with the chopped butter. Add 600 ml/ 1 pint water, and bake, covered, at 150 C, 300 F, Gas Mark 2, for 2¼-2½ hours. Remove the lid of the casserole to allow the potatoes to crisp and bake for a further 35-50 minutes. (With a longer baking time, you may need to add a little more water.)

If the stew is being made in advance, allow to cool and put the casserole into the refrigerator. Re-heat uncovered 20-30 minutes at 150 C as before.

LAMB AND KIDNEY PIE

Oysters were often used to enliven mutton; however, another traditional way of adding zest to meat was with anchovies, which I have used here and, in combination with rosemary, produce a different but equally rich result.

I have given enough pastry to cover an oval 900 ml/1½ pint pie-dish; if your dish is wider, you may need more.

The pastry can be made up to two days and the meat cooked a day in advance; because of the kidneys, however, it should be cooked not later than the day after it is bought. Allow about 1¾ hours for cooking the meat and 20-25 minutes to bake the pie.

Serve with crisp mashed potatoes (see page 113) or sliced potatoes baked with onions (see page 112), and/or green haricot beans or broccoli.

FOR 4-6

175 g/6 oz (1 largish) onion
3 cloves garlic
Long stem of rosemary (enough for 1½ tablespoonsful when chopped)
750-875 g/1½-1¾ lb meat from a leg of lamb (see page 55)
5 lambs' kidneys
Salt

Pepper
2-3 tablespoonsful oil
3 anchovies, or 6 fillets
225 ml/ 8 fl oz dry red wine
Milk for glazing

Flaky pastry made with:
175 g/ 6 oz plain white flour
Salt
40 g/ 1½ oz lard
75 g/ 3 oz butter

Peel and finely chop the onion and garlic. Wash, shake dry, and strip the leaves from the rosemary (pull downwards); dice very finely. Cut all the visible fat from the lamb, wash, dry, and chop into 3-4 cm/ 1¼-1½ inch squares. Pull the fat from the kidneys if necessary, skin (or wash if already skinned) and chop into 1½-2 cm/⅔-¾ inch pieces, discarding the tough central cores. Season the meat moderately with salt and more generously with pepper.

Fry the onion in 1½ tablespoonsful of the oil over medium heat for 3-4 minutes or until soft; add the garlic and fry for 2-3 minutes more or until the onion is starting to change colour; turn constantly and add more oil if necessary. Reduce the heat to very low and add the anchovies; sweat, stirring constantly, until dissolved. Remove from the heat and transfer the contents of the pan to a casserole.

Set the oven to 150 C, 300 F, Gas Mark 2.

Wipe the pan clean, add another tablespoonful of oil, and set over a medium heat. Sear the lamb on all sides (do not let it brown). Add and sear the kidneys. Add the rosemary and stir. Pour in the wine, raise the heat to high, and let it reduce to about half. Transfer to the casserole. Mix the meat with the onions and anchovies, cover, and bake for 1¾ hours or until the lamb is just tender. Leave to become cold. If cooked a day ahead, store in the refrigerator.

Set the oven to 225 C, 425 F, Gas Mark 7. Arrange the meat in the pie-dish. Roll out the pastry 4-5 mm/ less than ¼ inch thick. Lay a strip around the edge of the dish and cover the pie. Trim underneath the rim, stamp the edges, and make an air-hole in the middle. Paint with milk and bake 20-25 minutes, until golden.

LAMB SAUSAGES WITH ROSEMARY

Old recipes for sausages included a terrifying amount of fat: Queen Henrietta Maria (widow of Charles I) gave 1.8 kg/ 4 lb of butter or beef suet per leg of pork, and Eliza Smith a little later 900 g/ 2 lb suet per 450 g/ 1 lb lean meat. Neither, however, added starch, except that Eliza recommended bread steeped in cream if herbs were not available (though it is difficult to see why). In fact, sausages without a little fat and starch tend to be dry and heavy, which presents a problem to those wishing to satisfy the current demand for a low-fat, pure-meat product. Sometimes, marinating the meat solves it (see the venison sausages on page 211); here, however, I have added a little fat in the form of bacon and just 25 g/ 1 oz breadcrumbs, which have a remarkable effect in moistening and lightening the mixture. The breadcrumbs are also useful in absorbing a flavouring of wine.

Sausage-skins may have to be ordered from a butcher and bought in bulk; however, those which you do not need can be frozen. A large package may have a pronounced smell, but this entirely disappears after soaking and filling. One further word of warning: when filling sausages, at least with a forcing-bag, you need a sense of humour. You will see why when you try (it is not that it is difficult: it is actually very easy). If you prefer, do not use sausage-skins but form the meat into cakes for lamb-burgers.

The amounts below make 450 g/ 1 lb and include 275 g/ 10 oz lean meat from a leg of lamb. If you are making sausages, you will probably want to make more, in which case they can be increased; however, the quantities given mean that enough will be left on a whole or large half leg to roast or use for lamb and kidney pie.

As the skins are preserved in salt, they must be soaked for 24 hours before use. The sausages or burgers can be fried, grilled, or baked.

Serve with new potatoes and ratatouille or spiced spinach (pages 103 and 106).

275 g/ 10 oz meat from a leg of lamb, weighed after being trimmed of
all visible fat
¼ teaspoonful salt
Pepper
125 g/ 4 oz smoked streaky bacon
25 g/ 1 oz stale white bread, weighed without crust
2-3 sprigs rosemary (enough for 1 tablespoonful when chopped)
6-9 leaves fresh sage (enough for ¾ tablespoonful when chopped)
1 tablespoonful dry or medium-dry red or rosé wine
1¾-2 metres/ 5-6 feet sausage-skin for sausages
About 25 g/ 1 oz white flour for lamb-burgers
Oil for baking or frying

Sausage-making attachment to a mincer or a forcing-bag with a wide nozzle

Wash, dry, and check that all the fat has been cut from the lamb. Chop into pieces small enough to go through your mincer; season with salt and a moderate grinding of pepper. Trim the rind from the bacon and the crust from the bread; chop roughly. Mince finely.

Wash the rosemary and sage and shake or blot dry. Strip the rosemary stems (pull downwards) and chop very finely; finely chop the sage. Add to the minced meat with the wine and mix very thoroughly. Rinse the sausage-skin.

With a sausage-making attachment to your mincer, follow the instructions. To use a forcing-bag, insert the nozzle and cut the length of sausage-skin in half. Stretch one end of the skin over the mouth of the nozzle and push up most of the rest round it so that only a small piece protrudes. Twist the end, put the meat into the bag, and squeeze: use as much pressure as you can. When a length of skin the size of the sausage you want is filled, twist and cut the skin; check that the end is twisted for the next one and continue until you have used up all the meat.

For burgers, shape the meat into small flat cakes about the size of small beefburgers. Spread out the flour on a plate and roll to coat both sides; shake off any surplus.

To bake, pre-heat the oven to 230 C, 450 F, Gas Mark 8 and spread a little oil over the bottom of a baking tray. Prick sausages and turn both sausages and burgers to coat with oil all over. Bake for 15-20 minutes, turning sausages as they brown and burgers after 10-12 minutes. To grill, prick and coat with oil as for baking and set under a hot grill for 10-14 minutes, turning burgers after 7-8 and sausages as they brown. Fry over high heat until browned or very brown.

MICHAEL HJORT'S AROMATIC CHICKEN

Michael Hjort understands human nature: this is a really laid-back dish which takes hardly any time to prepare and is improved rather than otherwise if kept waiting.

Preparation took me 20 minutes, but at least 5 were accounted for by my going to pick the herbs in the garden. As to how long you can leave it, Michael says: 'It is almost impossible to overcook the dish. There is no advantage in eating it when it is only just ready . . .' The point is that the chicken is stewed in oil, which keeps it moist and succulent: the longer it cooks, the softer, creamier, and more impregnated with the sauce it becomes.

Initial cooking time is about 3 hours but depends on the size of the chicken. In his restaurant (he is chef/owner of Melton's, York), Michael serves it with new potatoes, but at home often only with French bread to mop up the sauce; it is also excellent with rice. Follow with salad.

FOR 4-6

3 large (but not outside) sticks of celery, preferably complete with leaves
2 heads garlic
2 or 3 sprigs rosemary or basil
5-6 good-sized sprigs of thyme
4-5 sprigs parsley
1 free-range chicken
Salt
Pepper
6 tablespoonsful virgin olive oil
2 tablespoonsful balsamic vinegar

Trim the root ends of the celery but do not cut off the leaves; wash, dry, and slice roughly. Peel the garlic; leave the cloves whole. If the parsley was bought, trim the ends of the stems; wash the herbs, shake off surplus moisture, and tie in a bunch with string. Wash the chicken inside and out; dry the outside, trim off any surplus fat round the cavity, and season lightly inside with salt and moderately outside with salt and pepper. Set the oven to 150 C, 300 F, Gas Mark 2. Put the chicken into a casserole with a tight-fitting lid, slip two or three of the cloves of garlic inside it, and surround with the celery and the rest of the garlic. Place the herbs on top, add the oil, sprinkle with the vinegar, and bake for 3 hours or longer.

CHICKEN BRAISED WITH CELERY AND ROSEMARY

This is designed simply to make the best of the flavour of a free-range chicken. The ingredients are similar to those for Michael Hjort's chicken (page 170); partly because of the predominance of garlic in his, however, the result is totally different. Sea salt and fresh rosemary are essential.

Cooking time is 1½-1¼ hours. Use the carcass for stock (see page 52).

Serve with Puy lentils (see page 189) and French, Kenya, or green haricot beans, or organically grown brown rice, the nutty taste and texture of which complements the dish perfectly, and follow with rocket or mushroom salad (pages 97 and 96).

FOR 4

3 large sticks celery
125 g/ 4 oz (1 large or 2 smallish) carrots
150 g/ 5 oz (1 medium) onion
4 cloves garlic
3 or 4 sprigs parsley
Bunch or several long sprigs rosemary (enough for 2 tablespoonsful when chopped)
2 bay leaves

1 lemon (zest only)
150 g/ 5 oz unsmoked streaky bacon
1.25-1.5 kg/ 2½-3 lb free-range chicken
Salt
Pepper
3 tablespoonsful oil
300 ml/ ½ pint dry white wine

Trim the root-ends and leaves from the celery; pare off any brownish streaks, wash, dry, and cut into slices 1 cm/ ⅓ inch thick. Peel and thinly slice the carrot; peel and finely chop the onion and garlic. Trim the ends of bought parsley stems, wash, and tie the parsley into a bunch. Wash and shake or blot the rosemary dry; strip off the leaves (pull downwards) and chop finely. Wash fresh bay leaves; scrub the lemon. Trim off the rind and dice the bacon. Untruss the chicken, remove the giblets, which are not needed for this recipe, and thoroughly wash and dry it inside and out; season lightly inside with salt and fairly generously outside with salt and pepper.

Set the oven 200 C, 400 F, Gas Mark 6. Warm 2 tablespoonsful of the oil in a wok or frying-pan over moderately high heat and brown the chicken lightly on all sides; baste the parts which do not touch the pan with the hot oil. Put both chicken and oil into the casserole. Wipe the pan clean, add the remaining 1 tablespoonful of oil and fry the onion and bacon for 2 minutes, still over moderately high heat; turn frequently. Add the garlic and continue to fry, turning constantly, for 2-3 minutes more or until the onion is just beginning to change colour. Add the rosemary and turn for 1-2 minutes; add the remaining vegetables and turn for another minute. Add the wine, bring just to the boil, and pour the contents of the pan over the chicken. Pare off two good-sized strips of lemon peel and add with the bay leaves and parsley. Cover and cook 1¼-1½ hours or until the chicken is very tender and no pink liquid emerges when it is pierced to the bone in the thickest part. Set the rice or lentils to cook when the chicken has been in the oven for 45 minutes. (The rice takes only 30 minutes to cook but should be left to dry for a further 10-15 minutes: see page 22.)

Carve and serve.

DAVID EYRE'S ROAST DUCKLING
STUFFED WITH PRUNES

David Eyre is chef and co-proprietor of The Eagle, London EC1, where most of the cooking is Mediterranean-inspired. 'I don't quite know why. It's silly really, because British dishes suit the climate far better. Perhaps the Mediterranean influence is just escapism.'

Roast duck is particularly inconvenient to serve in restaurants because, to melt the layer of fat underneath the skin, fairly long, slow cooking is required (this is one of David's private recipes: it is not on the menu at The Eagle). To give the melting process a head start but at the same time ensure that the duck does not dry out, I would normally recommend frying it before roasting: David, however, sears it by ladling hot fat over it, which is a very effective way of heating the surface without allowing the meat underneath to start cooking.

It is important to use large, juicy prunes for the stuffing. Do not forget the lemon peel, which counters their sweetness and adds an aroma which permeates the whole dish.

The prunes will need soaking before use: even the kind which are not supposed to need it should be soaked for 1-2 hours. As the cabbage has to be fried before the stuffing is mixed, it should be washed about an hour in advance so that it has time to dry. If you wish, the stuffing can be made a few hours ahead of time but should not be inserted into the duckling until just before cooking.

I have been generous with the amount of stuffing on the assumption that it is less annoying to have too much than too little.

The duck fat which will run during cooking is a bonus: use it for particularly delicious roast or fried potatoes.

Roasting time is 2-2½ hours.

Serve with roast potatoes and shallots or, in season, young broad beans and new potatoes.

FOR 3-4 (A 2-KG/ 4-LB BIRD IS ONLY ENOUGH FOR 3)

160 g/ generous 5 oz large prunes
185 g/ 6½ oz Savoy or other green cabbage
2 or 3 stems sage (enough for 1 tablespoonful when chopped)
2-2½ kg/ 4-5 lb free-range duckling, with giblets

1 medium carrot
2 medium onions, one of which should weigh about 150 g/ 5 oz
65 g/ 2½ oz unsmoked streaky bacon
65 g/ 2½ oz walnuts
5-cm/ 2-inch strip lemon peel
225 g/ 8 oz duck fat, bacon fat, or lard, in order of preference
Pepper
Salt

Set the prunes to soak according to the instructions on the packet, or for 1-2 hours if no-soak. Finely shred the cabbage, discarding the central stem and any thick pieces of stalk; wash and leave to dry in a colander. Pull the sage leaves from the stems; wash and leave to dry.

Remove the liver from the giblets; wash thoroughly, dry, and chop finely. Make stock for the gravy with the carrot, one of the onions (not the one weighing 150 g/ 5 oz, which is needed for the stuffing), and the rest of the giblets; leave it to simmer while the duckling cooks.

Prepare the stuffing. Peel and finely chop the second onion; finely chop the sage. Trim the rind from the bacon and dice (use scissors). Roughly chop or crush the walnuts. Wash and pare off a generous strip of lemon peel. Stone the prunes if necessary; if already pitted, cut in half. Blot any remaining moisture from the cabbage with kitchen paper. Warm 50 g/ 2 oz of the fat in a large pan and fry the cabbage over low heat for 6-7 minutes or until soft, turning often; take care not to let it brown. Mix with the prepared ingredients, including the duck liver and lemon peel, and a moderate seasoning of pepper. Wipe but do not wash up the pan in which the cabbage was fried.

Set the oven to 220 C, 425 F, Gas Mark 7. Thoroughly wash the duckling inside and out in running cold water; wipe dry with kitchen paper. Rub inside and out with a generous seasoning of salt and stuff loosely: if packed very tightly, the stuffing may not cook through. Pull the flap of skin at the neck-end over the opening, close the back, and truss or tie firmly with string. Then place the bird breast upwards in the pan in which you fried the cabbage. Heat the rest of the fat in a saucepan until it is just beginning to smoke and pour or ladle it quickly over the bird. The skin will blister slightly and turn white: return the fat to the saucepan, re-heat, and repeat until the duckling is opaque all over and faintly tinged with gold. Prick shallowly at intervals with a skewer or pointed knife so that the layer of fat underneath can escape; take care, however, not to pierce the flesh.

Transfer the duck to a rack set over a roasting-pan and roast for 15 minutes. Lower the oven heat to 180 C, 350 F, Gas Mark 4. Remove the bird from the oven, baste, and drain the fat from the pan: if the fat is not drained regularly, it may burn, which will make it unsuitable for re-use. David advises constant basting, but if the skin of the duckling is pricked, it will in effect baste itself. Roast for another 20 minutes; drain off the fat again. Continue to roast and drain every 15-20 minutes for a further 1½ -2 hours: total roasting time should be 30 minutes per 450 g/ 1 lb (this allows for removing the duckling from the oven for draining).

If you are planning to serve shallots and roast potatoes, put them into the oven when the duckling has an hour left to cook. Peel and cut the potatoes into moderate-sized pieces; peel and trim the tops of the shallots. Roll in the duck fat drained from the bird and either set on the rack round it or, if your oven is fan-heated (but not otherwise), put them in a separate pan lined with a thin film of fat.

When the duck is cooked, remove from the oven and leave in a warm place while you make the gravy (see page 178) or for at least 5 minutes. Do not take out the potatoes and shallots until the gravy is ready. Both ducks and geese are difficult to carve: slice the breast lengthways from end to end and if necessary turn the bird on its side to cut off the legs. Do not serve the wings, which carry virtually no meat.

ROAST GOOSE WITH ROAST POTATOES AND PLUM AND CHESTNUT STUFFING

Goose in Britain was traditionally eaten at Michaelmas (29th September), when the birds could be fattened in the fields after the harvest; it was also made into the famous Yorkshire and Christmas pies, which were enormous cold pies designed to last for weeks. The pastry of course became horribly stale but was not meant to be eaten; it merely served as a lid which could be lifted off when the pie was served and afterwards replaced to protect and preserve the meat. Such pies were often sent as Christmas presents (Dickens received one so large that he did not know what to do with it), but otherwise goose was never especially associated with Christmas. However, after cooking a turkey for Christmas dinner and a goose the very next day, I fear that I shall never choose turkey for Christmas again.

As between the two, only a few arguments go in favour of goose. One is that geese do not thrive in factory-farming conditions, so that even if they became more popular, most would probably be free-range. Partly for this reason, however, they are expensive – much more so than a comparable free-range turkey. In addition, they are uneconomic: like ducks, they carry less meat than their weight and appearance suggest. A 3.75-4 kg/ 8-8½ lb goose is only enough for 6; a 4.5-kg/ 9-lb one will feed 7-8. They are fatty, although you may count this as an advantage, since the fat (like duck fat) can be used for cooking. The barrier formed by their rib-cage means that stuffing tends not to cook inside them; they are also notoriously awkward to carve. However, to my mind at least, none of this counts against the taste. My turkey, which was free-range, organically fed, suitably stuffed, and carefully cooked, was pleasant Christmas fare; the goose was a feast.

An old goose is tough, although I am assured that you are unlikely to be supplied with a tough one, particularly at Christmas. Young ones should be plump over the breast; with free-range rearing, this is not infallible but the best guidance that I can give.

As the stuffing should be cooked separately, which I usually consider unsatisfactory, there is a case for serving the conventional apple sauce instead; however, stuffing is more festive and makes the meat go further. The chestnuts (which are dried) need soaking overnight; alternatively, you **can** pour hot water over them and leave them to soak for only 6 hours.

If you have a little goose fat independently of the goose, you can make and bake the stuffing the previous day and simply re-heat it with the goose. Cooking time for the goose is 2 hours-2 hours 15 minutes.

Serve with bread sauce (see page 184), roast potatoes, and cabbage, peas, Brussels-sprout tops, or Brussels sprouts with or without chestnuts (bearing in mind that by Christmas, sprouts tend to be soggy). Should there be any be any goose left over, it is very good cold with plum chutney (see page 215).

FOR 6

Plum and chestnut stuffing (see below)
1 lemon (zest only)
2 or 3 sprigs sage
3.75-4 kg/ 8-8½ lb goose
Salt
125 g/ 4 oz (1 smallish) onion
1 outside stick celery
40 g/ 1½ oz unsmoked streaky bacon
4 cloves
5 peppercorns
75 ml/ 2½ fl oz port
About 1.5 kg/3 lb floury potatoes
Pepper
Bread sauce (see page 184)

Make the stuffing. Set the oven to 225 C, 425 F, Gas Mark 7 (it is awkward to sear or fry a goose before roasting to melt the fat: using a hot oven is the next best alternative). Scrub the lemon; wash the sage. Wash or thoroughly wipe the goose inside and out, reserving the giblets. Remove the lumps of fat just inside the cavity, (if you have the goose the day before you cook it, remove and melt it down for the stuffing). Prick the goose all over, and rub the inside lightly and the outside fairly generously with salt. Place in a roasting tray on a rack, slice a strip of lemon-zest about 3 cm/ 1¼ inches long and 1 cm/ ⅓ inch wide and put into the cavity with the sage. Roast for 20 minutes. Remove from the oven, pour off and reserve the fat in the tray, and cover the bird with cooking foil. Turn down the oven to 180 C, 350 F, Gas Mark 4, and cook for 70 minutes; drain off the fat from the tray again after about 30 minutes. At the end of the 70 minutes, remove the cooking foil and roast uncovered for a further 30 minutes or until the goose is well-browned, very crisp, and runs only clear rather than pink juice when pierced to the bone over the breast with a knife.

After setting the goose to roast, prepare the ingredients for the gravy. Peel and finely chop the onion; trim, wash, dry, and finely slice the celery. Dice the bacon. As soon as you have fat drained from the goose to hand, put 1 tablespoonful of it into a medium-sized pan with a lid. Warm over medium heat, add the bacon and vegetables, and fry for 6-7 minutes or until the onion is starting to colour; turn frequently. Add the cloves and turn; add the peppercorns, turn, and add the port. Allow to cook for a few seconds and pour in 525 ml/ ⅞ pint water. Thoroughly wash and add the neck of the goose, bending it to fit the pan. Bring to the boil, skim, cover, and simmer until the goose is ready.

Put the stuffing into the oven when the goose has cooked for 45 minutes; start roasting the potatoes 15 minutes later. Peel the potatoes, cut into even-sized pieces, and season fairly generously with salt and pepper. If your oven is fan-heated, place them on a baking tray spread with goose fat; if not, turn them in the dripping underneath the goose and set them with it on the rack. Roast for about an hour, turning from time to time; if placed on the rack, they should also be basted. At this oven heat, they will come out gold rather than brown but, thanks to the fat, deliciously crisp.

When the goose is ready, take it from the oven but leave the stuffing and potatoes inside; if the potatoes were roasted on the rack with it, transfer them to a baking tray. Place the goose on a serving dish and leave in a warm place while you make the gravy or for at least 5 minutes. Drain the fat from the roasting tray, leaving the juices behind, and pour the stock into the tray through a sieve. Stir thoroughly and reduce for 1-2 minutes, either setting the tray over the ring or transferring the gravy to a saucepan. Take the stuffing and potatoes from the oven while the goose is being carved.

PLUM AND CHESTNUT STUFFING

75 g/ 3 oz dried chestnuts, soaked overnight or for 6 hours starting with
hot water
Salt
175 g/ 6 oz (1 medium/large) onion
1 large (outer) stick celery
225 g/ 8 oz red plums
5-6 sage leaves
1 small lemon (zest only)
5 cloves
50 g/ 2 oz unsmoked back bacon
The liver of the goose
150 g/ 5 oz (½ medium) Bramley apple
2½ tablespoonsful goose fat
1 tablespoonful port

15-cm/ 6-inch (900 ml/ 1½ pint) soufflé-dish

Put the chestnuts into a saucepan with rather more water than will
cover them, add a pinch of salt, and simmer 35-50 minutes or until
tender (if soaked overnight, they will take 35-45 minutes, but if for
only 6 hours a little longer). Drain and divide into halves: mash one
half to a purée and the other roughly.

Peel and very finely chop the onion. Trim the celery and pare off any
brownish streaks; wash, dry, and finely dice. Wash dry, and dice the
plums. Rinse the sage, blot dry, and chop into very narrow strips.
Scrub, dry, and finely grate about half the zest of the lemon over the
sage. Crush the cloves. Remove the rind from the bacon and dice; wash
and dry the goose liver and chop as finely as possible. Peel and coarsely
grate the apple; mix with plums.

Warm 2 tablespoonsful of the goose fat in a wok or frying-pan over
fairly low heat and fry the onion, celery, and bacon for 6-7 minutes or
until the onion is soft but not brown; turn often. Add the cloves, sage,
and lemon-zest and turn; add the goose liver and ½ teaspoonful of salt
and turn until the liver is opaque on all sides. Add the plums and apple
and continue to fry, turning constantly, 2-3 minutes more. Add the

chestnuts, turn to mix, and stir in the port. Lightly grease the soufflé-dish with goose fat, turn the mixture into it, spread smooth, and cover with cooking foil. Bake for 1 hour; remove the foil, drizzle about ½ tablespoonful more goose fat over the top, and cook for a further 15-20 minutes uncovered.

ROAST PHEASANT WITH CHESTNUT AND ORANGE STUFFING

As pheasants are not native to this country and were still a rarity in the early 18th century, neither Queen Henrietta Maria nor Eliza Smith gave any recipes for them. Hannah Glasse, whose book was published in 1754, gave several, but from her remark that they could be interchanged with chickens, it seems that it was not yet customary to hang them for any length of time: 'If you have but one pheasant, take a large fine Fowl about the bigness of the Pheasant, pick it nicely with the Head on, draw it and truss it with the Head turned as you do a Pheasant's . . . when roasted, put them both on a dish and no Body will know it' [*The Art of Cooking Made Plain and Easy*, p. 48]. 100 years later, Eliza Acton wrote: 'Unless kept to the proper point, a pheasant is one of the most tough, dry, and flavourless birds that is sent to table' and recommended that it should be hung 'as many days as it can without becoming really tainted' [*Modern Cookery*, 1856 ed., p. 287].

Whereas in my experience it was never easy to buy properly hung pheasants, it has now become officially impossible, since according to European regulations the maximum hanging time for birds is five days. Of course, you can still keep pheasants until they are high if you shoot (allow 7-12 days' hanging time, depending on the weather). Alternatively, give your butcher due notice and he may agree to hang the birds on your responsibility. However, if you buy an oven-ready pheasant, it will be, as Glasse says, not unlike chicken (actually, the nearest equivalent is guinea-fowl).

It may or may not be tough. My butcher says that to avoid complaints on this score, he always advises customers to braise rather than roast their pheasants. With this book in mind, I searched diligently for tough pheasants all through last autumn, but in vain. When I reported my failure, he said, 'Wait until after Christmas.' The chances are that the birds on sale were hatched the previous spring; in the autumn they are still tender, but they become tougher as the months go by. Young ones will have fat on the side of the breast which is gradually dispelled by the exercise of flying; also, the spurs on young cocks (which are not removed) will be short and round.

The traditional accompaniments to roast pheasant are bread sauce, fried breadcrumbs, watercress, and game chips: if serving an under-hung pheasant in this way, I suggest adding stuffing and/or a skewer of bacon for extra flavour. The chestnuts for the stuffing need soaking overnight or, if put into hot water, for at least 6 hours.

Cooking time is 40-60 minutes according to the size of the pheasant: this includes all accompaniments except stuffing and stock for the gravy.

One pheasant is just enough for 4 (no second helpings); cocks are larger than hens. Keep the carcass for soup (see page 57).

Either chestnut and orange stuffing (see below)
or 2 or 3 sprigs thyme plus an extra 15 g/ ½ oz butter
75 g/ 3 oz (1 small) onion
75 g/ 3 oz (1 medium) carrot
1 outside stick celery
1 bay leaf
275 g/ 10 oz unsmoked streaky but not very fatty bacon
15 g/ ½ oz butter
1½-2 tablespoonsful oil
4 peppercorns
150 ml/ ¼ pint claret
1 pheasant
Salt
Pepper
2 short or 1 long rasher unsmoked, thick-cut fatty bacon
½ tablespoonful (1 dessertspoonful) brandy
Watercress for garnishing an unstuffed bird
Bread sauce (see below)
Fried breadcrumbs (see below)

If you plan to stuff the pheasant, start by preparing the stuffing.

Set stock for the gravy to simmer. Peel and finely chop the onion and carrot; trim the celery, pare off any discoloured streaks, wash, dry, and slice. Rinse a fresh bay leaf. Remove the rind from 50 g/ 2 oz of the leaner, streaky bacon and dice. Warm the butter and 1 tablespoonful of the oil over medium heat and fry the onion, carrot, celery, and bacon 7-8 minutes or until the onion is gold; turn often, especially towards the end. Add the peppercorns and bay leaf, turn, and pour in the wine. Allow about half of it to boil away and add 300 ml/ ½ pint water. Reduce the heat, cover, and simmer very gently while the pheasant cooks.

Heat the oven to 225 C, 425 F, Gas Mark 7. Remove the piece of bacon over the breast with which pheasants are often sold and wash the bird inside and out with cold water; dry the outside. Season moderately with salt inside and out and lightly outside with pepper. If you are not stuffing it, wash the thyme and put into the cavity with a knob of butter; otherwise, stuff loosely. Spread a little oil over a shallow (not flat) baking tray small enough for the ends of a long skewer to rest on the edges and put in the pheasant. Cover the whole area of the breasts with the thick-cut, fatty bacon: this is to prevent them from becoming dry (the breast-meat should be served slightly rarer than the legs). Roast for 20 minutes per 450 g/ 1 lb plus 5 minutes. 10 minutes before it will be ready, remove the bacon from the breasts to allow them to brown. If you can resist it, throw it away (by now it will be somewhat burnt but deliciously crisp and pheasant-impregnated: I treat it as the cook's perquisite).

As soon as you have put the pheasant into the oven, set the milk to simmer for the bread sauce. Pick over the watercress, trim the stems, and wash; make breadcrumbs for the fried crumbs and bread sauce and prepare the game chips. Trim the rind from the rest of the bacon, roll up, and thread on a skewer. Set the skewer over the baking tray and put the game chips into the oven when the pheasant has 30 minutes left to cook. Add the crumbs to the milk for the bread sauce about 5 minutes before the pheasant will be ready; then make the fried breadcrumbs. Take the pheasant from the oven, set it on the serving dish, and surround with watercress. To make the gravy, drain excess fat from the tray, remove any fragments of stuffing which may have escaped and will probably be burnt, and add the stock through a sieve.

Discard the vegetables; scrape the tray so that any sticky juices on the bottom are incorporated with the stock, and transfer to a small saucepan. Add the brandy, bring to the boil over high heat, and reduce for 1-2 minutes.

CHESTNUT AND ORANGE STUFFING

50 g/ 2 oz dried chestnuts, soaked overnight or in hot water for 6 hours
Salt
50 g/ 2 oz shallot
75 g/ 3 oz button mushrooms
3 cloves
½ orange
40 g/ 1½ oz unsmoked streaky bacon
15 g/ ½ oz butter
1 tablespoonful oil
Pepper

Put the chestnuts into a small saucepan with rather more water than is needed to cover them, add a little salt, and bring to the boil. Skim and cook at a fast simmer 35-50 minutes, until tender (if soaked for only 6 hours, they will take a little longer). Drain and mash.

Peel and finely chop the shallot. Trim the ends of the mushroom stalks; wash and dry the mushrooms and dice finely. Crush the cloves; squeeze 1 tablespoonful of orange juice. Trim the rind from the bacon and dice finely.

Melt the butter in the oil over fairly low heat and fry the shallots and bacon for 2-3 minutes. Add the mushrooms, season lightly with salt and pepper, and continue to fry, turning often, for another 3-4 minutes or until the mushrooms have started to exude juice. Add the cloves and turn for a few seconds. Add and stir in the chestnuts. Remove from the heat and moisten with the orange juice.

BREAD SAUCE

The usual way of flavouring bread sauce is to use a whole onion stuck with cloves, which is removed before serving: instead, I have suggested chopping half an onion and leaving it in the sauce because it gives texture and a stronger flavour. This means that unless you do not mind serving whole cloves, you will either have to crush them or pick them out; another alternative is to tie them in a small piece of cheesecloth.

Very fresh bread will form doughy lumps if you try to grate it; however, the bread should not be stale enough to be hard.

50 g/ 2 oz onion
1 bay leaf
5 cloves
450 ml/ ¾ pint creamy milk
Salt
Pepper
75 g/ 3 oz slightly stale white bread, weighed without crust
15 g/ ½ oz butter
2 tablespoonsful double cream
Nutmeg

Peel and very finely chop the onion; rinse a fresh bay leaf. If you wish, crush the cloves (which, however, will affect the colour of the sauce). Put the cloves, onion, and bay leaf into a smallish saucepan with the milk, add a moderate sprinkling of salt and pepper, and bring just to the boil. Lower the heat and simmer until about 5 minutes before the pheasant is cooked. While it simmers, coarsely grate the bread. Unless crushed, pick out the cloves with a perforated spoon. Stir in the crumbs, butter, and cream, and sprinkle with a grating of nutmeg. Continue to simmer for 2-3 minutes and serve.

FRIED BREADCRUMBS

50 g/ 2 oz stale white bread, weighed without crust
Salt
Pepper
1 tablespoonful oil
25 g/ 1 oz butter

Finely grate the bread, season lightly with salt and moderately with pepper, and stir to mix. Set a plate lined with kitchen paper to hand by the cooker. Warm the oil and butter over medium heat and stir-fry the crumbs for 3-4 minutes or until evenly browned and crisp. Transfer from the pan to the paper-lined plate to drain off surplus fat before serving.

BRAISED PHEASANT WITH PISTACHIO NUTS AND CREAM

There are so many possibilities for braising pheasants that by the time I reached this one even my husband, whose appetite for them is almost inexhaustible, was complaining. This dish, however, has been regularly requested ever since – which suits me, since of all game dishes it is one of the quickest and easiest to prepare.

The carcass can be rinsed to remove the cream and used for soup (see page 57).

Allow about 25 minutes for preparation and 1 hour for cooking.

Serve with grilled polenta (page 23) or fried game chips (you cannot bake them as on page 111 without a second oven, since the temperature needed is much higher than for the pheasant) and French, Kenya, or green haricot beans.

FOR 4

3 sticks celery (not outside)
75 g/ 3 oz shallots
1 lemon (zest only)
2 sprigs rosemary
125 g/ 4 oz lean, lightly smoked bacon chop
1 pheasant
Salt
Pepper
1-2 tablespoonsful oil
40 g/ 1½ oz pistachio nuts
15 g/ ½ oz butter
1½ scant teaspoonsful fennel seeds
150 ml/ ¼ pint milk
150 ml/ ¼ pint double cream

Trim the leaves and root-ends of the celery; pare off any brownish streaks, wash, dry, and slice finely. Peel and finely chop the shallots. Scrub the lemon and pare off two or three good-sized strips of peel. Wash the rosemary, strip the leaves from one of the stems (pull downwards), and finely chop (if you do not mind the leaves whole, omit chopping). Trim the fat from the bacon chop and cut into strips 2-3 mm/ ⅛ inch thick, 1 cm/ ⅓ inch wide, and 2cm/ ¾ inch long. Wash and dry the pheasant inside and out; season moderately inside and out with salt and lightly outside with pepper.

Warm the oil in a wok or frying-pan and toss the nuts briefly over medium heat to crisp them; remove with a perforated spoon and reserve. Raise the heat to high and sear the pheasant on all sides. Place in a casserole which fits it fairly closely, arrange the strips of bacon round it, and put the butter and the remaining sprig of rosemary into the cavity. Leave the oil in the pan. Set the oven to 180 C, 350 F, Gas Mark 4. Replace the pan over medium heat and fry the shallots and celery for 5-7 minutes or until the shallots are changing colour; turn constantly. Add the lemon-zest, fennel seeds, and rosemary (chopped or in spikes) and turn. Add the milk and pour the contents of the pan over the pheasant. Cover and cook for 45 minutes. Raise the heat to 200 C, 400 F, Gas Mark 6, add the cream, and cook uncovered for 10 minutes. Add the nuts, cook for another 5 minutes, and serve.

ROAST PARTRIDGES WITH PUY LENTILS AND MUSHROOMS

It used to be the custom to serve partridges distinctly 'high': Eliza Acton directed, 'Let the birds be hung as long as they can possibly be kept without becoming offensive' [*Modern Cookery*, 1856 ed., page 288]. However, as they have a distinctive but delicate flavour which long hanging overlays, and, assuming that they are young, are very tender, it seems to me that the limit on hanging time laid down by the recent regulations is in their case an advantage. Their delicate flavour also indicates simple treatment: in this recipe I have given a stuffing of only mushrooms and thyme, with no other ingredient except salt, pepper, and a little bacon for larding, which is usually sold with the bird (like other game, with the exception of duck, they carry very little fat). If you have the choice, the British type of partridge has more flavour than the French. Young birds suitable for roasting can be distinguished after plucking by soft legs and large breasts: in fact, all those I have bought recently have been young and tender, but if you are in doubt or simply want a different, more original way of serving them, see page 190.

The conventional way to serve roast partridges is as for pheasants, with fried breadcrumbs, bread sauce, and game chips (see pages 185, 184, and 111); with the plain mushroom stuffing, however, an excellent alternative is Puy lentils with mushrooms (below) and polenta chips (page 24). Accompany bread sauce and game chips with Brussels sprouts or cabbage; lentils and polenta chips should be followed by salad.

Polenta has to be made in advance; the stuffing can be prepared up to 24 hours ahead of time if you wish. Allow 30 minutes for roasting the birds plus an extra 10-15 for simmering lentils.

FOR 4 (1 PARTRIDGE EACH)

275 g/ 10 oz small brown or chestnut mushrooms, preferably organically grown
Small bunch thyme (enough for 2 teaspoonsful leaves)
2 tablespoonsful oil
25 g/ 1 oz butter

Salt
Pepper
4 plump partridges
2 rashers fatty, thick-cut bacon for larding if not supplied with the birds

To make the stuffing, trim the mushroom stalks close to the caps; wash, dry, and finely slice the mushrooms. Wash the thyme and strip off the leaves (pull down the stems; pick off the top leaves or those on short, subsidiary stems individually). Warm the oil and butter over low heat and add the mushrooms; season moderately with salt and pepper and sweat, turning constantly, for 2 minutes or until they run juice; add the thyme and sweat 2-3 minutes more or until some of the juice has been absorbed. Remove from the heat. If you are planning to serve the partridges with lentils, set the lentils to cook (see below); alternatively, prepare breadcrumbs, bread sauce, and potatoes.

Set the oven to 225 C, 425 F, Gas Mark 7. Untuck the legs of the partridges, remove the bacon with which they are sold from the breasts, and wash inside and out. Dry, season lightly with salt inside and out and outside with pepper, and stuff loosely. Set on a baking tray, replace or add half a rasher of bacon over the breasts, and roast 30 minutes; remove the bacon after 20 to allow the breasts to brown. Serve with the juices from the pan as gravy. While the partridges cook, prepare game chips and sprouts or cabbage or make salad and cut out polenta chips.

Puy Lentils with Mushrooms

50 g/ 2 oz shallots
125 g/ 4 oz chestnut mushrooms, if possible organically grown
75 g/ 3 oz unsmoked, streaky bacon
125 g/ 4 oz Puy lentils
1/2 small lemon
15 g/ 1/2 oz butter
1 tablespoonful oil
1 tablespoonful port
Salt

Peel and finely chop the shallots. Trim the mushroom stalks: wash, dry, and dice the mushrooms. Remove the rind from the bacon and dice finely. Rinse the lentils. Squeeze 3 teaspoonsful lemon juice.

Melt the butter in the oil over very low heat and sweat the shallots and bacon, turning fairly often, for 8-10 minutes or until both are soft. Add the mushrooms and sweat for another 5-6 minutes; add a little more oil if necessary. Add and cook away the port. Add the lentils, turn thoroughly, and pour in 480 ml/ 16 fl oz water. Raise the heat and bring to the boil; boil briskly for 2 minutes, reduce the heat, cover, and simmer for 30 minutes. Add 1 teaspoonful salt and simmer 5-10 minutes more or until soft (the time they take varies, partly according to how long they have been stored). If the partridges are not quite ready, remove the lentils from the hob, keep covered, and re-heat gently when needed. Raise the heat slightly to cook away surplus liquid if necessary. Stir in the lemon juice and serve.

PARTRIDGES BRAISED WITH FIVE-SPICE POWDER AND ORANGE

I owe the idea of this to Sean Wood and Benedict Gorman at 15 North Parade, Oxford, where they use the spicing to make partridge paté. As partridges are expensive, I felt that most people in a domestic situation would rather serve them whole than as paté and so did not plan to include the recipe; however, it lingered in the mind and finally I adapted it into the following, which is sympathetic and gentle, not in the least cloaking the taste of the partridges but giving it new emphasis and interest.

You can easily buy the five-spice powder ready prepared, but since the spices lose their flavour and aroma very quickly after grinding, I suggest making your own, which for the small quantity needed scarcely takes two minutes. All the components are fairly widely available except one, Sichuan peppercorns; green peppercorns, however, can be substituted.

One of the attractions of the dish is that even allowing for making the powder, very little preparation is needed; cooking time is 65 minutes.

Serve accompanied by rice fried with pistachio nuts, which can be prepared while the partridges cook (see below), and Kenya, French, or green haricot beans and/or rocket salad.

FOR 2

Five-spice powder:
3 cloves
5 green peppercorns
½ small or ⅓ large star anise
⅕ teaspoonful fennel seeds
¼ teaspoonful ground cinnamon

4-5 sprigs thyme (enough for 2 teaspoonsful leaves)
1 large or 2 small oranges
2 partridges
Salt
1 tablespoonful oil

4 teaspoonsful plain white flour
3 tablespoonsful port
1 teaspoonful set honey
2 tablespoonsful double cream

20 cm/ 8 inch casserole about 7.5 cm/ 3 inches deep

For the powder, pound the first four spices very finely in a mortar; stir in the cinnamon.

Wash, dry, and pull the leaves from the thyme (pull down main stems; pick off the top leaves and those on subsidiary stems individually). Scrub and dry the orange(s). Pare off two strips of zest about 4 × 2 cm / 1 ½ × ¾ inch, taking care to peel thinly: if much pith is removed, it will be difficult to squeeze efficiently. Squeeze 225 ml / 7½ fl oz juice: if the orange(s) yield slightly less (but it must be only a little less) the quantity can be made up with water.

Set the oven to 180 C, 350 F, Gas Mark 4. Wash the partridges inside and out; dry, and season moderately inside and out with salt. Warm the oil over high heat and sear the partridges very quickly on all sides. Remove from the heat and put into the casserole; leave the oil in the pan. Set the pan over medium heat, add the thyme, and turn; add the spices and turn for a few seconds. Add the flour off the heat and stir until amalgamated; return to the heat and add the port, orange juice, and zest. Bring to the verge of boiling, pour over the partridges, cover, and bake 55 minutes. Uncover, baste thoroughly with the sauce, and cook uncovered for a further 10 minutes. Place the birds on a serving plate, pour the sauce into a smallish saucepan, removing the orange-zest, and add the honey. Boil over medium heat 1-1½ minutes until slightly thickened and reduced, add the cream, and return to the boil. Pour some over the birds and serve the rest separately. Arrange the rice round the partridges.

RICE WITH PISTACHIO NUTS AND RAISINS

Set the rice to cook 15-20 minutes after putting the partridges into the oven.

FOR 2

125g / 4oz brown Basmati or other long-grain brown rice
Salt
15 g / ½ oz raisins
About ¾ tablespoonful port
25 g / 1 oz shallot
1 tablespoonful oil
25 g / 1 oz pistachio nuts

Turn the rice into a sieve, rinse thoroughly under the cold tap, and put into a medium-sized saucepan which can be covered. Add a pinch of salt and 250 ml / 8 fl oz water. Bring to the boil, stir, and simmer very gently for 30 minutes. While it cooks, set the raisins to soak in the port.

After 30 minutes, turn off the heat but leave the rice on the warm hob, covered, in the saucepan. Peel and finely chop the shallot. Warm the oil over medium heat and fry the shallot 1-2 minutes or until golden, turning constantly. Add the nuts and stir; add the raisins and port. Add the rice and stir briefly but thoroughly. Return to the covered saucepan until you are ready to serve.

Roast Pigeons Stuffed with Apple and Raisins

Rearing pigeons used to be a popular amateur activity, since the birds need no ground-space, were cheap to feed, and also regarded as exceptionally pleasant and virtuous: 'Pigeons lead a peaceful, social life . . . and under any conditions are distinguished for cleanliness, simplicity and innocence, qualifications in which they afford an example worthy of imitation' [*The Poultry Yard, Garden and Farm*, pub. E. Lloyd, 1854-5]. To Londoners used to the pigeons living off garbage on every roof-top, this may seem hard to believe; however, it may be of some reassurance to know that those shot for food are almost certainly from the country.

There are various different kinds of pigeon, but all are virtually indistinguishable in terms of eating quality. Although not classified as game (and therefore available throughout the year) they have a strong, distinctive gamey flavour. For this reason you might not want to eat them every day, but plump ones, which are probably young birds, are juicy and tender when roasted, and both the young and not-so-young can be braised or turned into an exceptionally rich-tasting salmi (see next recipe).

Roast pigeon (in contrast to salmi) is a quick dish, since the birds take only 12-15 minutes to cook. Serve rather rare with oven-chip potatoes (page 111) or sliced potatoes baked with onion (page 112) and braised celery (page 104) and/or French, Kenya or green haricot beans.

FOR 2

20 g/ ¾ oz raisins
3 tablespoonsful port
2 plump pigeons
Salt
Pepper
25 g/ 1 oz streaky unsmoked bacon plus 1 preferably thick-cut fatty rasher
75 g/ 3 oz (1 small) onion
3 leaves sage

25 g/ 1 oz walnuts
50 g/ 2 oz (½ medium) Cox apple
15 g/ ½ oz butter
1 tablespoonful oil

Set the raisins to soak in 1 tablespoonful of the port; leave 15-20 minutes. Wash the pigeons inside and out, dry, and season moderately with salt inside and out and lightly outside with pepper. Remove the rind and dice the bacon finely (use scissors). Peel and finely chop the onion; wash, dry, and finely chop the sage. Finely chop or coarsely crush the nuts. Peel and dice the apple.

Pre-heat the oven to 225 C, 425 F, Gas Mark 7; prepare and put in the potatoes, which take 30 minutes.

Fry the onion and bacon in the butter and oil over medium heat, turning constantly, for 2 minutes; add the apple and fry 2-3 minutes more or until the onion is soft. Add the sage and turn; add the port-soaked raisins, stir, and cook away most of the liquid. Stir in the nuts and remove from the heat.

Stuff the pigeons, inserting the stuffing loosely; set on a baking tray and cover the breast of each with half the rasher of fatty bacon. Roast 10 minutes; remove the bacon and roast 3-5 minutes more. Serve with gravy made from the pan juices quickly brought to the boil with the remaining 2 tablespoonsful of port and a very slight scattering of salt.

SALMI OF PIGEONS WITH MUSHROOMS AND JUNIPER BERRIES

The popularity of pigeons (for the table) in the eighteenth century is illustrated by Eliza Smith and Hannah Glasse, who gave numerous recipes for them, including (between them) pigeon paté, pigeon bisque, roast, grilled, and boiled pigeons, pigeon pudding, pigeon pie, pigeons baked in breadcrumbs, as rissoles, in jelly, stoved, and stewed in various ways. One so-called stew (perhaps Glasse borrowed from Smith, as the recipes are very similar) is in fact a salmi, flavoured with pickled mushrooms and oysters, lemon, and white wine.

Salmis are traditionally partly baked or roasted and then the cooking finished by simmering in a strongly flavoured sauce. Eliza Acton gave two recipes for game birds, one (British) plainer, and the other (French) in which the predominant flavour was sherry or Madeira; among several offered by the Victorian chef Francatelli, the most desirable and luxurious was partridges flavoured with truffles.

Glasse and Smith thickened their sauce by adding egg yolks; Acton used flour. Francatelli, presumably for the sake of flavour, did not add anything but relied on reduction. In order to keep the meat tender, both he and Eliza Acton also altered the earlier method and entirely cooked it before adding it to the sauce. I have followed his example in both respects: I admit that the consistency of the sauce is improved by flour but instead have suggested making a purée using some of the vegetables with which it is flavoured.

The salmi can be made either with plump pigeons tender enough to be roasted or with skinnier ones more suitable for simmering or braising. The meat is juicier and has more taste in itself when roasted but at the same time the sauce is one of the liveliest ways that I have found of serving older, tougher birds.

If the meat is to be roasted, the stock for the sauce can be simmered up to 24 hours in advance; simmered meat will be moister if served on the day it is cooked but can be kept until the next day if necessary.

The stock takes 50-55 minutes to simmer and the sauce 30 minutes.

Serve with polenta (see page 23) and either a separate vegetable or French, Kenya, or green haricot beans.

FOR 4

Stock or ingredients for simmering the pigeons
125 g/ 4 oz (1 smallish) onion
75 g/ 3 oz (1 largish) carrot
1 outside stick celery
4 pigeons
Salt
2 cloves
4 peppercorns

For roasting the pigeons
4 short rashers streaky bacon

Sauce
125 g/ 4 oz (1 smallish) onion
75 g/ 3 oz (1 largish) carrot
1 outside stick celery
275 g/ 10 oz chestnut or button mushrooms
5-6 sprigs thyme (enough for 2 teaspoonsful leaves)
8 peppercorns
1 teaspoonful juniper berries
50 g/ 2 oz unsmoked streaky bacon
25 g/ 1 oz butter
1½ tablespoonsful oil
2 tablespoonsful red-wine vinegar
142 ml/ ¼ pint claret
450 ml/ ¾ pint pigeon stock
1 level tablespoonful redcurrant jelly
2 tablespoonsful double cream

To make the stock and simmer the pigeons

Peel and finely chop the onion; peel and finely slice the carrot; trim the celery, pare off any brownish streaks, wash, and slice finely. Put into a saucepan with a lid. Wash and dry the pigeons inside and out. If the meat is to be roasted, slice the breasts from the carcasses as close to the breast-bone as possible (only the breasts are served in the salmi, but as virtually all the meat on pigeons is over the breast, this is not wasteful). Flatten the carcasses by loosening the breast-bone and add to the vegetables in the saucepan. Unless to be served directly, cover the breasts with foodwrap and store in the refrigerator until needed. If the pigeons are to be simmered, season moderately inside and out with salt and put them whole into the saucepan. Add the cloves, peppercorns, and 900 ml/ 1½ pints water or enough to just cover and bring to the boil. Skim, cover, and simmer 50-55 minutes or until the whole pigeons are tender. If for immediate use, strain and measure the stock but do not cut up the pigeons until the sauce is ready. If made in advance, strain the stock and leave to cool; cover and store both the birds (uncarved) and the stock in the refrigerator.

To make the sauce
Peel and finely chop the onion; peel and finely slice the carrot; trim the celery, pare off any brownish streaks, wash, and slice finely.

Wash and dry the mushrooms and cut off the stalks level with the caps. Trim the bottoms of the stalks, removing as little as possible, and dice. Slice the caps fairly thickly; keep each separate. Wash the thyme, blot dry, and pull off the leaves (pull down main stems; pick off top leaves individually). Crush the peppercorns; bruise the juniper berries. Remove the rind from the bacon and dice.

Warm 15 g/ ½ oz of the butter and ½ a tablespoonful of the oil in a wok or frying-pan over medium heat and fry the celery, carrot, onion, bacon, and mushroom stalks 8-10 minutes or until the onion and bacon fat are gold, turning constantly. Add the pepper and berries and turn; add the vinegar and stir. Add the claret and stock, bring to the boil, and simmer, covered, for 30 minutes. Pour into a smallish saucepan through a sieve and press as much of the contents through the mesh as you can.

To roast the pigeon breasts and finish the salmi
While the sauce simmers, set the oven to 225 C, 425 F, Gas Mark 7. Lightly season the pigeon breasts with salt, lay on a baking tray, and cover each with half a rasher of bacon. Start cooking them when you have finished sieving the sauce: roast 12-15 minutes.

Set the sieved sauce to simmer for 12 minutes; while it cooks, cut the breasts as neatly as you can from the simmered pigeons. Fry the mushroom caps: warm the rest of the butter and 1 tablespoonful of oil over medium heat and fry, turning constantly, for 4-5 minutes or until they have exuded and re-absorbed their juice and are slightly crisp. Raise the heat under the sauce and allow it to reduce for 2-3 minutes.

Add the mushrooms and stir in the jelly. If the pigeon breasts were simmered, add and simmer for 2 more minutes to warm them through before adding the cream; if roasted, stir in the cream and bring just to the boil before adding the meat. Turn off the heat, add the breasts, and leave for about a minute. Serve with the polenta.

BRAISED MALLARD STUFFED WITH THYME AND ALMONDS

The mallard is the largest and commonest of several kinds of wild duck eaten in Britain (the others are wigeon and teal). Like any duck, it is fatty: since the fat tends to go rancid in a relatively short time, it is hung for only a couple of days, which means that, although it has a pronounced gamey or wild taste, it does not develop the strong flavour traditionally associated with game. It also has a reputation for toughness which I must confess that I have found justified on occasion; however, if you choose a plump, young one, it will be as tender as a partridge. If roasted, it should be served very rare, before the meat has set; alternatively, it can be braised.

To roast, prick, fry and stuff the duck as below and roast for 30 minutes in a pre-heated oven at 200 C, 400 F, Gas Mark 6; drain off the fat as it cooks and serve with the juices from the pan rather than sauce, plus oven chip potatoes (page 111) or sliced potatoes baked with onions (see page 112) and braised celery (page 104).

With braised duck, which needs only the simplest accompaniments, I suggest plain, organically grown brown rice followed by a green or rocket salad (see page 97).

To avoid the risk of rancidity, the duck should be cooked within 24 hours of purchase. You can make the stuffing in advance but preferably not the previous day, since it tends to lose some of its flavour and aroma if kept. For braising, cooking time is just over 2 hours plus 10-12 minutes for frying.

One duck is enough for 2: if you cook only one, halve all the quantities but, unless you have a casserole which fits it closely, add a little water (up to 75 ml/ ⅛ pint) to the claret for the sauce.

FOR 4

4 or 5 sprigs parsley (enough for 1 tablespoonful when chopped)
Small bunch thyme (enough for 1 tablespoonful leaves)
50 g/ 2 oz whole (unblanched) almonds
1 large or 2 small oranges (zest only)
225 g/ 8 oz (2 smallish) onions
2 small inner and 1 outer stick celery
225 g/ 8 oz (2 medium) Cox apples
25 g/ 1 oz butter
3 tablespoonsful oil
About 2 teaspoonsful milk
2 mallards, preferably plump
Salt
Pepper
300 ml/ ½ pint claret
1 tablespoonful or a little more fresh apple juice (optional)

Casserole about 21-24 cm/ 8½-10 inches across and about 9 cm/ 3½ inches deep

Trim the ends of the stems of bought herbs; wash and thoroughly dry the parsley and thyme. Finely chop the parsley; strip the leaves from the thyme (pull downwards: pick off top leaves or those growing on subsidiary stems individually). Crush the almonds in a mortar: most of them should be reduced to a fairly fine powder, but a few larger pieces will add interest to the stuffing. Scrub, dry, and finely grate the zest of the orange(s). Peel and very finely dice one of the onions; fairly finely chop the other and set aside. Trim the leaves and root ends from the celery; wash and blot dry. Finely dice the inner stick; slice the outer one and set aside. Peel, quarter, core, and dice one of the apples.

Warm the butter and 1 tablespoonful of the oil over medium heat in a largish wok or frying-pan and fry the apple, the diced (but not the chopped) onion and the inner sticks of celery, turning constantly, for 5-6 minutes or until the onion is just changing colour. Remove from the heat; stir in the orange-zest, herbs, and almonds and moisten with the milk. Transfer to a bowl and wash or wipe the pan clean.

Wash and dry the ducks inside and out, prick the skin all over, and season moderately inside and out with salt and lightly outside with pepper. Warm the remaining 2 tablespoonsful of oil in the pan over low heat and fry the mallards, turning fairly often, for 10-12 minutes; baste as you fry and turn them on their sides as well as their breasts and backs. After 10-12 minutes, they should still only be very slightly coloured but will have run an appreciable amount of fat (probably 2-3 tablespoonsful).

Set the oven to 150 C, 300 F, Gas Mark 2. Stuff the ducks: add the stuffing loosely. If there is slightly too much, as there may be if they are small, leave a little of it rather than packing it in very tightly. Pour 300 ml/ ½ pint of water into the casserole, add the ducks (breast upwards), cover, and cook for 25 minutes.

Peel, core, and dice the second apple and put into a saucepan with the remaining prepared onion and celery. Add the claret and bring just to boiling point. Remove the casserole from the oven, drain off the water, with more fat which will have run, and pour the hot wine over the ducks. If you are cooking only one duck in a casserole which does not fit it fairly closely, add up to 75 ml/ ⅛ pint water to allow for evaporation during cooking. Tuck the apple and vegetables which were heated with the wine round the sides, cover, return to the oven, and cook for 80 minutes; check after 30 minutes to ensure that the casserole still contains plenty of liquid and add a little more wine if necessary. Uncover, raise the heat to 180 C, 350 F, Gas Mark 4, and bake for a further 20 minutes, or until the ducks are a rich brown.

Place the birds on a serving dish and slowly pour the liquor from the casserole into a smallish saucepan through a sieve, skimming off as much of the fat on top as you can. Slightly crush the vegetables in the sieve with the back of a spoon so that all the liquid and a little purée to thicken the sauce goes through. Set the saucepan over a high heat, bring to the boil, and boil 1½ – 2 minutes, until the sauce is slightly reduced and thickened. Serve separately.

HARE STEWED WITH PORT

With its rich smell and deep, thick sauce, jugged or stewed hare is a mandatory dish for anyone who likes the flavour of game. The traditional 'jugged' hare is so called because it was steamed in a jug set in a pan or cauldron of simmering water over the fire, like a pudding (which suited poachers, who were usually too poor to afford ovens); a similar effect, however, is given by stewing it in a casserole in the oven. Some cookery writers (although not Eliza Smith or Mrs Beeton) thickened the sauce at the end with its blood, but I prefer the flavour given by a purée of the accompanying bacon and vegetables.

To develop its characteristic, gamey flavour, a hare needs to be hung (before skinning and paunching) for about a week, although the time needed varies according to the weather. It will probably already be skinned and jointed when you buy it; otherwise, a butcher will certainly do it for you.

The accomplished impression given by the finished dish is deceptive, since preparation is actually very quick and easy: assuming that the hare is already cut up, you can have it in the oven in 20-25 minutes. Cooking time is 2-2¼ hours.

Serve with new or sliced potatoes baked with onions (page 112) and Brussels sprouts or braised celery (page 104).

A moderate-sized hare, weighing about 1.8 kg/ 4 lb after skinning and paunching, is enough for 8; a small one weighing about 1.3 kg/ 2½ lb will serve 6: if yours is small, scale down the quantities below proportionately.

1.8 kg/ 4 lb hare, skinned and jointed
Salt
Pepper
2 sticks celery
175 g/ 6 oz (2 medium) carrots
350 g/ 12 oz (3 smallish) onions
6 cloves garlic
6-7 sprigs each thyme and parsley
4 bay leaves
1 lemon

225 g/ 8 oz unsmoked streaky bacon
20 g/ ¾ oz butter
4 tablespoonsful oil
12 cloves
7.5-cm/ 3-inch stick cinnamon
225 ml/ ⅜ pint port
1 tablespoonful redcurrant jelly (optional)

Casserole about 23 cm/ 9 inches across and 10 cm/ 4 inches deep

Wash the meat thoroughly in cold water, dry with kitchen paper, and season fairly generously with salt and pepper.

Trim the leaves and root-ends from the celery; pare off any brownish streaks, wash, and slice thinly. Peel and finely slice the carrots, onions, and garlic. Trim the ends of bought thyme and parsley stems and wash; wash fresh bay leaves. Scrub the lemon and pare off 3 or 4 sizeable slices of the zest. Cut long rashers of bacon into two or three pieces.

Warm the butter with 1 tablespoonful of the oil in a large wok or frying-pan over fairly high heat and sear the pieces of hare on all sides (you will almost certainly have to do this in two sessions). Put half into the casserole; set the rest aside. Wipe the pan clean and lower the heat to medium. Add the rest of the oil and fry the onions for 2-3 minutes; add the garlic and fry 3-4 minutes or until the onion is just starting to change colour; turn constantly. Add the cloves and cinnamon and turn for 30 seconds. Add the lemon-zest and turn; add the port and cook half of it away. Remove from the heat.

Set the oven to 150 C, 300 F, Gas Mark 2. Place half the bacon over the hare in the casserole, sprinkle with half the celery and carrot, and pour in some of the port, onion and other flavourings from the pan, distributing them evenly over the meat. Arrange the rest of the hare on top, adding any juice which it may have run, and repeat with the rest of the ingredients. Lay the herbs on top, cover, and bake about 1¼ hours; baste the top layer of meat with juices from the bottom of the casserole and bake another 45-60 minutes or until the hare is very tender but not falling apart.

Reduce the oven heat to very low (90 C, about 200 F, Gas Mark ¼). Take the hare from the casserole and pour the rest of its contents into a smallish saucepan through a sieve. Wipe the casserole, put back the pieces of hare, moisten with just a very little of the gravy in the saucepan, and return to the oven to keep warm. Remove the thyme-stalks and bay leaves from the sieve and press as much of the bacon and vegetables through it as you can. Bring the thickened gravy in the saucepan slowly to the boil, stirring continuously. It should be as thick as custard; if necessary, reduce it by boiling over medium heat. You can now either leave it as it is or sharpen and sweeten it with 3 teaspoonsful lemon juice and 1 tablespoonful redcurrant jelly. (Taste before adding them: I prefer it without.) Arrange the joints of hare on the serving dish, glaze with some of the sauce, and distribute the rest over the top of each serving.

NICHOLA FLETCHER'S
QUICK-ROAST VENISON

The lean of venison has no marbling of fat. Young venison is very lean overall and such fat as it carries is low in saturates. It is therefore healthier than other kinds of red meat, but needs to be cossetted if it is not to dry out during cooking. As Nichola Fletcher, who owns a deer-farm and is well known as an expert on venison, points out, the lack of marbling means that the food eaten by the deer has little effect on taste; in fact, farmed and wild deer have much the same diet, but even if they did not, their meat would taste very similar. The quality of the meat from the different types of deer (red, fallow and roe) is also very similar, although the size of joints varies. The only two factors which seriously affect quality are the age of the deer and hanging. An old deer will be tough: even long hanging will not make it suitable for frying or roasting. Young meat is tender whether farmed or wild, hung or not, but the deep, rich taste which characterises venison is only acquired after 2-3 weeks' hanging. Age can be assessed (after purchase) by the sinews; if thick and tough, use the meat for stews, pasty, or sausages. How long it has been hung is almost impossible to judge until it has been cooked: smell may be a guide, although it is misleading to say this since even long-hung meat in good condition smells very little. Most supermarkets and butchers, however, sell it under-hung, partly for the same reason as beef (cost) and partly because many customers prefer the milder flavour; if you want it full and rich, either go to a knowledgeable dealer, or order directly from a supplier.

This recipe is for young, tender, well-hung venison, which needs only the very simplest cooking. Nichola always serves meat of this class when she has visitors, partly because, as she says, they would be disappointed if she gave them anything else, but also because cooking it is so quick and easy. In her list of ingredients, she specifies sirloin: however, a cheaper cut which is sometimes available is a piece of leg known as the 'silver' (part of the silverside), which can be cooked in exactly the same way. If possible, buy the meat complete with the outer skin, which can be used for the stock; otherwise, ask for some venison bones and trimmings, or make and reduce the gravy for beef on page 152.

Redcurrant jelly can be used instead of rowan jelly, but you will need a little less because it is sweeter.

The stock can be made up to 3 days in advance; allow 3-4 hours for it to simmer. The cooking and resting time for the venison is 25-35 minutes.

Serve with new potatoes and glazed carrots, courgettes, or green salad.

FOR 4

Stock
50 g/2 oz shallots
75 g/3 oz (1 largish) carrot
1 stick celery
50 g/2 oz unsmoked streaky bacon
4 juniper berries
Skin from the venison, or venison bones and trimmings
15 g/½ oz butter
1 tablespoonful oil
3 cloves
6 peppercorns
150 ml/¼ pint dry red wine
2 or 3 sprigs parsley
2 or 3 sprigs thyme
2 bay leaves

Venison
900 g/2 lb venison sirloin
25 g/1 oz butter
1 tablespoonful oil
12 juniper berries
1 heaped tablespoonful rowan jelly
300 ml/½ pint dry red wine
150 ml/¼ pint venison (or beef) stock
Salt
Pepper

Stock

Peel and finely chop the shallots; peel and finely slice the carrot. Trim, wash and dry the celery; slice finely. Dice the bacon. Bruise the juniper berries in a mortar; rinse and dry the skin or trimmings.

Warm the butter and 1 tablespoonful of the oil in a wok or frying pan over medium heat. Add the prepared vegetables and bacon and fry, turning constantly, for 5-7 minutes or until light brown; add the juniper berries, cloves, and peppercorns, turn, and pour in the wine. Allow about half of it to cook away, add 450 ml/¾ pint water, and transfer to a saucepan. Add the venison trimmings with just enough extra water to cover if necessary; wash and add the herbs and bring to the boil. Skim, reduce the heat to a gentle simmer, and cook for 3-4 hours. Strain; if made in advance, leave to cool and refrigerate. Before use, set over high heat and reduce by about one third.

Venison

Set the oven to 225 C, 425 F, Gas Mark 7. Wash and dry the venison. Warm the butter and oil in a large frying-pan over a fairly high heat until the butter is starting to turn gold. Sear the meat on all sides. Transfer to a small roasting pan and tip the hot fat over the top; do not wash up the pan. Cook the venison for 10-12 minutes, then turn off the oven, open the door briefly to reduce the heat inside, shut it again, and leave the venison for 15-20 minutes if you like it rare, or for 25-30 minutes if you prefer it cooked more.

While the meat rests, crush the juniper berries. Return the frying-pan to medium/high heat, add the berries, jelly, and wine, and stir to mix thoroughly. When the jelly has dissolved, add the stock; then reduce until only a small amount of deep, ruby-red sauce is left. Leave until the meat is ready.

When the meat has rested, add the pan-juices to the sauce and bring to the boil; taste, season as necessary, and strain. Serve with the meat, which should be cut into thick chunks rather than thin slices so that the flavour can be fully appreciated.

VENISON PASTY WITH CORIANDER SEEDS AND THYME

The flavourings I have used for this pasty give a light, slightly orange-like, aromatic result which contrasts with the stronger, gamier taste of Sean and Benedict's sausages (see page 211). It is designed for briefly hung meat: it neither suits nor is necessary with full-flavoured venison hung for two weeks or more.

If you are using stock, allow 1-2 days for marinating the meat, 2-2¼ hours for cooking it, and 30 minutes for baking the pie; the stock, if you make it, takes 3-4 hours to simmer. The pastry can be made up to 2 days and the meat cooked a day in advance; the stock can also be simmered a day ahead.

Serve with boiled, or mashed potatoes and broccoli, French, Kenya, or green haricot beans or salad.

FOR 6-8

Marinade
125 g/ 4 oz (1 smallish) onion
1 outside stick celery
125 g/ 4 oz (2 small) carrots
3 or 4 sprigs thyme
8 peppercorns
2 teaspoonsful coriander seeds
2 tablespoonsful oil
1 tablespoonful red-wine vinegar
300 ml/ ½ pint claret
1.5 kg/ 3 lb shoulder or haunch of venison

Stock
The bone from a haunch of venison
125 g/ 4 oz (1 smallish) onion
75 g/ 3 oz (1 largish) carrot
1 outside stick celery
4 peppercorns

Pasty

125 g/ 4 oz shallots
5-6 sprigs thyme (enough for 1 tablespoonful leaves when stripped)
2 teaspoonsful coriander seeds
1.5 kg/ 3 lb venison and its marinade
Salt
Pepper
65 g/ 2½ oz white flour
25 g/ 1 oz butter
3 tablespoonsful oil
1 tablespoonful red-wine vinegar
180 ml/ scant ⅓ pint venison stock (optional)
200 ml/ ⅓ pint claret
Puff or flaky pastry made with 225 g/ 8 oz flour (see page 20)

3-pint pie-dish

Marinade
Peel and finely chop the onion. Trim the ends of the celery; wash, dry, and slice finely. Peel and thinly slice the carrot. Wash the thyme. Bruise or lightly crush the peppercorns and coriander seeds in a mortar.

Warm the oil in a wok or frying-pan over medium heat and fry the onion, celery, and carrot for 6-7 minutes or until the onion is light brown; turn frequently. Add the peppercorns and coriander seeds and turn; add the vinegar, turn, and pour in the wine. Bring to the boil, add the thyme, and leave until cold. Wash and dry the meat, pour the marinade over it, turn, and cover. Leave for 1-2 days in the refrigerator, turning from time to time.

Stock
Saw the bone into lengths which will fit a saucepan. Peel and finely chop the onion; peel and thinly slice the carrot. Trim, wash, and slice the celery. Put the bone and vegetables into a saucepan with a lid, add the peppercorns, and cover with water. Bring to the boil, put on the lid, and simmer 3-4 hours. Strain; if made ahead of time, cover and store in the refrigerator or somewhere cool.

Pasty

Peel and finely chop the shallots. Wash, dry, and pull the leaves from the thyme (pull downwards: pick off top leaves and those growing on short stalks individually). Crush the coriander. Take the meat from its marinade, dry it, and chop it into 3-4-cm/ 1¼-1½-inch chunks. Season fairly generously with salt and pepper and roll in the flour: coat it very thinly, however, and shake off all the surplus.

Set the oven to 150 C, 300 F, Gas Mark 2. Melt the butter in 2 tablespoonsful of the oil in a wok or frying-pan over high heat and sear the meat quickly all over: you will probably have to do this in two sessions. Put the meat into a casserole. Wipe the pan, add the rest of the oil and the shallots and fry them over medium heat for 3 minutes or until just beginning to colour. Add the coriander and stir; add the thyme and stir. Add the vinegar and pour in the marinade liquor through a sieve. Add the stock or the same amount of water (180 ml/ scant ⅓ pint) with the wine. Bring just to the boil, pour over the meat, cover, and bake 2-2¼ hours or until tender. Leave to become cold: if made in advance, store overnight in the refrigerator.

Set the oven to 225 C, 425 F, Gas Mark 7. Put the meat into the pie-dish, roll out the pastry to a thickness of 5-6 mm/ ¼ inch, cut and stick strips round the rim of the dish, and cover the pie. Trim underneath the rim and make an air-hole in the middle; stamp the edges, and bake for 25-30 minutes or until golden.

PLAIN VENISON PASTY

This will be boring if you make it with mild meat, but with the deep, subtle, bitter-sweet flavour of long-hung venison it needs nothing except red wine and a little shallot.

If you have the bone from the haunch, use it for stock (see previous recipe).

The pastry can be made up to 2 days and the meat cooked 24 hours in advance. Cooking times are 2-2½ hours for the meat, and 25-30 minutes for the pastry.

Serve with boiled or crisp mashed potatoes and Brussels sprout-tops, Brussels sprouts, or carrots.

FOR 4

50 g/ 2 oz shallots
750 g/ 1½ lb shoulder of venison
Salt
Pepper
35 g/ scant 1½ oz white flour
15 g/ ½ oz butter
1½-2 tablespoonsful oil
225 ml/ ⅜ pint claret
225 ml/ ⅜ pint venison stock (optional)
Puff or flaky pastry made with 175 g/ 6 oz flour (see page 20)

22- by 15-cm/ 8½- by 6-inch (900 ml/ 1½ pint) pie-dish

Peel and finely chop the shallots. Wash, dry, and chop the meat into 2.5-cm/ 1-inch pieces; remove any tough tendons. Season fairly generously with salt and pepper and roll in the flour. Melt the butter in 1 tablespoonful of the oil over high heat and sear the meat quickly on all sides. Put into a casserole, wipe the frying-pan (although it should be clean), and add the remaining ½ tablespoonful of oil. Fry the shallots over medium heat for 2½-3 minutes or until golden, turning constantly; add a little more oil if necessary. Pour in the wine and an equal quantity (225 ml/ ⅜ pint) water or venison stock, bring to the boil, and pour, with the shallots, over the meat. Cover and cook at 150 C, 300 F, Gas Mark 2 for 2-2¼ hours or until tender. Allow to cool.

Set the oven to 225 C, 425 F, Gas Mark 7. Transfer the meat to the pie-dish. Roll out the pastry to a thickness of 5-6 mm/ ¼ inch, damp the edges of the dish, and cover the pie. Make an air-hole in the middle, stamp the edges, and bake for 25-30 minutes.

SEAN AND BENEDICT'S SPICED VENISON SAUSAGES

At 15 North Parade, Oxford (where Sean and Benedict are the chefs), you can sit in the dining-area and watch your sausage cooking for dinner, but to see it made means visiting the restaurant fairly early in the morning. When I arrived, at about 10 am, Sean was making redcurrant sorbet; someone else was shaping loaves of bread (everything, including preserves and biscuits for cheese, is made on the premises) and Benedict was stirring the purplish-red venison mixture for the sausages in a tub. As he filled the sausage-skins, I wondered how much practice one needs to become as adept as he is: none of his skins broke, he twisted the ends as lightly as if for boiled sweets, and the sausages when made were firm and even, curling spontaneously into a horse-shoe shape as he put them down. His are very large, each one being a generous portion; because of marinating, however, they are surprising light although containing no starch and virtually no fat.

Benedict uses a haunch, but meat from the shoulder (which is cheaper) is also suitable. You may have to buy the sausage-skins in bulk, but the surplus can be frozen; alternatively, omit the skins and use the sausage-meat for venison-burgers.

Allow 1-2 days for marinating the meat, 24 hours for soaking the skins, and 2-3 minutes for frying or 7-10 for baking the sausages.

Serve with elderberry or blackcurrant gravy or plum chutney (page 215), creamed celeriac, and baked or mashed potatoes or polenta (pages 113 and 23).

FOR 6-8

Marinade
1 leek
125 g/ 4 oz onion
1 outside stick celery
75 g/ 3 oz (1 largish) carrot
2 tablespoonsful oil
2 teaspoonsful juniper berries
2 teaspoonsful peppercorns
2 cloves
2 teaspoonsful allspice
2 tablespoonsful red-wine vinegar
375 ml (½ bottle) claret
1.5 kg/ 3 lb haunch or shoulder of venison

Sausages
About 3 metres/ 10 feet of sausage-skins
25 g/ 1 oz shallots
Small bunch thyme (enough for 3 tablespoonsful leaves)
1 teaspoonful peppercorns
1 teaspoonful juniper berries
1 clove
2 teaspoonsful green peppercorns
1.5 kg/ 3 lb venison, marinaded
Salt
1 teaspoonful allspice
3 teaspoonsful Dijon mustard
Red-wine vinegar
2 tablespoonsful port

Sausage-making attachment to a mixer or a forcing-bag with a wide nozzle

Marinade
Trim the root-end and leaves from the leek, peel off the outer layer, and slice finely; wash and leave on kitchen paper to dry. Peel and very finely chop the onion. Wash, dry and finely slice the celery; peel and thinly slice the carrot.

Warm the oil in a wok or frying-pan over the medium heat and fry the prepared vegetables for 7-8 minutes or until the onion is light brown; turn frequently. Add the juniper berries, peppercorns, and cloves and turn for 30-40 seconds; add the allspice, continue to turn for a few seconds more, and add the vinegar. Remove from the heat, pour in the wine, and leave until cold.

Wash, dry, and chop the meat into large pieces, removing any tough sinews and all traces of fat. Marinade, covered, in the refrigerator for 24-48 hours.

Sausages
Set the sausage-skins to soak for 24 hours before making the sausages. Drain and rinse before use.

Peel and finely chop the shallots. Wash and pull the leaves from the thyme (pull downwards: pick off top leaves and those growing on short stems individually). Grind or crush the peppercorns, juniper berries, and clove; roughly crush the green peppercorns. Take the meat from its marinade and chop into chunks of a size which will go through your mincer; reserve the marinade. Season the meat lightly with salt, mix with all the ingredients except the green peppercorns, and mince. Add the green peppercorns and mix thoroughly.

If you have an attachment to your machine, make the sausages according to the instructions. To make them with a forcing-bag, cut the soaked skin into 45-60-cm/ 18-25-inch lengths, insert the nozzle into the bag, and stretch one end of a length of skin over the mouth. Push more skin over the nozzle until only a short piece remains and twist the end. About two-thirds fill the bag with meat, squeeze out a sausage of the size you want, twist firmly, and cut. Twist the end of the skin again and repeat until all the meat is used.

Alternatively, shape the meat into burgers, which should be thick enough to be juicy: without fat, thin ones tend to be dry.

For the same reason, i.e. that they tend to dry out, frying or baking suits the sausages better than grilling; for burgers, I recommend frying. To bake sausages, heat the oven to 225 C, 425 F, Gas Mark 7 and cover the bottom of a baking tray with oil. Prick the sausage-skins and bake for 15 minutes or until brown. To fry sausages or burgers, prick sausage skins and warm 2 tablespoonsful of oil over fairly high heat. Fry 2-2½ minutes, or until sausages are brown and burgers almost black. Stand back a little, since the water content of the mixture may cause spitting. Although almost black on the outside, the burgers should be slightly rare in the middle; sausages will be juicier if not fried too dark.

BLACKCURRANT GRAVY

For this, you need the water in which you boiled the celeriac (or, if you have any, a little vegetable stock).

150 ml/ ¼ pint of the venison marinade
75 ml/ ⅛ pint celeriac-water or vegetable stock
1 scant tablespoonful blackcurrant jelly

Strain the marinade. Bring the stock to the boil, remove from the heat, and add the jelly; stir until dissolved. Add 150 ml/ ¼ pint of the marinade, return to the boil, skim, and reduce over medium heat for about 1 minute.

PLUM CHUTNEY

As well as the sausages, this is excellent with cold goose or cheese. If put into sterilized jars and stored in a cool place, it will keep for over a year.

Allow 2-2½ hours for simmering the ingredients and at least 8 weeks for the chutney to mellow before serving. As vinegar will in time attack metal, metal tops to the jars should be lined with greaseproof paper.

MAKES 900 G/ 2 LB

750 g/ 1½ lb red plums
225 g/ 8 oz (2 medium/small) onions
2 cloves garlic
2.5-cm/ 1-inch piece fresh ginger
6 cloves
1½ teaspoonsful ground cinnamon
1 teaspoonful allspice
1 teaspoonful salt
125 g/ 4 oz raisins
225 g/ 8 oz soft brown sugar
150 ml/ ¼ pint red-wine vinegar
225 g/ 8 oz (1 medium) Bramley apple

2 x 1-lb jam-jars with fitted tops

Wash, blot dry, and chop the plums into eighths; put into a saucepan. Peel and very finely chop the onions, garlic, and ginger, rejecting any fibrous patches on the ginger; add to the pan. Crush and add the cloves with all the other ingredients except the apple; peel, coarsely grate or very finely chop, and add the apple. Stir thoroughly and simmer over the lowest possible heat for 2-2½ hours or until thick. Sterilize the jars, tops, and a tablespoon as on page 148; dry the jars and tops in the oven and fill the jars, using the tablespoon, while they are still warm. Seal and keep for at least 8 weeks.

SWEET DISHES

SUMMER PUDDING WITH RASPBERRY SAUCE

Part of the popularity of summer pudding springs from the fact that it is a genuine pudding and, since it contains no fat, it is relatively healthy. It is also a particularly attractive way of serving small quantities of soft fruit.

You can use a mixture of any three kinds of currant or berry provided that it gives contrast and includes at least one fairly sharp flavour. Over time, I must have tried almost every possible combination: two very good ones are raspberries and gooseberries with strawberries or blackcurrants, but even better (which makes late- rather than mid-summer pudding) are raspberries, blackberries, and blueberries.

The pudding is simple but presents one problem: sometimes the fruit juice, which is supposed to soak right through the bread, refuses to do so although there is plenty of juice. The cause seems to be the lack of absorbency of certain types of bread, since it usually happens with the sort of close-textured sliced white bread which never goes stale but retains its moisture even unto mould. The bread should be fairly stale and dry: I suggest unsliced brown bread, which is more porous and in my view goes better with the taste of the fruit than white. The usual and infallible remedy, however, is either to have a little extra fruit juice to apply to the bald patches or make a sauce to pour over the pudding: hence the raspberry sauce below, which not only serves a cosmetic purpose but adds an extra touch of luxury to the pudding.

If possible, use wild blackberries, which are sharper than the cultivated varieties.

The pudding must be weighted for 24 hours in the refrigerator before serving. Allow 2 hours for the raspberries to steep for the pudding and 1 hour for the sauce.

Accompany with whipped cream.

FOR 6-8

Pudding

200 g/ 7 oz raspberries
125 g/ 4 oz caster sugar
225 g/ 8 oz blackberries
225 g/ 8 oz blueberries
150-175 g/ 5-6 oz fairly stale brown (not wholemeal) bread, weighed
without crusts

Sauce

200 g/ 7 oz raspberries
50 g/ 2 oz caster sugar
¹/₂ lemon

2-pint pudding basin

Pudding

Pick over the raspberries, wash, and leave to drain. Sprinkle with
25 g/ 1 oz of the sugar and leave for about 2 hours.

Pick over and wash the blackberries and blueberries, shake off surplus
water, and put into a saucepan with the rest of the sugar. Set over very
low heat, stirring gently at the beginning, for about 5 minutes or until
the sugar has melted and the fruit is submerged in juice. Leave to cool.

Cut the bread first into 8 or 9 thin slices, removing any crust, and
then into strips; if you like, cut a circle to fit the bottom of the basin.
Line the basin with the bread, leaving enough to cover the top.

Mix the raspberries with the stewed fruit and turn into the basin.
Cover with bread and a saucer which fits into the top. Put a weight on
top of the saucer (e.g. a full pot of jam) and refrigerate for 24 hours.
To turn out the pudding, slide a knife around the edge of the basin,
place the serving plate upside-down over the top, and invert; tap the
bottom of the basin smartly and remove.

Sauce

Pick over, wash, and drain the raspberries. Sprinkle with the sugar and
leave to steep for an hour. Squeeze and add 1 teaspoonful lemon juice.
Press through a sieve. Pour about half over the pudding and serve the
rest separately.

SUMMER FRUIT SALAD

This is based on a recipe given by Eliza Acton for a salad of strawberries, red and white currants, and red and white raspberries. (Why is it now impossible to buy white raspberries? Many years ago, I used to pick them by the basketful in the woods: are they so very uneconomic?) At first, having bought some delicious red eating-gooseberries in Wales, I intended to use them to replace the white fruit; however, as the only ones I could find in London were bland and woody-tasting, I have slightly changed the nature of the original and added blackberries and peaches instead, which means making the salad late in the season, when the blackberries are ripe. If at all possible, use wild ones: the cultivated ones look magnificent but seldom have much flavour. I am resigned to the fact that the strawberries will probably be tasteless and have included them chiefly for their appearance.

Make sure that the berries are firm and not over-ripe; the peaches should give slightly to the touch.

Allow at least 4, and preferably 6-8 hours for the fruit to macerate. The berries should also be left for an hour or so to dry after washing.

FOR 4-6

225 g/ 8 oz raspberries
225 g/ 8 oz strawberries
125-175 g/ 4-6 oz blackberries
2 peaches
25 g/ 1 oz caster sugar
1 glass medium-dry red or rosé wine

Carefully pick over the berries and remove any which are squashed or mouldy. Wash and leave to dry in a colander for at least an hour. Peel and fairly thinly slice the peaches. Put all the fruit into a serving bowl, sprinkle with the sugar, and pour the wine over it gently. Cover and allow to macerate in the refrigerator 4-8 hours. Serve chilled.

AHMED KHARSHOUM'S CHOCOLATE MOUSSE WITH COFFEE SAUCE

Ahmed, who is chef at a discreet restaurant in North London (Granita, London N1), understands how to raise a simple dish to distinction with details. In this, the raisins soaked in heated brandy are decisive; the sauce is also masterly, the flavour of the coffee being just strong enough to balance the richness of the chocolate.

The chocolate should be about as bitter as Meunier Chocolat Patissier, which I recommend; do not use very bitter chocolate such as Valrhona. It must, however, be cooking chocolate, which contains more fat than ordinary chocolate and is less likely to become gritty when heated.

As the eggs are used raw, be particularly careful to ensure that they are fresh; do not serve the mousse to children or to anyone vulnerable.

The mousse should be chilled overnight, but not made more than one day in advance.

Allow 30 minutes for the raisins to infuse for the mousse and the flavourings in the milk for the sauce.

FOR 8-10

Mousse
1½ tablespoonsful brandy
75 g/ 3 oz large raisins
250 g/ 9 oz medium-bitter cooking chocolate
125 g/ 4 oz butter
4 size 2 eggs

Sauce
1 vanilla pod
Scant tablespoonful finely-ground expresso coffee
300 ml/ ½ pint milk
4 size 2 eggs (yolks only)
125 g/ 4 oz white sugar

18 cm/7 inch soufflé-dish, or similar size oval dish

Mousse

Warm the brandy, mix with the raisins and leave to infuse for at least half an hour. Line the dish with cooking foil which overhangs sufficiently for you to remove the mousse to a flat serving dish if you wish. Chop the chocolate and butter into small pieces, place in a bowl in a saucepan of water over low heat, and stir until the chocolate is almost melted. Remove the bowl from the heat and continue to stir until the chocolate is perfectly smooth. Separate the eggs (see page 17); beat the yolks into the chocolate and whip the whites until they are close-textured and stiff enough to stand in peaks when lifted from the whisk but not beaten to the point where they exude liquid. Gently fold them into the chocolate. Turn the mixture into the dish, cover, and chill overnight.

Sauce

Score the vanilla pod lengthwise to release the seeds. Put it with the coffee and milk into a smallish saucepan and heat to just under boiling point. Leave for about 30 minutes. Strain through a very fine sieve or a jelly-bag. The vanilla pod can be used again: wash, dry, and store in an air-tight jar.

Separate the eggs and beat the yolks with the sugar. Gradually pour the flavoured milk into them, stirring continuously. Return mixture to the milk-saucepan (or put into any smallish saucepan) and set over low heat, stirring continuously, for 3 minutes or until the top of the mixture is smooth and the custard has thickened sufficiently to coat the back of a spoon. Remove from the heat; continue to stir for a moment or two. Serve warm or chilled (but do not re-heat or the custard will curdle).

RICE PUDDINGS

Some people love and some loathe rice puddings; others avoid them because they think of them as fattening. I love them, and like every true enthusiast never tire of evangelizing. I am well aware that for someone who hates milk (like my daughter) they are a lost cause, but to those who are worried about weight I can point out that they contain no added fat and not much sugar, so that an entire pudding for 3 or 4 is under 1,000 calories, i.e. only 200-300 calories per portion. They are much healthier as an accompaniment to fruit than cream; alternatively, you can flavour them in any number of ways. They are also the laziest pudding known to the cook: all they involve is putting the ingredients (which, except with some flavourings, do not need preparation) into a dish or saucepan, and stirring every now and again.

The basic recipe is 50 g/ 2 oz pudding rice, 75 g/ 3 oz sugar, and 1 ¼ or 1 ½ pints of milk; this can either be simmered for 1 ¼-1 ½ hours or baked for 3 hours. Much of the point of baked puddings is the skin; also, as usual with baking, the flavour is slightly more concentrated. Simmered ones, on the other hand, are lighter and often work better with flavourings. The first of the two given here should be simmered; the second can be cooked either way.

BROWN RICE PUDDING

The *raison d'être* of rice pudding is that short-grained white rice releases its starch into the liquid in which it is cooked to give a thick sauce. As brown rice does not release its starch nearly so readily, it did not seem surprising that short-grain brown rice was not marketed; however, it has recently become available. When I first tried it, the result was a failure because it scarcely softened at all; the secret turned out to be not to add sugar until it is tender. It makes a pudding which is nutty and fudge-like rather than creamy and so far as I am concerned the best of all.

This pudding takes 1 hour 50 minutes to 2 hours to simmer, or 1 hour 45 minutes to 2 hours to bake.

Serve hot.

FOR 3-4

50 g/2 oz brown short-grain rice
750 ml/1¼ pints milk
(If you wish, 300 ml/½ pint of the milk can be skimmed milk)
75 g/3 oz soft dark brown sugar

To simmer, rinse and put the rice into a saucepan with 600 ml/1 pint of the milk, bring just to the boil, and simmer very gently for 1½ hours, stirring from time to time and often towards the end. Add the sugar and the remaining 150 ml/¼ pint milk, stir and simmer for another 20-25 minutes.

To bake, set the oven to 150 C, 300 F, Gas Mark 2; rinse and put the rice into a pie- or soufflé-dish with 600 ml/1 pint of milk, and bake 1½ hours, stirring every half hour. Stir in the remaining milk and bake 15 minutes more; add and stir in the sugar and bake for another 15-20 minutes.

SAFFRON AND VANILLA RICE

This is sweetened more than plain rice pudding to bring out the flavour of the vanilla.

Do not use powdered saffron, which has very little flavour. The vanilla pod or pods (which are expensive) can be used again, although they will give less flavour the second time round.

Serve hot.

FOR 3-4

50 g/2 oz pudding rice
125 g/4 oz caster sugar
900 ml/1½ pints whole, i.e. unskimmed milk
1 large or 2 small vanilla pods
2 g (½ small packet) saffron threads

Rinse the rice under the cold tap, put into a saucepan with the sugar and 1 pint of the milk, and bring just to the boil. Stir, lower the heat, and cook at a very gentle simmer for 30 minutes, stirring occasionally. Slit the vanilla pod(s) lengthways to release the seeds, and add with the saffron; stir and simmer for another 15 minutes. Add the rest of the milk, sprinkle in the saffron, stir thoroughly, and cook at just under a simmer for a final 15 minutes, stirring often.

Wash and thoroughly dry the vanilla pod(s), and store in an air-tight jar.

ORANGE AND HAZELNUT TART

I owe the idea of this tart to Tim Jones of the Patisserie Bliss, whose products, over the long period during which I have been a customer, have fully lived up to the name. The only item with which I have ever been disappointed was a hazelnut tart (in fairness, he warned me that it was experimental and refused to be paid). The recipe below is my attempt at improvement. The filling is very crisp and tastes as if it were made with honey

Use unskinned, whole hazelnuts, which will have more flavour than blanched or chopped ones (ready-chopped ones will also not give the required variation in texture). With the nuts, the pastry base should be very thin: I have therefore recommended using only 125 g/ 4 oz flour.

The dough for the pastry can be made and, if you wish, the tart tin lined up to two days in advance: either wrap the dough or cover the tin with foodwrap and store in the refrigerator.

Although obviously best when first baked, the tart will stay crisp even outside a tin for several days.

FOR 6-10

Shortcrust pastry made with:
125 g/ 4 oz plain white flour
1 teaspoonful caster sugar
Pinch of salt
25 g/ 1 oz butter
25 g/ 1 oz lard
Squeeze lemon juice
1 tablespoonful plus 1 teaspoonful cold water

185 g/ 6½ oz unskinned whole hazelnuts
110 g/ generous 3½ oz slightly salted butter
2-cm/ ¾-inch piece cinnamon stick
1 scant teaspoonful coriander seeds
1 orange (zest only)
150 g/ 5 oz caster sugar
1 tablespoonful brandy
2 tablespoonsful double cream

Heat the oven to 200 C, 400 F, Gas Mark 6. Roll out the pastry to fit a 22-cm/8½-inch tart tin and line the tin. Cover all over with cooking foil, including the rim, weigh down with baking-beans if possible, and bake for 10 minutes. Remove the beans and foil and bake for a further 5 minutes or until the pastry is just beginning to colour. While the pastry cooks, spread out the nuts on a baking tray and bake for 8-10 minutes or until slightly browned. Allow to cool a little. Turn down the oven to 180 C, 350 F, Gas Mark 4. Roughly chop the butter and set over low heat until just, or almost melted; take care not to let it brown. Pound the cinnamon and coriander to a powder in a mortar. Add about 150 g/ 5 oz of the nuts and crush unevenly, leaving a few larger pieces. Wash, dry, and finely grate the zest of the orange. Stir the crushed nuts and spices, whole nuts, orange zest, sugar, brandy, and cream into the butter. Turn into the pastry case and bake for 25-30 minutes, until the top of the tart begins to turn pale brown at the edges. Serve cold.

TIM JONES'S LEMON TARTS

So far as I am concerned, these are the *only* lemon tarts. The recipe, like all of Tim's, is the very model of simplicity: the filling consists only of eggs, lemon, single cream, and surprisingly little sugar, with none of that horrible concoction known as lemon curd. As the small amount of sugar indicates, it is bracingly sharp; this is balanced, however, by the sweet pastry.

Tim's tarts are larger than the standard patty-tin size; you can either use ordinary patty-tins for smaller ones or make one large tart.

The cream should be very fresh: if it is near the end of its date, it is more likely to curdle.

Baking time is 15 minutes.

MAKES ABOUT 20 SMALL TARTS OR ONE LARGE TART SUFFICIENT FOR 8-10

Sweet pastry (see page 20) made with:
225 g/8 oz plain white flour
Salt
125 g/4 oz butter
125 g/4 oz caster sugar
4 size 2 eggs (yolks only)

2 large or 3 small lemons (enough for 150 ml/¼ pint juice)
4 size 2 eggs
60 g/2¼ oz caster sugar
142 ml/¼ pint fresh single cream

2 patty-tins or 22-cm/8½-inch tart tin

Roll out the pastry 2-3 mm/⅛ inch thick if for small tarts, or 4-5 mm/ less than ¼ inch for the large tart. Line the tin or patty-cases.

Set the oven to 225 C, 425 F, Gas Mark 7. Scrub and dry two of the lemons; finely grate the zest of 1½. Squeeze 150 ml/¼ pint juice. Separate the eggs (see page 17). Beat the yolks and sugar to a cream (the whites are not needed for this recipe). Stir in the lemon juice. Add and stir in the cream, fill the tart or tarts at once, and bake for 15 minutes or until the filling is set and the pastry golden.

WHITE CHERRY AND ALMOND TART

White cherries (which are actually yellow tinged with red) are firm-textured and sharper than the red or very sweet black varieties and make a tart with an almost refreshing intensity of flavour.

I have accompanied them not only with an almond filling, but almond pastry, which is deliciously short and melting but difficult to roll (although easily patched) and breaks easily: if you prefer, use ordinary shortcrust pastry made with an egg yolk and 2 teaspoonsful caster sugar.

The pastry can be made up to 2 days in advance.

Serve (cold) with single cream.

FOR 6-8

Almond pastry (for pastry, see page 20) made with:
50 g/ 2 oz ground almonds
125 g/ 4 oz plain white flour
2 teaspoonsful caster sugar
75 g/ 3 oz butter
1 size 2 egg yolk
1 tablespoonful water

400 g/ 14 oz white cherries
½ large lemon
65 g/ 2½ oz butter
150 g/ 5 oz caster sugar
125 g/ 4 oz ground almonds
185 g/ 6½ oz redcurrant jelly

21-cm/ 8½-inch fluted china tart dish

Pick over the cherries, wash, and leave to dry. Set the oven to 200 C, 400 F, Gas Mark 6. Line the tart dish with the pastry, cover all over with cooking foil, and blind-bake for 10 minutes. Remove the foil and bake for a further 10-12 minutes, until light brown. Leave to cool.

Squeeze the half-lemon. Put the butter into a small saucepan and set over low heat until just melted: immediately stir in the sugar, then the almonds. Add just enough lemon juice to bring the mixture to a soft paste; reserve the rest of the juice. Spread the almond filling evenly over the pastry base.

Stone and halve the cherries and arrange over the filling: set in tight circles with each half very slightly overlapping the next. Bring the redcurrant jelly to the boil with 3 teaspoonsful lemon juice and boil for 20 seconds. Pour over the top of the tart, making sure that all the cherries are completely covered. Allow to cool before serving.

PLUM TART WITH PORT AND CINNAMON

The traditional English pie with fruit underneath the pastry is simpler to make than a tart and (since cooks were not always skilful) was therefore favoured so long as there were servants in the kitchen to bake and serve it hot; now, however, tarts which can be made ahead of time and served cold are more practical. I have found no way of presenting cooking plums which does them such justice as the following. When possible, use Victorias, which are sharp and full-flavoured.

With the acidity of the plums, a fairly rich pastry cream is needed; similarly, the smoothness of the cream and texture of the plums call for very crisp, well-browned pastry.

The same recipe without port or spices can be used for a greengage tart, which is also excellent. You can make the pastry and, if you like, line the tart tin up to two days ahead: wrap the dough or cover the tin with foodwrap and store in the refrigerator.

It is essential to eat the tart on the day it is made, since the pastry will become soggy and the spices lose their flavour if it is kept for more than a few hours.

FOR 6-8

__Shortcrust pastry (see page 19) made with:__
Either 175 g/ 6 oz plain white flour or 75 g/ 3 oz each plain white and
wholemeal flour
Pinch salt
40 g/ 1½ oz butter
40 g/ 1½ oz lard
2 teaspoonsful caster sugar
1 teaspoonful lemon juice

3 size 2 eggs (yolks only)
65 g/ 2½ oz caster sugar
20 g/ ¾ oz plain white flour
150 ml/ ¼ pint milk
142 ml/ ¼ pint double cream
450 g/ 1 lb Victoria or other cooking plums
125 g/ 4 oz soft brown sugar
4 tablespoonsful port
2½-cm/ 1-inch piece cinnamon stick
3 cloves
Squeeze lemon juice

Set the oven to 200 C, 400 F, Gas Mark 6. Roll out the pastry to a thickness of about 5mm/ ¼ inch. Line a 22-cm/ 8½-inch tart tin; trim off surplus pastry, cover all over with cooking foil, including the rim, and weigh down with baking-beans if available. Bake for 10 minutes; remove the beans and foil and bake a further 15-18 minutes or until well coloured.

Make the pastry cream. Separate the eggs (the whites can be used for soufflés (see pages 63 and 65) or meringues). Whisk the yolks with the sugar; whisk in the flour by degrees. As the mixture is thick, the whisk may stick, in which case stir thoroughly with a spoon. Heat but do not boil the milk and cream. Pour into the egg mixture by degrees, whisking continuously. Transfer to the saucepan in which you heated the milk and bring to the boil: stir continuously and watch carefully, since whisking will mean that the mixture is already frothy. As soon as it boils, lower the heat to a simmer; simmer for 3½ minutes, stirring continuously. Allow to cool a little and pour into the pastry case.

Wash, halve, and stone the plums as tidily as possible. Put into a saucepan with the sugar, port, cinnamon, and cloves (leave the spices whole); set over gentle heat and simmer for 7-10 minutes or until the plums are just soft but not disintegrating. Remove them with a perforated spoon: shake them slightly over the pan to drain off any surplus juice. Arrange over the cream; leave the juice in the pan. At this stage, the tart will not look very decorative, as the plums are squashy and may be rather ragged; however, its appearance will be transformed by the glaze. Set the pan containing the juice over fairly high heat until the liquid is thick and reduced to about 4 tablespoonsful. Add a squeeze of lemon juice, bring back to a sharp boil, and remove from the heat. Spoon over the tart, taking care to cover the top completely, including the fruit. The whole surface will now be a glistening dark red. Serve cold with yoghurt or whipped cream.

DAMSON AND WALNUT CRUMBLE WITH ARMAGNAC

Crumble may be humble pie in that it is far quicker and easier to make (and cheaper) than pastry; however, I could not complete a book on the best of British cookery without including this, which is a seasonal treat and (since I love damsons) one of my favourite puddings. The crumble crust is as light and crisp as pastry, the damsons baked for just long enough to be juicy but retain their freshness, and their rich flavour deepened by the Armagnac.

Stoning the damsons is a chore, but otherwise the pudding takes only 10-15 minutes to prepare and 20-25 to bake; provided that you use a proper pie-dish with sloping sides and do not overcook it, it is foolproof. The point of the pie-dish is that the crust will cover a wider area than the fruit, which means that the crumble absorbs less juice and that the juice is less likely to bubble over it, which destroys its crispness. Serve with cream or crème fraîche.

FOR 4-6

450 g/ 1 lb damsons
250 g/ 9 oz caster sugar
½ tablespoonful Armagnac
50 g/ 2 oz walnuts or walnut pieces
40 g/ 1½ oz plain white flour
40 g/ 1½ oz plain wholemeal flour
Pinch of salt
50 g/ 2 oz butter straight from the refrigerator

900-ml/ 1½-pint tapered pie-dish, measuring 24 cm/ 9½ inches × 19 cm/ 7½ inches at the outside edges

Pick over the damsons, discarding any which are over-ripe and squashy. Wash, halve and stone; mix with 150 g/ 5 oz of the sugar and the Armagnac, and put into the pie-dish.

Set the oven to 180 C, 350 F, Gas Mark 4. Crush the walnuts very finely and mix with the flours, salt, and remaining 100 g/ 4 oz sugar. Cut the butter into very small pieces and rub it into the mixture with your fingers until it is like breadcrumbs (or work it in gently with a spoon). Distribute in a thick, even layer over the fruit, spreading it right to the edges of the dish. Very lightly smooth the top and bake 20-25 minutes; remove from the oven at the first sign of fruit juice bubbling up at the edges. Serve hot or warm.

You can re-heat it the next day: bake at the same temperature (180 C, 350 F, Gas Mark 4) for 12-15 minutes. Once it has been started however, the juice will almost certainly over-run the crust at the edges.

BLACKCURRANT TART

As I have included recipes for blackcurrant fool and ice-cream, I had not originally meant to give one for blackcurrant tart as well; however, when I made one the other day to use up some spare blackcurrants, I was reminded that it is actually one of the best fruit tarts in the repertoire.

The pastry can be made and, if you wish, rolled out and the tart tin lined up to 2 days in advance; wrap the dough or cover the tin with foodwrap and store in the refrigerator.

Serve with single cream or crème fraîche.

Shortcrust pastry (see page 19) made with:
125 g/ 4 oz plain white flour
50 g/ 2 oz plain wholemeal flour
Pinch salt
25 g/ 1 oz lard
50 g/ 2 oz butter

300 ml/ ½ pint milk
3 size 2 eggs (yolks only)
225 g/ 8 oz caster sugar
25 g/ 1 oz plain white flour
142 ml/ ¼ pint double cream
275 g/ 10 oz blackcurrants
3 or 4 mint leaves (optional)
Dusting of icing sugar

22-cm/ 8½-inch tart tin

Set the oven to 200 C, 400 F, Gas Mark 6. If the tart tin is not already lined, roll out the pastry to 3-4 mm/ ⅛ inch thick. Line the tin, trim off surplus dough, and cover all over, including the rim, with cooking foil. Weigh down with baking-beans if you have any and bake for 10 minutes; remove the foil and bake for a further 15-18 minutes, until the pastry is an even, light brown. Leave to cool.

Make pastry cream. Heat the milk in a smallish saucepan; take care not to let it boil. Separate the eggs (see page 17) and whisk with

75 g/ 3 oz of the sugar until smooth; whisk or beat in the flour until the mixture is perfectly homogenous. Pour in the milk gradually, stirring continuously. Return the mixture to the milk-saucepan and bring to the boil over low heat, still stirring continuously (watch carefully, since the whisking will mean that the surface is already frothy). Reduce the heat slightly and simmer for 4 minutes; stir constantly. Leave to cool until lukewarm; stir at intervals to prevent the custard from setting. While it cools, whisk the cream until thick and fairly stiff but not so stiff that it stands in peaks when lifted on a spoon or the whisk. Fold into the custard gradually but thoroughly (do not add the custard to the cream). Spread in an even layer over the pastry.

Pick over, wash, and top and tail the currants; put into a smallish saucepan with the remaining 150 g/ 5 oz of the sugar. Rinse and add the mint leaves if you are using them; tuck under the currants to ensure that they are submerged. Set over very low heat, shaking gently from time to time, for 4-5 minutes or until the sugar has melted and the currants are submerged in juice. Pour into a sieve set over a bowl to catch the juice; remove the mint. Distribute the drained currants as evenly as possible over the pastry cream. Return all but 1 tablespoonful of the juice to the pan, set the pan over high heat, and boil for 70-90 seconds, until very thick and just starting to caramelize. Remove from the heat, throw in the reserved tablespoonful of juice, which will instantly lower the temperature and prevent further caramelization from taking place (otherwise, cooking will continue in the hot pan), and immediately spoon over the currants. When completely cold, dust the top of the tart with icing sugar.

BLACKCURRANT AND MINT FOOL

Before the vitamin C content of blackcurrants was known (which was not until this century), their intensity of flavour meant that they were relatively unpopular: if used sparingly, however, they make particularly delicious fool or yoghurt-cum-cream ice. I have combined yoghurt with cream for both fool and ice, not to reduce their fat and cholesterol content but because the addition of yoghurt gives a cleaner, fresher taste. If the yoghurt is tart, you may need to add a little more sugar.

You can make the fool up to 2 days in advance.

Serve with Lemon Shortbread (page 242) or amaretti.

FOR 6

225 g/8 oz blackcurrants
2 or 3 leaves applemint or spearmint
100 g/ 3½ oz caster sugar
200 g/ 7 oz mild, whole-milk yoghurt
142 ml/ ¼ pint double cream (not extra-stiff)

Pick over and wash the blackcurrants; rinse the mint leaves. Put both into a small saucepan with the sugar. There will be a little water clinging to the currants after washing: do not add more. Set over very low heat, stirring from time to time, until the sugar has melted and the juice started to run. Raise the heat slightly and continue to cook 3-4 minutes, until the fruit is soft and submerged in liquid. Pass through a sieve, pressing out as much of the pulp as possible. Leave until cold.

Stir the yoghurt into the purée; if it will not mix smoothly, sieve again. Whip the cream until thick but not very stiff (stiffly whipped cream will not mix smoothly) and fold in until homogenous. Chill for at least 3 hours before serving.

BLACKCURRANT ICE WITH BLACKCURRANTS OR BLACKCURRANT SAUCE

Blackcurrants are probably better known for sorbets or water rather than cream-type ices, but I have not given recipes for water ices in this book because you cannot obtain a professionally fine, smooth texture without an ice-cream machine; however, the following, studded with whole blackcurrants or served with the currants stewed as a sauce, is if anything even better. Like blackcurrant fool, the ice itself is fairly mild, but the sauce or currants in it add interest and strength of flavour without being overwhelming. My preference is for the sauce, but as the stewed blackcurrants do not freeze satisfactorily, freezing them in the ice may be more convenient.

The ice will retain its flavour for at least three weeks, although it is best if eaten within a few days.

For serving immediately, allow 5½-6¼ hours' freezing-time; for defrosting in the refrigerator, 3-3¾ hours.

Serve with Lemon Shortbread (see page 242) or *amaretti*.

FOR 6

*400 g/ 14 oz blackcurrants for an ice with blackcurrant sauce or
375 g/ 13 oz for an ice with currants frozen into it
3 leaves apple or spearmint
225 g/ 8 oz caster sugar
200 g/ 7 oz mild, whole-milk yoghurt
142 ml/ ¼ pint double cream (not extra-thick)*

Wash and pick over 225 g/ 8 oz of the blackcurrants; wash the mint leaves. Put into a small saucepan with 175 g/ 6 oz of the sugar (do not add water) and set over very low heat while the sugar melts and the juice starts to run. Raise the heat slightly and cook for 3-4 minutes or until the fruit is soft and submerged in liquid. Sieve, pressing as much pulp through the mesh as possible. Leave to become cold. Stir the yoghurt into the purée and sieve again. Whip the cream until thick but not stiff and fold in gently but thoroughly. Turn into a pudding-basin or other heat-proof bowl and freeze 3-3½ hours or until the ice has set round the outside but is still liquid in the middle.

If you are going to mix blackcurrants into it, prepare them as soon as you have put it into the freezer. Wash, pick over, and top and tail 150 g/ 5 oz currants; take care to remove any brown fragments of leaf. Put them into a small saucepan with the remaining 50 g/ 2 oz sugar and set them over a very low heat until the sugar has melted, as before. Raise the heat slightly and cook for 2-3 minutes, until just soft but still whole. Allow to cool and chill in the refrigerator.

When the ice is frozen round the outside, set ready an egg-whisk and freezer-container with a lid. It is a good idea to cool the container by holding it upside-down under the cold tap (but keep the lid on to ensure that the inside stays dry). Take the ice from the freezer and whisk it smooth thoroughly but quickly: this breaks up the ice-crystals but speed is necessary because if they melt, the point of whisking is lost. It may also mean that the added blackcurrants sink to the bottom, although as the mixture is thick this will probably not happen. Stir in the chilled blackcurrants, transfer to the container, cover, and return at once to the freezer. The ice will be ready to serve in 2¼-2¾ hours.

To serve with blackcurrant sauce, whisk and re-freeze as above without the added blackcurrants; prepare the sauce within 24 hours of serving. Top, tail, pick over, and wash 175 g/ 6 oz currants, add 50 g/ 2 oz sugar, and stew as before. Chill (covered) until you are ready to eat the ice: pour some of it over the individual portions and serve the rest separately.

GOOSEBERRY FOOL

Isabella Beeton noted of gooseberries: 'in this country especially, there is no fruit so universally in favour.' At that time, nearly 200 varieties were cultivated, many of which were the red and white rather than green types. People who could not afford the sugar and butter or cream needed for making them into jam or puddings favoured the sweet sorts; a great many were used for wine, known as 'Poor Man's Champagne' (and supposedly widely used to adulterate real champagne).

Isabella's recipe for gooseberry fool was similar to mine, except that she used milk, or milk and cream instead of whipped cream, which must have given a rather liquid result. Yoghurt can also be used, but gives a less rich flavour; you can also freeze the fool, perhaps with a little more sugar, into ice-cream.

Serve with very thin ginger or almond biscuits.

FOR 4

450 g/1 lb medium-ripe green gooseberries
125 g/4 oz sugar
142 ml/¼ pint double cream

Pick over the gooseberries, wash, and shake in a colander to remove surplus liquid. Put into a saucepan with the sugar (do not add water) and set over very low heat until the sugar has melted and they have started to run juice. Raise the heat slightly and cook until the fruit is soft and submerged in liquid. Press through a sieve, using the back of a spoon to force as much of the pulp through as possible. Leave until cold.

Whip the cream until it is thick but not so thick that it stands in peaks. Stir the gooseberry purée into it gradually (not *vice versa*). Serve chilled.

To make ice-cream, use an extra 15 g/½ oz sugar (i.e. 140 g/4½ oz, instead of 125 g/4 oz) and follow the instructions for freezing on page 238.

ELIZA ACTON'S VERY SUPERIOR WHIPPED SYLLABUB

Early recipes for syllabub suggest that it was a stiff, frothy liquid rather than whipped solid. Isabella Beeton gave two recipes, one made with frothed milk which was obviously a drink, and the other for a thicker mixture made with straight cream and topped with whipped cream; however, she said that this could be converted to a stiff syllabub by using only whipped cream.

The recipe below is the only one which I have given in, or nearly in, its original form. The mixture is thick rather than as stiff as perhaps you may wish but tastes wonderful. Eliza recommended making it the previous day, but it is delicious served merely after chilling. If you make it in advance (you can actually keep it for at least 2 days) you will find liquid at the bottom, which I suggest stirring in for the sake of flavour.

Serve with very thin, crisp almond bisuits.

FOR 8-10

100 g/ 3½ oz caster sugar
1 lemon
4 tablespoonsful Armagnac
4 tablespoonsful medium-dry sherry, e.g. Amontillado
284 ml/ ½ pint double cream

Put the sugar into a large bowl. Scrub, dry, and finely grate the zest of the lemon over the top. Mix thoroughly so that the sugar is an even yellow. Squeeze 2 tablespoonsful of lemon juice, add with the other ingredients, and whisk until stiff (it will not, however, be stiff enough to stand in peaks). Chill before serving.

TIM JONES'S HAZELNUT CAKE

I have already referred, perhaps rather unfairly, to a hazelnut tart from Tim Jones's Patisserie Bliss: this cake sets the record straight. Tim is an architect, and applies architectural principles to his baking, keeping his recipes as basic as possible but paying the utmost attention to cooking standards and the quality of ingredients. The cake could not be simpler but will suffer if you do not use high-quality, unskinned nuts, which have more flavour than blanched or ready-ground ones; you should also use the freshest possible free-range eggs. As it contains nothing else except a minimum of sugar, with no added fat, it is rich but very light, and, as cakes go, healthy. It is perhaps at its best served alone with coffee, but is also the ideal accompaniment to fresh raspberries or Summer Fruit Salad (page 220); alternatively, serve it with plain whipped cream (as the cake itself is delicately flavoured and only slightly sweet, flavoured, sweetened cream overwhelms it).

Cooking time is 1 hour.

FOR 8-10

150 g/ 5 oz whole hazelnuts
Groundnut oil for greasing
6 size 2 eggs
65 g/ 2½ oz caster sugar
Salt
Icing sugar for sprinkling (optional)

20-cm/ 8-inch cake tin

Heat the oven to 200 C, 400 F, Gas Mark 6. Put the nuts into a baking tray and toast 8-10 minutes, until slightly coloured; allow to cool a little and grind, or, if you have no grinder, pound to the consistency of flour in a mortar (pounding is not nearly such hard work as it sounds because the nuts crush easily after being toasted).

Re-set the oven to 120 C, 250 F, Gas Mark ½. Line the base of the cake tin with cooking foil and grease both tin and foil with groundnut oil. Separate the eggs (page 17). Beat the yolks with the sugar until homogenous; add a pinch of salt to the whites and whip until close-textured and stiff enough to stand in peaks when lifted from the whisk. Fold first the nuts and then the egg yolks into the whites; make sure that the yolks are thoroughly incorporated. Put immediately into the oven and bake for 60 minutes. Turn upside-down on a rack and leave in the tin until cold. If you like, sprinkle a little icing sugar over the top.

LEMON OR ORANGE SHORTBREAD WITH HAZELNUTS

The hazelnuts go better with orange flavouring than lemon; I like them with either, but you may prefer to omit them with lemon.

MAKES 12-16 FINGERS

150 g/ 5 oz butter, if possible at room temperature
50 g/ 2 oz caster sugar
1 orange or lemon
Pinch salt
50 g/ 2 oz whole, unskinned hazelnuts
75 g/ 3 oz ground rice
125 g/ 4 oz plain, fine white flour

18-cm by 18-cm/ 7-inch by 7-inch square baking tin about 2.5 cm/ 1 inch deep, or a round baking tin of similar size

Set the oven to 190 C, 375 F, Gas Mark 5. If the butter is not already soft, chop it into small pieces and work it with a wooden spoon until creamy. Beat in the sugar (beat only enough to mix). Scrub and dry the orange or lemon: finely grate and add the zest. Add the nuts, ground rice, and flour, and stir until incorporated: do not, however, beat or stir more than necessary. Line the baking tray with cooking foil, fill with the mixture, and press into an even layer about 12 mm/ ½ inch thick; make sure that the top is flat and smooth, without protruding nuts. Bake 18-20 minutes or until pale gold. Allow to become cold and cut into fingers.

BREAD AND BUTTER PUDDING

I f ready-made versions were not sold in supermarkets, I should have said that this was a forgotten delight. Longish cooking makes it unsuitable for restaurant presentation; nor is it an obvious choice for dinner-parties. However, it is relatively convenient to serve at home, since it should be prepared an hour or so in advance and thereafter needs no attention; furthermore, if the bread is carefully cut and the top baked saffron gold, it looks surprisingly festive and elegant.

The following is loosely based on an early eighteenth-century recipe from *The Compleat Housekeeper* by Eliza Smith. Eliza Smith (d. circa 1732) spent over thirty years employed by 'fashionable and noble Families'; not much more is known about her, but she described the contents of her book as 'Directions. . . for dressing after the best, most natural and wholesome Manner, such Provisions as are the Product of our own country' and deplored the fact that French cooking in Britain was already gaining popularity.

In her recipe, the pudding was made with three pints of cream (it was evidently for 16-20 people) and baked in a puff pastry case. I have replaced the pastry with a crisp collar of bread and reduced the amount of cream to 142 ml/¼ pint; the custard can be made with only milk, but a proportion of cream enormously improves the texture.

The original flavouring of orange-flower water is delicious; however, an excellent alternative is orange peel and cinnamon. If you want to add extra zest, soak the raisins in brandy. If possible, use bread which is two to three days old. Fresh bread is difficult to cut neatly; it may also curl rather than standing up round the edge of the dish.

The pudding should be left to soak 1-2½ hours before baking; cooking time is 40-55 minutes.

FOR 6-8

100 g/ 3½ oz slightly salted butter
Either *2 × 5 cm/ 2-inch strips orange peel and 2.5-cm/ 1-inch piece*
cinnamon stick
or *1 scant tablespoonful orange-flower water*
600 ml/ 1 pint milk
142 ml/¼ pint double cream (not extra thick)

40 g/ 1½ oz raisins
50 g/ 2 oz currants
1 tablespoonful brandy (optional)
185 g/ generous 6½ oz ordinary stale white bread (do not use enriched
bread or French loaves)
4 size 2 eggs (yolks only)
75 g/ 3 oz caster sugar
Sprinkling of nutmeg

Unless the butter is already soft, take it out of the refrigerator and chop it into small pieces. To flavour the pudding with orange peel and cinnamon, wash and dry an orange, pare off the peel, and add to the milk with the cinnamon and cream. Heat the milk but do not let it boil; cover and leave to allow the flavours to infuse. If you are using brandy, pour it over the raisins; scatter the currants on top.

Trim the crust from the bread and cut very thinly as for sandwiches, buttering before cutting. For a really tidy, elegant pudding, divide the slices lengthways into fingers. Lightly butter a 16-cm/ 6½-inch, 9-cm/ 3½-inch deep soufflé-dish or other ovenproof dish not more than 20 cm/ 8 inches in diameter. Arrange very slightly overlapping slices or fingers of bread round the dish; place two or three more over the bottom. Cover with the currants and raisins, plus any brandy which has not been absorbed.

Separate the eggs: use the whites for soufflés (see pages 63 and 65) or meringues. Whisk together the yolks and sugar; then gradually whisk in either the flavoured milk and cream (throw away the orange peel and cinnamon) or plain milk and cream with the orange-flower water. Pour the custard-mixture into the dish, taking care not to displace the bread round the sides. Grate in a generous sprinkling of nutmeg and arrange the rest of the bread over the top, butter-side up. Cover with a plate and leave 1-2½ hours.

Bake at 150 C, 300 F, Gas Mark 2, for 55 minutes or until the bread is gold but not brown. Check to ensure that it is set by inserting a knife into the middle. Serve hot or warm.

MINCE PIES

Mincemeat derives its name from the fact that at one time it actually contained meat: Henrietta Maria and Eliza Acton used tongue, Eliza Smith veal, and Isabella Beeton beef. Hannah Glasse, instead of including meat in her mince, added a layer of it to her pies, together with a sprinkling of fresh citron- and orange-zest. In the recipe below, I have followed her example in suggesting adding fresh orange- or lime-zest just before baking: lime in particular adds interest and intensity to the flavour.

Mincemeat

If you prefer mincemeat without suet, omit it: use only 4 tablespoonsful of brandy and add a small knob of butter or brandy butter (see page 249) to the pies before baking.

The mincemeat should be kept for about 2 weeks before use: if put into sterilized jars (see page 148), it can be kept for 6.

MAKES 1.75 KG/ 3½ LB

10 cloves
75 g/ 3 oz whole (unblanched) almonds
75 g/3 oz walnuts
225 g/ 8 oz raisins
225 g/ 8 oz currants
225 g/ 8 oz shredded vegetable suet (optional)
225 g/ 8 oz sultanas
8 tablespoonsful Armagnac (or 4 if you are not using suet)
1 large orange (zest only)
1 large lemon
225 g/ 8 oz (1 medium) Bramley apple
2 level teaspoonsful ground cinnamon
225 g/ 8 oz soft dark brown sugar

Grind or crush the cloves to a powder. If you are using suet, chop or crush the nuts into fairly even small pieces; if not, crush most of them about as finely as coarse breadcrumbs but leave some larger pieces. Put them into a mixing-bowl with the raisins, currants, suet, and sultanas: if the sultanas are stuck into a mass, moisten them with the brandy and add at the end, when you will be able to separate them relatively easily with a spoon (this is quicker than pulling them apart individually). Scrub and dry the orange and lemon; finely grate the zest of both and add. Squeeze and add 3 tablespoonsful of lemon juice. Peel and coarsely grate the apple; add and mix. Add the cloves, cinnamon, and sugar, and mix again. Add the brandy; mix thoroughly. Keep for 2 weeks.

Pies

Traditionally, the pies are made with puff or flaky pastry, but I suggest shortcrust, which is less rich.

For a dozen pies 6.5 cm/ 2½ inches in diameter, pastry made with 225 g/ 8 oz of flour is just enough but means re-rolling every scrap of dough: using 275 g/ 10 oz is more comfortable.

MAKES 12 6.5-CM/ 2½-INCH PIES

3 limes or 2 oranges (zest only)

Shortcrust pastry (see page 19) made with:
275 g/ 10 oz white flour
50 g/2 oz lard
75 g/ 3 oz butter

225-275 g/ 8-10 oz mincemeat without suet
or 275-350 g/ 10-12 oz mincemeat with suet
Butter or brandy butter

Scrub, dry, and finely grate the lime- or orange-zest. Roll out the pastry to a thickness of 2-3 mm/ ⅛-inch. If you have two round pastry-cutters, one to fit the tops of the indentations of your pastry-tin and one a little larger (for the bottoms of the pies), cut out the bottoms and place them in the tin; however, you may find it easier to lay the pastry over the tin in a sheet, press it into the indentations, and then cut round them, leaving a small margin of pastry on which to stick the tops. Gather up the trimmings, which you will need for the tops.

Set the oven to 225 C, 425 F, Gas Mark 7. Fill each pie with ½-¾ tablespoonful of mincemeat (if it contains suet you should use more than if it does not because the suet will melt). Add a small knob of butter to the top if the mincemeat is without suet and sprinkle with lime- or orange-zest. Re-roll the pastry and cut out the tops. Moisten the edges of both tops and bottoms with cold water and cover the pies, pressing the edges firmly together. Make an air-hole in each one, stamp the edges if you wish, and bake for 15 minutes, until light brown. Do not over-bake or the pies may be dry.

CHRISTMAS PUDDING

Our ancestors boiled their puddings in floured cloths rather than basins: this meant that the puddings were spherical, which looked very impressive, although it must have made them difficult to serve.

The following recipe is a relatively light, delicately flavoured pudding which (if you have room to eat it) goes well after goose.

The bread for the crumbs should be moderately stale: fresh bread forms doughy lumps when grated.

The pudding is better if mixed 1-2 days in advance to give the flavours time to develop.

Allow 3½ hours for boiling two small puddings or 7 hours for one big one. The whole quantity will just fit into a 1.5-litre/ 2½-pint pudding-basin; for half-sized ones, half-fill two basins. Serve with brandy butter or brandy cream; personally, I much prefer brandy cream.

FOR 5-6 OR 10-12

3 size 2 eggs
150 g/ 5 oz muscovado sugar
125 g/ 4 oz shredded suet
6 cloves
50 g/2 oz whole (unblanched) almonds
50 g/ 2 oz stale white bread, weighed without crust

75 g/ 3 oz (2 small) carrots
100 g/ 3½ oz (1 small) Cox or similar sweet apple
1 lemon (zest only)
75 g/ 3 oz mixed candied citron and lemon peel
25 g/ 1 oz crystallized ginger
1 teaspoonful ground cinnamon
Moderate pinch of salt
50 g/ 2 oz currants
175 g/ 6 oz raisins
175 g/ 6 oz sultanas
1 tablespoonful Cointreau
6 tablespoonsful brandy plus 1-2 tablespoonsful to pour over pudding
75 g/ 3 oz plain white flour
1 teaspoonful bicarbonate of soda

Beat the eggs and sugar until perfectly smooth and add the suet. Crush and add the cloves; chop the nuts moderately finely and add (do not crush, since the pieces should be of an even size). Finely grate and add the bread; peel, grate finely, and stir in the carrots and apple. Scrub and grate the zest of the lemon over the mixture. Finely dice and add the peel and ginger. Add and thoroughly mix all the other ingredients, leaving the flour and soda until last.

Generously butter the sides of the pudding-basin or basins; for easy turning-out, cut a circle of cooking foil to fit into the bottom, which should also be buttered. Transfer the pudding to the basin(s). Cover with more cooking foil, secure the foil round the rim with string, and tie up the basin like a parcel, with a loop on top if you like, so that you can lift it out of the pan. Put the basin into a saucepan with a lid: the pan should be large enough for water to be poured down the side. Fill the pan to within 4 cm/ 1½ inches of the top for a large pudding or three-quarters full for small ones, and bring fairly slowly just to the boil (it is preferable to avoid letting water splash over the top of the pudding in case any seeps inside). Reduce the heat to the lowest possible simmer, cover, and simmer for 3½ or 7 hours according to size, refilling the saucepan with boiling water from the kettle if necessary. With the foil and lid, the pudding will continue to steam even if there is not much water; however, the pan must not run dry. The pudding is ready when a knife inserted into the centre comes out clean, as for a cake.

Run a knife round the edge of the basin before turning it out; turn out, pour 1-2 tablespoonsful of brandy over the top, and set it alight. (This is not just cosmetic, since the burnt brandy adds considerably to the flavour.)

BRANDY CREAM

FOR 6

50 g/ 2 oz caster sugar
284 ml/ ½ pint double cream
2 tablespoonsful brandy
2 tablespoonsful sherry

Whip all the ingredients together until stiff.

BRANDY BUTTER

FOR 4-5

125 g/ 4 oz butter
100 g/ 3½ oz icing sugar
2½ tablespoonsful brandy

Beat the butter and icing sugar until very light and fluffy; then beat in the brandy by degrees.